JAMES LEE RAY is professor of political science at Florida State University. He has served as director of the International Affairs program since 1985 and as director of the Peace Studies program since 1987. Ray has taught at the State University College at Fredonia, New York, and at the University of New Mexico, where he served as chair of the political science department from 1982 to 1984. Author of *The Future of American-Israeli Relations* and *Global Politics*, he has published articles in *International Interactions, International Organization, International Studies Quarterly*, and *The Journal of Conflict Resolution*. Ray's current research focuses on regime transitions and their relationship to foreign policies and international politics.

Democracy
and International Conflict

Studies in International Relations

*Charles W. Kegley, Jr.,
and Donald J. Puchala, General Editors*

Democracy
and
International Conflict
An Evaluation
of the Democratic Peace Proposition

James Lee Ray

UNIVERSITY OF SOUTH CAROLINA PRESS

A few paragraphs from chapter 1 have appeared previously in the author's contribution to *Controversies in International Relations Theory,* edited by Charles Kegley, Jr., copyright 1995. They are reprinted with permission from St. Martin's Press, Inc. Roughly the latter half of chapter 2 has been published as "Global Trends, State-Specific Factors and Regime Transitions, 1825–1993," *Journal of Peace Research* 32 (February 1995): 49–64, and is reprinted here with permission from the editor of that journal. Finally, chapter 3 is an extended and revised version of "Wars Between Democracies: Rare, or Nonexistent?" *International Interactions* 18, no. 3 (1993): 251–76, and portions of that chapter appear here with permission from Gordon and Breach Science Publishers.

© 1995 by the University of South Carolina

Published in Columbia, South Carolina by the
University of South Carolina Press

Manufactured in the United States of America

99 98 97 96 95   5 4 3 2 1

Library of Congress Cataloging-in-Publication Data

Ray, James Lee.
   Democracy and international conflict : an evaluation of the
democratic peace proposition / James Lee Ray.
     p.   cm. — (Studies in international relations)
   Includes bibliographical references and index.
   ISBN 1–57003–041–3
   1. Peace. 2. Pacific settlement of international disputes.
3. Democracy. I Title. II. Series.
JX1952.R333 1995
909.82'9—dc20   95–4339

Contents

Tables and Figures

Preface

Perhaps the best answer to the question "How long did it take you to write that book?" is "My whole life." It is certainly true that any author draws upon, consciously or subconsciously, the relevant experiences and impressions of his or her entire life in the process of writing a book. Still, in retrospect, I feel that I started working on this book while listening to shortwave radio broadcasts from Radio Moscow after Mikhail Gorbachev came to power in the Soviet Union in the middle of the 1980s. At that time, Radio Moscow began to broadcast on a regular basis commentaries on issues in the Soviet Union and in international politics suffused with what can accurately be described as enthusiasm for political and economic liberalism that I found rather astonishing. Almost equally astonishing were the continual denunciations of dictatorship in general, and of Stalin in particular. I found these broadcasts especially amazing in light of my memories of broadcasts from Radio Moscow to which I had listened with some regularity in the 1960s. Then, the broadcasts were so steeped in Marxist-Leninist ideology that I found myself alternately amused by the extreme views that were expressed and impressed at how differences between the ideology on which those commentaries were based and the predominant ideology in the United States and the rest of the "free world," with which I was admittedly more familiar and sympathetic, could produce such starkly contrasting evaluations of and opinions about global political issues. But, in the 1980s, I became equally impressed by what a different place the world could be if the relationship between the United States and the Soviet Union (both armed with nuclear weapons) based on passionate ideological antagonism were replaced by a relationship between those two countries based on mutual respect for political as well as economic liberalism, which the broadcasts I heard on Radio Moscow at that time suggested to me was possible.

Whether reform in Russia will in fact create the basis for a lasting and friendly relationship with the United States is an interesting question. But the potential for democracy to ameliorate international conflict that dramatic changes in the Soviet Union helped bring to my attention may be substantial regardless of the fate of reforms in Russia. In this book I focus especially on relationships between democratic states and on the proposition that such states will not initiate international wars against each other because they are democratic. I evaluate the theory and evidence in favor of that proposition and conclude that the present state of that theory and evidence suggests that greater attention should be paid to global trends in regime transitions, to the question of just how many exceptions to the rule that democracies do not initiate international wars against each other exist, and to the necessity, in light of the extent to which both wars and democracies are rare, to supplement the evidence from analyses of large numbers of cases with intensive analyses of individual and particularly crucial cases. The latter chapters of the book take modest steps toward each of these goals.

The list of people who have generously provided me comments, criticisms, and advice on this project at various stages is somewhat embarrassing in length. Stuart Bremer, Bruce Bueno de Mesquita, James Caporaso, Steve Chan, Tom Cusack, Larry Diamond, Paul Diehl, William Dixon, Michael Doyle, Dan Geller, Nils Petter Gleditsch, Ted Robert Gurr, Patrick James, Ram Krishnan, Alan Lamborn, Jack Levy, Zeev Maoz, Glenn Mitchell, George Modelski, Lawrence Mohr, John Owen, Dan Reiter, R. J. Rummel, Bruce Russett, Philippe Schmitter, J. David Singer, Max Singer, Randolph Siverson, Harvey Starr, Kevin Wang, Michael Ward, and Spencer Weart all devoted time and effort to all or parts of the book in manuscript form. The length of this list is embarrassing both because it is so long that readers might justifiably wonder why I needed so much help and because I fear it is probably too short, as I may have forgotten some who also deserve my gratitude. I apologize for that and of course accept responsibility for errors or shortcomings that those "unknown soldiers" as well as the people I have named specifically did their best to save me from. This project was also supported by a grant from the United States Institute of Peace, although the opinions, findings, and conclusions or recommendations in the book are mine and do not necessarily reflect the views of the United States Institute of Peace. Charles Kegley encouraged me to begin this project several years ago, and several people at the University of South Carolina Press kept encouraging me through some times when they must have wondered whether they would ever see a completed manuscript. Finally, I want to thank Cam, Alex, and Nicholas for their patience and support through all the months I have worked on this project, which is especially impressive in light of the fact that Cam, at least, realizes that the next project begins today.

Democracy
and International Conflict

Chapter 1

Theory and Research on the Democratic Peace Proposition
A Critical Review

The basic idea that autocracy or dictatorship is an important cause of war that can be eliminated by democracy, because democratic states will have peaceful relationships with each other, has philosophical roots that antedate the middle 1980s and the end of the Cold War by about two hundred years. The current literature on the democratic peace proposition gives primary credit for the idea to Immanuel Kant, for an essay published in 1795 titled "Perpetual Peace." Kant was "probably the most powerful and consistent exponent and champion of the doctrine of human freedom that has ever lived," according to John Bourke (1942, 25). Even more to the point in the present context, he is, in the opinion of Chris Brown (1992, 14), "the greatest of all theorists of international relations."

The Philosophical Roots
of the Democratic Peace Proposition

The essence of Kant's argument that democracy is an important force for peace is contained in the following oft-quoted passage from "Perpetual Peace":

> [The] republican constitution . . . provides for this desirable result, namely, perpetual peace, and the reason for this is as follows: If (as must inevitably be the case, given this form of constitution) the consent of the citizenry is required in order to determine whether or not there will be a war, it is natural that they consider all its calamities before committing themselves to so risky a game. (Among these are doing the fighting themselves, paying the costs of the war from their own resources, having to repair at great sacrifice the war's devastation, and, finally, the ultimate evil that would make peace itself better, never being able—because of new and constant wars—to expunge the burden of debt.) By contrast, under a nonrepublican constitution, whose subjects are not citizens, the

easiest thing in the world is to declare war. Here the ruler is not a fellow citizen, but the nation's owner, and war does not affect his table, his hunt, his place of pleasure, his court festivals, and so on. Thus, he can decide to go to war for the most meaningless of reasons, as if it were a kind of pleasure party, and he can blithely leave its justification (which decency requires) to his diplomatic corps, who are always prepared for such exercises. (Kant 1795, 113)

Although this passage has the advantage of ornate, archaic language and evokes the respect appropriate to its accumulated years in existence, it does contain assertions and implications about the relationship between regime type and international conflict that are debatable. The basic argument is that the public and public opinion in democracies (or republics) are pacifistic, while autocratic leaders are bellicose or warlike. But history is rife with examples (one of which, the Spanish-American War, we will examine in some detail in chapter 5) of public opinion seeming to support aggressive policies that lead to war.[1] Then, too, many of the reasons that Kant provides for believing that the general public and public opinion will be pacifistic are not persuasive. Citizens (in a democracy, or in any state, for that matter) are likely to be opposed to decisions for war, Kant tells us, because "they are doing the fighting themselves." But in most wars, only a small proportion of the population, usually young males not typically very influential politically, actually get involved in the fighting. The citizenry in a republic, Kant tells us, will be against war because they must pay the costs of war from their own resources. But there are also profits to be made from wars, and jobs created by them, and in any case it is unlikely that most citizens in most countries base their attitudes about any given war on precise calculations of economic profit or loss for themselves because, for most, those calculations are difficult or impossible to make.

"Repairing the sacrifice of war's devastation" is only likely to be a compelling consideration if one is convinced that such devastation will occur and/ or that the war under consideration will be lost. In fact, though, wars do not consistently bring devastation to the states that fight them, and on the eve of many wars the general publics on at least one and sometimes both sides are quite convinced that the preponderance of devastation will be wreaked on the *other* side. As for the "ultimate evil" of the burden of debt created by "new and constant wars," one must consider, in evaluating the impact of this factor on the public's thinking in prewar crises, the number of wars fought, according to their defenders, to eliminate future wars, or at least to make it unnecessary to fight even larger and more costly wars in the future.

Kant may also be guilty in this prominent passage of exaggerating the distinction between democratic and autocratic leaders with respect to their usual wartime experiences. The rulers in a democracy may, as Kant puts it, be "fellow citizens." But it is rare for the leaders, or the vast majority of the ruling class, to suffer directly from war's deprivations in either democracies or autocracies. In other words, war does not often directly affect the "table," "hunt," or "places of pleasure" (such as golf courses or yachts) of, say, American presidents or British prime ministers any more that it affects those of autocratic leaders.

Nevertheless, Kant's "Perpetual Peace" is an important symbolic as well as substantive source of inspiration for advocates of the democratic peace proposition, increased in its influence by the work of Michael Doyle (1983a, 1983b, 1986). Kant may well deserve credit, for example, for the shape of contemporary thought regarding the relationship between regime type and international conflict because of his emphasis on international law as a source of peace among republics. Kant's argument in this respect shares important points with the cultural, as opposed to the structural, explanation of the democratic peace, both of which we will examine below. In fact, Doyle (1983a, 230) argues explicitly in his exposition of Kant's work that Kant believed that "as republics emerge . . . and as *culture* [emphasis added] progresses, [it] sets up the moral foundations for the liberal peace." Doyle goes on to point out that Kant's work suggests that "domestically just republics, which rest on consent, presume foreign republics to be also consensual, just, and therefore deserving of accommodation." This foreshadows important arguments in the contemporary literature on the democratic peace proposition in, for example, Rummel (1979), Russett (1993), and Dixon (1994).

Three additional points about the relationship between regime type and international conflict from the work of Kant, later stressed by Doyle, deserve mention here because of their impact on later work. One involves the relationship between democratic and nondemocratic states. According to Doyle (1983b, 324–25, 337), "The very constitutional restraint, shared commercial interests, and international respect for individual rights that promote peace among liberal societies can exacerbate conflicts in relations between liberal and nonliberal societies . . . [L]iberalism does appear to exacerbate intervention against weak nonliberals and hostility against powerful nonliberal societies."[2] From this strain in Kantianism, perhaps, comes the insistence in current literature that democratic states are not less war prone in general than nondemocratic states, that it is only in relationships with each other that their pacific characteristics emerge. Doyle (1983a, 219) also stresses that "differing domestic regimes do affect the quantity of resources available to the states," thus pointing the way toward an argument that democratic states are likely to be particularly effective combatants in international war, an argument that we will consider below. Finally, Doyle emphasizes a third source of peace among democracies, in addition to domestic law and constitutionalism (which corresponds roughly to the stress on the impact of structures in later work), and international law (which serves to strengthen cultural inhibitions also pointed out by current work on the democratic peace). This third source received scant attention in the recent empirical work on democratic peace, until recently. Kant argued, according to Doyle (1983a, 231), that "*cosmopolitican law,* adds material incentives to moral commitments . . . [T]he 'spirit of commerce' sooner or later [takes] hold of every nation, thus impelling states to promote peace and to try to avert war." Kant here was stressing the pacifying impact of free trade among nations. "Avoiding a challenge to another liberal state's security or even enhancing each other's security by means of alliance naturally follows economic interdependence" (Doyle 1983a, 231).

Hegel and the Democratic Peace Proposition

Another source, generally underappreciated, of inspiration for contemporary work on the democratic peace proposition is Georg William Friedrich Hegel, "the most important philosopher of the 19th century" (Johnson 1991, 811). The relevance of Hegel to that contemporary work has been pointed out most forcefully, albeit indirectly, by Francis Fukuyama (1989, 1992), who in turn has emphasized the role of Alexander Kojeve. Kojeve was a "French-Russian philosopher who taught a highly influential series of seminars at Paris's *Ecole Pratique des Hautes Etudes* in the 1930s" (Fukuyama 1992, 65–66). Kojeve's central thesis in those seminars was that Hegel was right when he argued that in 1806 ideological evolution had reached an end point "beyond which it is impossible to progress further." "Hegel saw in Napoleon's defeat of the Prussian monarchy at the Battle of Jena the victory of the ideals of the French Revolution, and the imminent universalization of the state incorporating the principles of liberty and equality" (Fukuyama 1989, 4–5).[3]

To say that Hegel's prediction regarding the "imminent universalization" of liberal values was rather premature would be somewhat akin to asserting that Adolf Hitler was rather biased against Jews. (It would be, in other words, an understatement.) Why it turned out to be so premature is a point to which we will return shortly. Let us turn first, though, to the alleged (by me) relevance of Hegel's prediction to contemporary research and writing on the democratic peace proposition.

Hegel's prediction is relevant primarily because that research and writing has been inspired to an important extent by the end of the Cold War, which has restored confidence in the idea that Hegel did much to originate, i.e., that democracy (or liberalism) is the wave of the future. For example, certainly one of the more important recent documents regarding the democratic peace proposition is *Grasping the Democratic Peace* by Bruce Russett (1993). Significantly, the subtitle of that book is *Principles for a Post–Cold War World.* In the first paragraph of the book Russett asks: "Does the post–Cold War era represent merely the passing of a particular adversarial relationship, or does it offer a chance for fundamentally changed relations among nations?" It is soon clear that this question is mostly rhetorical, for a major theme of the book is that the end of the Cold War does make possible a revolutionary renovation of the global political system. It would be impossible to generate such enthusiasm without confidence that democracy will become significantly more prevalent in the international system than it has been up to this point. This does not mean that Russett, or other supporters of the democratic peace proposition, necessarily buy into Fukuyama's (1989) thesis regarding the "end of history," or the idea that democracy is on the verge of becoming universal. But the hope that international politics may be in the process of being changed to a revolutionary extent must be based, for adherents to the democratic peace proposition, on some confidence that democracy will become universal, or nearly so, among the major powers in the international system.

Although it is probably unlikely that Russett was inspired directly or consciously by Hegel, surely it is optimism about a global trend toward democracy that has inspired much of the work and perhaps even more of the interest in that work on the democratic peace proposition. That enthusiasm is most clearly exemplified, perhaps, by Max Singer and Aaron Wildavsky in *The Real World Order* (1993, 194), who declare that the "traditionalists" (by which they mean "realists") have not fully grasped how much the world will be changed "by the new reality of no war among the democratic great powers. Relations among these countries will not be influenced by the need for military allies. Nor will they be concerned with the balance of military power among groups of democracies . . . [D]emocracy is a basis for peace among the great powers . . . [D]emocracy is a basic long-term hope for achieving general peace."

Hegelian ideas about the potential universalization of liberal values are an important source of inspiration for current work, too, on the democratic peace proposition, because faith or confidence in such ideas is about the only defense logically possible against one fundamental realist critique of the idea that democracy has the potential to revolutionize global politics. As John Mearsheimer (1990, 53) points out, "[T]he possibility always exists that a democracy will revert to an authoritarian state. Liberal democracies must therefore worry about relative power among themselves. . . . Lamentably, it is not possible for even liberal democracies to transcend anarchy." How else can defenders of the democratic peace proposition, and of its importance to the future of international politics, respond to this point except with a partially Hegelian argument that it is too possible that liberal democracies will be able to transcend anarchy, if they can be confident that democracy is the wave of the future and is secure at least among the most powerful states in the international system?

In short, the potential for democracy to have a revolutionary, pacifying impact on global politics is a function of two of its alleged characteristics as a political phenomenon. The first is its ability to modify relations between states, at least if they are democratic. This might be referred to as the Kantian aspect of the democratic peace proposition. The second is its ability to diffuse through-out the international system, or at least to its largest, most powerful states. This is its Hegelian dimension. So far, the literature on the democratic peace propo-sition has focused primarily on the allegedly pacifying power of democracy. But the interest in that potential has been heightened by the end of the Cold War because its end makes plausible what Hegel originally suggested about two hundred years ago, that liberal values will become universal or at least clearly predominant.[4]

The Postponements of Universal Liberalism

But, as we have noted, Hegel in retrospect seems to have been seriously premature in his prediction to that effect. A lot of water has gone over the dam, so to speak, since 1806. The year 2006 is approaching, and liberal values are still a significant distance from being universally accepted.

In simple, even partly tautological terms, Hegel's expectations about the "imminent" universalization of democratic or liberal values involved a sub-stantial underestimation of the strength of antiliberal ideologies, both of which, ironically enough, Hegel helped to inspire. Hegelian thought, according to Torbjørn Knutsen (1992, 149), "provided Continental (that is, European as op-posed to Anglo-Saxon liberal) conservatives with a set of concepts and a sense of purpose which allowed them to comprehend the dramatic social changes they could not prevent." Thus inspired, conservative European leaders like Metternich, and then Bismarck, fought a rearguard action against liberal values and mass participation that was at least partially successful. "The Enlighten-ment project and its attendant visions of progress, industrialization, and mass participation gradually emerged as the dominant vision of the nineteenth cen-tury," according to Knutsen (1992, 153). But Knutsen also acknowledges that "the collapse of the anti-Enlightenment edifice . . . did not result in the clear victory of liberalism." In fact, in 1914, more than one hundred years after Napoleon's victory over the Prussians at the Battle of Jena, liberal France and its liberal allies Great Britain and ultimately the United States were on the verge of a life-and-death struggle with the successor to the defeated Prussian state, led by the Kaiser.

So Hegel's estimate that "history ended" in 1806 was premature first be-cause he underestimated the strength of conservative antiliberal forces in the nineteenth century. It turned out to be doubly premature (at least—who knows what will happen in the twenty-first century?) because he underestimated the strength-to-be of radical antiliberal forces in the twentieth century. And, to repeat, Hegel made an important, if mostly unwitting, contribution to this strain of thought, also, because Karl Marx, an "outstanding product of . . . Hegelianism," according to Paul Johnson (1991, 812), "transformed Hegel's intellectual engineering into a system of social engineering, with incalculable consequences for the 20th century."

In defense of Marx (and Marxism), it should be pointed out that whereas "liberals look to a union of republican *governments* pursuing peaceful policies, radicals focus on democratic pressure against aggression from ordinary citizens," and that this makes it possible to argue that "Marxian theory is more robustly deliberative and democratic than liberal conceptions, since the sustenance of dissident movements, lacking state power, requires clear political argument, internal discussion, and reflection" (Gilbert 1992, 11).[5]

However, it is clearly more difficult to argue that Marxism-Leninism turned out to be more democratic than liberal conceptions, certainly as it came to be interpreted and implemented by Joseph Stalin. And Stalin had interesting similarities and connections to the other major-power post–World War I menace to liberal and democratic values in international politics, Adolf Hitler. By 1929, "Stalin had acquired a pupil [and] admirer . . . in the shape of Hitler" (Johnson 1983, 61). "Hitler learned from Lenin and Stalin," according to Johnson (1983, 296) "how to set up a large-scale terror regime." "Hitler remained to the end a socialist" and in his bunker in 1945 voiced his regrets that "he had not exterminated the German nobility, that he had come to power 'too easily,' not unleashing a classical revolution, 'to destroy elites and classes,' that he had supported Franco in Spain instead of the Communists." Finally, he regretted his leniency, "his lack of the admirable ruthlessness Stalin had so consistently showed and which invited one's 'unreserved respect' for him" (Johnson 1983, 413). In sum, then, the twentieth century proved a difficult one for advocates of liberal values because of effective opposition from conservative opponents and then from radicals such as Stalin and Hitler.

Liberals versus Realists in the Academic Field of International Politics

The leader of liberal forces against their ideological antagonists in the early part of the twentieth century was Woodrow Wilson. Wilson can be seen as the founder of "idealism" in the field of international relations and, in a way, as the founder of the field itself. "President Wilson became the world's most influential statesmen in the aftermath of the First World War. His arguments dominated the new utopian discipline of International Relations" (Knutsen 1992, 196–97). Those utopian arguments emphasized the liberal faith in reason, public opinion, individual liberty, democracy, international law, and international organization. In the United States, the "dominant approach" among American scholars of international politics "was to embrace what was international and to condemn what was national, and to evaluate events of that day by reference to the extent to which they conformed to the standards established by international legal norms and the League of Nations" (Dougherty and Pfaltzgraff 1990, 6).

This utopianism or idealism received a devastating blow from events surrounding the onset of World War II and the predominant interpretation of those events after the war. One of the major lessons that was apparently learned by American theorists of international relations from the process leading to World War II was that regime type does not matter. In other words, from a realistic point of view (and ultimately the neorealistic perspective as well), a state is a state is a state, and for the purpose of understanding the foreign policies of states, or how they interact, one need not and/or should not focus on what type of political regimes the states have.

The denunciation of the idea that democracy is a force for peace that is a fundamental aspect of modern realism in international political thought was launched even before World War II, in *Twenty Years' Crisis* by E. H. Carr. Carr (1939, 143) acknowledges that "the victory of the democratic countries in 1918 created an almost universal opinion that democracy was the best form of government." But one of the more effective, best-remembered passages in this book is a critique of "Wilsonians" and the tendency of "English-speaking peoples," that is, the United States and Great Britain, to identify what is in their own national interest with "universal right." Carr (1939, 79–83) explains that "theories of international morality are . . . the product of dominant nations or groups of nations. For the past hundred years, and more especially since 1918, the English speaking peoples have formed the dominant group in the world; and current theories of international morality have been designed to perpetuate their supremacy."

Carr (1939, 79) here justifiably emphasizes the validity of the point that "theories of social morality are always the product of a dominant group which identifies itself with the community as a whole." But he also exemplifies, and makes his own contribution to, the discrediting of the Wilsonian idea that democracy is a key to peace that became an important feature of realism as it emerged from World War II.

The antidemocratic bent of realism was solidified by the founder of modern realism. In the first edition of *Politics among Nations,* Hans Morgenthau (1948, 187) explained that "when in the course of the nineteenth century democratic selection and responsibility of government officials replaced government by aristocracy, the structure of international society, and with it, of international morality, underwent a fundamental change." A democrat or a Kantian might anticipate that this assertion is a prelude to the development of a thesis to the effect that democratically elected leaders face effective ethical constraints with which aristocratic leaders, whose positions of power are theirs by birthright, are not forced to deal. But Morgenthau's argument is to the contrary. "Where responsibility for government is widely distributed among a great number of individuals with different conceptions as to what is morally required in international affairs" (i.e., in democratic regimes), Morgenthau (1948, 189) asserts, "international morality as an effective system of restraints upon international policy becomes impossible." In short, in Morgenthau's view, "the democratic selection and responsibility of government officials destroyed international morality as an effective system of restraints."

But probably the most effective and influential realistic argument against the idea that democracy is a pacifying factor of importance appeared in *Man, the State and War* by Kenneth Waltz, appearing in 1954. An essential thesis of that still-influential book is that the "second image, the idea that defects in states cause wars among them" (Waltz 1954, 83) is fundamentally flawed. In a chapter that still bears close scrutiny by liberals or neoliberals in danger of overconfidence, Waltz (1954, 101) points out that in 1791 Thomas Paine asserted with respect to the French Revolution that "Monarchical sovereignty, the enemy of mankind, the source of misery, is abolished. . . . Were this the case throughout Europe . . . the cause of war would be taken away." Waltz (1954, 118) traces the evolution of this argument to Woodrow Wilson, who, in his message to Congress asking for a declaration of war against Germany, stated that "a steadfast concert for peace . . . can never be maintained except by a partnership of democratic nations." The basic problem with all these arguments of the second image type, according to Waltz, is that they assume that the conflicting units can be "perfected," though perfection is impossible for states as well as men. Waltz concludes: "A world full of democracies would be forever at peace, but autocratic governments are warlike. . . . *Capitalist* democracies actively promote war, *socialist* democracies are peaceful. Each of these formulations has claimed numerous adherents, and each adherent has in turn been called to task by critics and by history" (Waltz 1954, 121).

Waltz goes on to point out that the hopes that *socialism* would bring peace to humankind were dashed by divisions and conflicts among socialist states, such as Tito's split with Stalin. In criticism of the idea that democracy has important pacifying potential, he points out not divisions and conflicts among democratic states but aggressive American policies with respect to Mexico, Spain, and the Philippines and argues that "the optimism of nineteenth century liberals was confounded by the First and Second World Wars" (Waltz 1954, 121). Although the inconsistency of disparaging the peace-producing potential of socialist states by pointing to conflicts among them—while expressing equally skeptical opinions about the pacifying potential of democratic states because of their conflict proneness vis-à-vis autocratic states—is apparent to contemporary readers familiar with the thesis about peace among democratic states, Waltz is nevertheless correct in his assessment that the liberal faith in democracy as a key to peace was severely damaged by the First and Second World Wars. World War I was fought, according to the leader of what became the most powerful state in the victorious coalition, to make the world safe for democracy. It failed to do that, and its failure became obvious quite rapidly. Perhaps even more important, Adolf Hitler was elected democratically. That turn of events can be interpreted, and rather clearly has been historically, as devastating to the idea that democracy is a guarantor of peace.

The democratic election of Hitler is in fact an important reminder of the limits of democracy as a force for peace (as well as of the importance of the Hegelian dimension of the democratic peace proposition). But that example is also arguably a shaky foundation for the rejection of the pacifying potential of democracy (and of other liberal principles) that the process leading to World War II, and the war itself, seems to have produced among theorists of international relations and more broadly. Hitler's rise to power might have, as logically, been utilized as an example in support of the idea that autocracy, especially in major powers, is dangerous and destabilizing. Instead, for reasons I will not guess at here, the historical lessons learned by international relations theorists about the relationship between regime type and international conflict focused more intently on the democratic process that brought Hitler to power rather than the thoroughly antidemocratic regime he established and through which he carried out his foreign policies that were crucial to the onset of World War II.

The Emergence
of the Democratic Peace Proposition

After World War II, which autocratic regimes such as those in Germany, Japan, and Italy did so much to foment, one might have anticipated a priori that in reaction there would be in the academic world of international relations a theoretical thrust focusing on autocracy as a fundamental cause of war. But nothing of the sort occurred. Idealist critics of the emerging realist paradigm restricted themselves to arguments that ethical and legal norms were not irrelevant to international politics, that international organizations like the United Nations deserved support, and that conciliatory policies were at least a useful complement to the hard-line policies typically advocated by realists. The burgeoning conflict with the Soviet Union, coming so soon after the brutal struggle with Germany, Japan, and Italy did not constitute a nurturing environment for idealist or liberal ideas in the realm of international politics.

Early Quantitative Studies of the Impact of Democracy on Conflict

Nevertheless, the advent of the quantitative approach in the field of international politics did involve a smattering of attention to the idea that regimes of different types have systematically different kinds of foreign policies. Much of this was inspired by James Rosenau's (1966) article on "Pre-Theories," which specified that size, wealth, and type of political system were the most fundamental distinctions among states for any attempt to understand the differences in their foreign policies. Even before that article appeared, though, Michael Haas (1965) reported that democratic countries have less conflictful relationships than nondemocratic countries. In roughly the same time period, Maurice East and Philip Gregg (1967), Steven Salmore and Charles Hermann (1969), Dina Zinnes and Jonathan Wilkenfeld (1971), and Maurice East and Charles Hermann (1974) all reported strikingly similar findings, i.e., that democratic states have less conflict-ridden foreign policies than do nondemocratic states. In 1976, Michael Sullivan (1976, 136), in a thorough integrated review of quantitative research in international politics up to that point, concluded that "evidence . . . does exist [that] lends credence to the argument of democratic theorists who see 'good' flowing from open, democratic systems. For the most part, open systems engage in less overall conflict . . . than do closed systems, both in the long and short run."

There are several reasons that this rather substantial body of research on the impact of regime type on international conflict has been largely ignored in the recent literature on the democratic peace proposition. First, the articles and chapters in question were published some twenty years ago. Second, they focused on conflict proneness rather than war proneness. (In other words, they focused almost exclusively on violence and conflict below the level of international war.) But perhaps the most important reason is that the research from this era did not focus on the relationship *between* democratic states, and the findings did not therefore conform to the generally accepted notion in the current literature that democratic states are as conflict prone as other kinds of states.

There was an intriguing exception to this focus on national level analyses that was apparently originally published in 1964 and then republished in 1972 by Dean Babst. (At the time Babst was an associate research scientist at the New York State Narcotic Addiction Control Commission. The note at the end of the article in *Industrial Research* asserts that "he has been studying war and peace for several decades and has had several articles published in the field of peace research.") Despite the fact that the article was published in a source far removed from mainstream peace research or international politics outlets and despite its brevity, this article is in its way rather surprisingly sophisticated. First, Babst's source of data on international war was Quincy Wright's *A Study of War* (1942). Second, Babst develops a rather detailed operational definition of "democracy" based on four indicators: "legislative and national finances controlled by a legislature . . . chosen by majority vote from at least two opposing choices," "administrative control of the government by an executive chosen by majority vote," "a secret ballot and . . . freedom of the press," and "the country must have been independent" (Babst 1972, 55). Having developed these reasonably operational criteria for international wars and democracy, he concludes that "no wars have been fought between independent nations with elective governments between 1789 to 1941" (55). He discusses such "close calls" as the War of 1812, the American Civil War, and the Boer War. He even calculates the statistical probability that no democratic governments would end up opposing each other in World War I (with thirty-three independent participants), and World War II (with fifty-two independent participants). Finally, he closes with due attention to the Hegelian portion of the democratic peace proposition having to do with the global trend toward "elective governments."[6] Babst's effort is most modest, perhaps, on the theoretical dimension. The only explanation he offers for the absence of war between elective governments is contained in one brief phrase to the effect that "the general public does not want war, if it can choose" (55).

Babst's article was probably rescued from obscurity by Melvin Small and J. David Singer in "The War-Proneness of Democratic Regimes, 1816–1965" (1976),[7] even though the clear purpose of Small and Singer was to discredit Babst's conclusion. They report that between 1816 and 1965, international wars involving democracies lasted about as long and involved about as many battle deaths as wars that involved only undemocratic states.[8] They acknowledge that, with a couple of debatable exceptions (which will be discussed in chapter 3), there have been no wars between democratic states. But they conclude that this was probably owing to the fact that "war is most likely between neighbors" and the fact that "bourgeois democracies do not border upon one another very frequently" (Small and Singer 1976, 64).

However, the argument (and possibly not a well-supported argument: see note 8) that wars involving democratic states have not been significantly different, with respect to their length and number of battle deaths, from wars involving only autocratic states is at best only tangentially relevant to an evaluation of the hypothesis regarding the rates at which different types of political regimes become involved in war (the national level proposition) or the rate at which they become involved in wars against each other (the dyadic level notion). Small and Singer were aware of at least some of these problems (see p. 61 of their work). Even if democratic states had been, over the time period analyzed, 99 percent less likely to become involved in wars than autocratic states and 100 percent less likely to become involved in wars with each other, the wars in which they did become involved might still have been equivalent in length and severity to those involving only autocratic states. In addition, Small and Singer conclude that democracies do not border upon one another very frequently from a rather cursory review of a partial list of bordering democratic states. They do not estimate what proportion of democratic pairs of states border on each other compared to the analogous portion of undemocratic states. They could not; data on contiguity among states of the international system had not yet been generated. But they assert that "as we can see from this listing, the incidence of geographic contiguity between democratic states is quite small" (Small and Singer 1976, 67), even though in fact it is not possible to see anything of the sort because no basis of comparison is provided.

In fact, Nils Petter Gleditsch (1993, 21) demonstrates quite persuasively that for most of the time period from 1816 to 1986, "the average distance between democracies was well *below* the system distance and for the period after World War II the two distances are roughly the same." So, according to Gleditsch, "the idea that democracies tend to be particularly far apart can be dismissed out of hand." Gleditsch is dealing with the geographic relationship between pairs of states in terms of the distance between the capitals, which is not precisely the notion that Small and Singer (1976) had in mind when they speculated about the extent to which democratic states are contiguous. But utilizing a measure of proximity or contiguity from the Correlates of War project, which more closely approximates the concept that Small and Singer (1976) address, Bremer (1992, 1993) has demonstrated quite convincingly that the absence of war between democratic states cannot be accounted for by a lack of contiguity among them. In other words, even when contiguity is controlled for, the relationship between regime type and the probability of international wars between pairs of states that Bremer reports persists.

Rummel's *Understanding Conflict and War*

According to Gleditsch (1992, 371), "so persuasive was [Small and Singer's] article that for a long while" no one pursued the idea presented by Babst. Actually, the notion of peaceful relationships between democratic states was discussed in some detail (obviously independently of Babst) in Peter Wallensteen's *Structure and War* (1973), and R. J. Rummel was hard at work producing five volumes of *Understanding Conflict and War,* a major theme of which was the pacifistic potential of democracy, and the specific proposition, in volume 4 (published in 1979) that "a necessary condition of violence between two states is that at least one be totalitarian or authoritarian" (278).

In volume 1, Rummel develops the philosophical, epistemological, even metaphysical underpinnings of his theory of international conflict, called "intentional humanism." In volume 2, he develops the concept of the conflict helix applicable in his view to conflict ranging from that between two persons to international war. In volume 3, he compares his theory of conflict to all others and claims that his is superior to or subsumes all others. In volume 4, he addresses international relations in particular. He develops his theory explicitly, presenting thirty-three specific, interrelated hypotheses. The two of greatest interest in the current context are "Freedom inhibits violence" and "Libertarian systems mutually preclude violence." In this volume, Rummel also summarizes the findings of previous research regarding each of his thirty-three hypotheses. Finally, in volume 5, Rummel derives the major policy prescription from his multivolume effort, which is "promote freedom" (Ray 1982b).

Because the major thesis of these five volumes involves the pacifying potential of democracy (or more specifically, "libertarianism") and because there has recently been so much attention paid to the democratic peace proposition, one might reasonably infer that *Understanding Conflict and War* is one of the major influences and inspirations of the literature on that proposition. Such is not the case. In his recent essay on that literature, for example, Gleditsch explains that the proposition regarding the absence of wars between democracies was ignored for years because it "seemed to be based . . . on rather raw empiricism," and he cites Rummel as an example of such "raw empiricism." Obviously, he did not have in mind the three volumes of theoretical development building up to the fourth volume of *Understanding Conflict and War,* in which the proposition regarding the lack of violence between "libertarian" states is presented. Nor did Randall Schweller (1992, 235) have that elaborate theoretical development in mind when he asserts that "the data-driven nature of much of the literature may explain the lack of consensus among the studies of regime type and war." (He does not cite *Understanding Conflict and War.*) James Dougherty and Robert Pfaltzgraff in *Contending Theories of International Relations* (1990) (the subtitle of which is *A Comprehensive Survey*) do in fact present one of the most comprehensive surveys of the North American literature on international relations in existence. They point out "Kenneth Waltz states . . . a broadly shared view when he asserts that democratic states are more peaceful than nondemocratic ones" (336).[9] They go on to observe that "it is now axiomatic that no conflict between or among states escalates to war unless at least one is an authoritarian or totalitarian state." But the only sources they cite in support of that statement are three pieces on arms races by Paul Diehl. They never cite *Understanding Conflict and War* on this or any other point. T. Clifton Morgan (1993) reviews quite comprehensively proposed theoretical explanations of the lack of war between democratic states; he does not cite or discuss *Understanding Conflict and War.* Rummel (1989, 234) himself has admitted, "I was not prepared . . . for [*Understanding Conflict and War*] being so widely ignored."

Why it has been so widely ignored is a sociology of knowledge question.

Perhaps Rummel's arguments were simply too long and complex to catch on. Perhaps so few people were willing to pay for five volumes that his arguments never got the attention they arguably deserved. Or, as I have speculated elsewhere (Ray 1995a), perhaps the emergence of the key volume 4 at the time that the Cold War was being reborn (in 1979), combined with Rummel's reputation as, shall we say, outside the ideological mainstream of the profession, prevented his thesis from being seriously considered. In any case, that Rummel's magnum opus has been largely ignored is quite clear, with results for the shape of the current debate regarding the democratic peace proposition that I will allude to below.

But what were Rummel's ideas, as developed in *Understanding Conflict and War,* about the pacifying potential of democracy, or "libertarianism." First, he does stress the importance of *economic* institutional arrangements within a society and the corrupting influence of power on autocratic leaders in a way that is not often reflected in other sources on the democratic peace proposition. When he specifically addresses the extent to which democratic or libertarian states are more peaceful than autocratic states, both in general, and in their relationships with each other, he focuses intently on the role of public opinion and interest groups on foreign policy. For example, with regard to the proposition that "freedom inhibits violence," he argues that "libertarian states have natural inhibitions on involvement in violence: the responsiveness of elected leaders to domestic interest groups or public opinion, which ordinarily will oppose violence, tax increases and conscription." He goes on to say that "domestic interests set limits and libertarian leaders lack the power or the will to take violent initiatives or make moves escalating violence, unlike their authoritarian or totalitarian counterparts" (Rummel 1979, 292). The contrast with the role of public opinion in autocratic states plays a key role in Rummel's argument. For example, with respect to another of his thirty-three basic propositions, "Political distance most affects totalitarian states," he argues that "totalitarian states are coercively unified by an enforced definition of the true and just by an ideology. . . . Competition with this formula is not permitted, critical assessments are not allowed" (294).

With respect to his key proposition that "libertarian systems mutually preclude violence," he first argues, again, that "totalitarian and authoritarian states are the source of military violence. Power is centralized and in the hands of a small group or a leader. Control over the communications media can be used to direct and intensify public opinion against another state: domestic interest groups can be controlled: and dissidents in the elite can be jailed" (277–78).

In contrast, according to Rummel, "in open systems . . . initiating a war or military action is usually precluded by the restraint of public opinion and opposition of interest groups." He adds that "between libertarian states there is a fundamental sympathy of their peoples toward each other's system, a compatibility of basic values, an existence of cross-pressures and overlapping groups and organizations, and a diffusion of power and interests" (278).

There is in Rummel's argument in *Understanding Conflict and War* a strong Kantian stress on the role of pacifistic public opinion and interest groups in making democratic (or libertarian) states peaceful, and it is vulnerable to all the criticisms cited earlier in this chapter on Kant's argument on this point.[10] There are elements of both the structural and the cultural theses regarding the democratic peace proposition we will discuss below. Public opinion and the potential opposition of specific groups in Rummel's reasoning are *restraints* making it less likely that democratic states will go to war, both in general and against each other, in a manner congruent with the discussion of restraints, or constraints in structural arguments regarding the democratic peace. His emphasis on the sympathy between peoples in democratic systems and the compatibility of their basic values resonates with later arguments that are categorized as the cultural explanation of the democratic peace.

Contemporary Theory and Evidence Regarding the Democratic Peace Proposition

Another reason that Rummel's *Understanding Conflict and War* has received so little attention in recent literature on the democratic peace is that it has been perceived as superseded, or at least conveniently summarized in a couple of later articles in the *Journal of Conflict Resolution,* which I will, somewhat arbitrarily to be sure, treat as the starting point of the most recent literature on the democratic peace proposition.[11] In the first article, "Libertarianism and International Violence" (1983), Rummel focuses on three hypotheses: (1) libertarian states will not be violent toward each other, (2) the more libertarian two states, the less their mutual violence, and (3) the more libertarian a state, the less its violence. The first hypothesis, regarding the absence of violence and war between libertarian states, has been widely accepted. The second, regarding the relationship between the degree of libertarianism exhibited by two states and the degree of violence between them, has been mostly ignored. The final hypothesis, regarding the assertion that the more libertarian a state is, the less violence it will be involved in, has been discredited in the eyes of what seems almost unanimous opinion.

For his data analyses, Rummel (1983) uses Freedom House data to place states on a scale from "politically free" to "politically nonfree." He measures conflict on a scale operationalized in terms of events data; it runs from accusations and denunciations in the category of negative communications to war and the number killed in the category of military violence.

Rummel generates scores on "libertarianism" and conflict for all pairs of independent states from 1976 to 1980. He finds no cases of violence between libertarian states, and this finding has not really been challenged, although later studies such as that by Maoz and Russett, 1992, do report cases of "use of force" between democratic states. (This difference occurs primarily because of differences in the operationalizations of "libertarianism" and "democracy" in the two pieces.) His findings here do share a problem with later studies that I will discuss in more detail below. Rummel calculates whether or not the lack of violence between democratic or libertarian dyads is statistically significant. His units of analysis are dyad-years. Those dyad-years obviously do not constitute independent events, or cases. Yet the N, or the total number of cases Rummel uses to calculate the significance tests is 62,040, or the number of dyad-years observed.

In order to test his hypothesis that greater libertarianism will correlate negatively with amounts of foreign violence on both the national and the dyadic level of analysis, Rummel (1983) analyzes the relationship between his indices of libertarianism and foreign violence in contingency tables. He finds in both cases that libertarianism is "significantly" correlated in a negative direction with the *degree* of foreign violence experienced by states or pairs of states from 1976 to 1980. (I emphasize *degrees* of foreign violence for reasons that will soon become apparent.) His analysis of dyad-years again is based on observations that are not independent, even though the significance tests on which he relies were based on the assumption that the observations are independent.

This article prompted two papers, by Steve Chan (1984) and Erich Weede (1984), respectively, which successfully challenged Rummel's proposition that libertarianism correlates negatively with *degrees* of foreign violence, even though neither of them directly tested that idea. Chan analyzes the relationship between regime type and the dichotomous variable of war involvement. Overall, he finds that "the unfree [dyad] years have had less then their expected share of wars. In other words, contrary to the view that freedom discourages war, the evidence points in the direction that it is associated with more war" (Chan 1984, 632). Weede (1984) analyzes the relationship between regime type and international conflict in the years from 1960 to 1980. Like Chan, Weede focuses only on war involvement, not *degrees* of violence experienced by states. His main conclusion is that democratic states were about as frequently involved in war as other states were in the 1960s and the 1970s.

The articles by Chan and Weede, along with some more recent findings, constitute an important part of the core of findings leading to the continually repeated assertion that while democratic states do not fight wars against each other, they are as war prone and conflict prone as autocratic states. Jack Levy (1988, 661–62), for example, in the same piece in which he makes the oft-quoted observation that "the absence of war between democracies comes as close as anything we have to an empirical law in international relations," also asserts that "the evidence is conclusive that democratic states have been involved, proportionately, in as many wars as non-democratic states." Nils Petter Gleditsch (1992, 369–70) asserts that there is "now a near-consensus" that there is little difference in the amount of war participation between democracies and non-democracies (Rummel being the major dissenter here). Harvey Starr (1992, 43) declares in virtually identical terms that "research on this question has been nearly unanimous in finding that democracies are as war prone as nondemocratic states. Only Rummel has dissented from this result." Bruce Bueno de Mesquita and David Lalman (1992, 148) join the chorus of those who claim that "democracies are no less likely to participate in interstate wars . . . than are other states." Finally, Maoz and Russett (1993, 624) assert most broadly and emphatically that "there is something in the internal makeup of democratic states that prevents them from fighting one another *despite the fact that they are not less conflict prone than nondemocracies*" (emphasis in original).[12]

The casual, or even the careful, reader might quite understandably conclude that Rummel is a voice in the wilderness calling out against the virtually unanimous opinion and overwhelming evidence that democracies are not less war prone or conflict prone than nondemocratic states, even though they do not fight wars against each other. It is surprising (or perhaps not really surprising, since the work has been so widely ignored) to find that Rummel (1979, 292) himself asserts explicitly in the fourth volume of *Understanding Conflict and War* that "libertarian states are often involved in . . . violence against the initiatives of nonlibertarian states. Therefore, in general, I do not expect that there will be a correlation between libertarianism and the *frequency* [emphasis added] of involvement in war or violence." Recall that it is exactly the *frequency* of involvement that both Chan (1984) and Weede (1984) analyzed, even though they both realized and acknowledged that Rummel's national level hypothesis regarding the relationship between regime type and conflict focused on the impact of libertarianism on *degrees* or *severity* of violence, not frequency of war involvement.

Ironically, there is quite a bit of evidence that both Rummel and his critics may be wrong on this point. Some evidence suggests that democratic states are less prone to violence, escalation, and war than undemocratic states in general, not just in their relationships with each other and not just in the *degrees* of violence in which they become involved. For example, Daniel Geller (1985) analyzes a sample of thirty-six nations designed to be representative of all nations in the world. The book focuses to a large extent on the idea that "regime structure is a principal factor in the explanation of foreign policy behavior." He also argues that "regimes whose actions must satisfy a large and varied number of interests are presumably more constrained than regimes which must satisfy only a few" and that "regimes which stand for election relatively frequently are more constrained than regimes whose authoritative positions are fixed for relatively long intervals" (Geller 1985, 63). (In short, his arguments are very similar to those made on behalf of the structural version of the democratic peace proposition that we will discuss in more detail below.) And one of the principal findings of this careful study is that "generally, foreign conflict varied negatively with regime constraint, whereas foreign cooperation revealed a positive association to constraint" (181). That relationship between conflict and regime characteristics tends to disappear when "strain," or domestic conflict, is controlled for. But this might happen because (as with Maoz and Russett, 1992, which we will discuss below), the amount of instability in a regime intervenes in the relationship between regime type and foreign conflict. If this is the case, then controlling for instability would eliminate the relationship between regime characteristics and foreign conflict, without suggesting that those characteristics do not have an important impact on foreign conflict.

Interestingly, additional evidence that democracies are less conflict prone in general, and not just in their relationships with each other, is presented by Zeev Maoz and Nasrin Abdolali (1989), whose declaration that "nation-level analyses reveal that . . . politically free . . . polities are neither more conflict prone nor less conflict prone than nonfree polities" constitutes the core of the research findings, along with those of Small and Singer (1976), Chan (1984), and Weede (1984), upon which the consensus that democratic states and autocratic states are no different in their war proneness rests. But Maoz and Abdolali acknowledge that there are exceptions to this general finding. For example, they report that "the proportion of disputes in which [democracies] participate that escalate to war is significantly lower than that of nondemocratic polities" (1989, 18). This finding covering the years from 1816 to 1976 is not dependent upon the kinds of states with which democracies become involved in those disputes.[13]

T. Clifton Morgan and Valerie Schwebach analyze militarized interstate disputes from 1816 to 1976 and focus on differentiating between those disputes that end in war and those that do not. They report that "domestic political structures can serve to create a constraining influence on the belligerent impulses of state leaders." They *also* emphasize that the effect of those structures "is felt through a reduction in the probability that the state will opt for war and *does not appear to depend on the domestic structure of the opponent*" (Morgan and Schwebach 1992, 318). In other words, they specifically analyze the impact of the interaction term focusing on the *combination* of regimes involved in disputes, and they find that that term has no effect over and above the additive impact of each regime involved in a dispute.

Similarly, Bueno de Mesquita and Lalman (1992, 158) analyze a set of European militarized interstate disputes (compared to interactions involving randomly associated European states) and hypothesize that disputes involving democracies will be more likely to end up in negotiations or preserving the status quo rather than in the use of force. They find that the regime type of both states *independently* increases the likelihood of force being avoided. In other words, negotiations, or preservation of the status quo are more likely if either the initiator *or* the target is democratic; it is not necessary that they *both* be democratic.

Kevin Wang, Noh Soon Chang, and James Ray (1992) focus on determinants of the probability that targets in militarized interstate disputes from 1816 to 1976 will use force. The basic finding is that democratic targets are less likely to use force than nondemocratic targets. *And* this is true regardless of the initiator's regime type. "In other words," Wang et al. point out, "we cannot state that the effect of the target's level of democracy or its likelihood of escalation varies according to the initiator's level of democracy" (14).

Finally, most comprehensively, and pertinently, Stuart Bremer (1992) focuses on all pairs of states in the international system each year from 1816 to 1965 in an attempt to find which types of dyads are most likely to produce an international war. He reports that "war onset in undemocratic dyads is about 4 times as likely as between mixed (i.e., one democratic, one undemocratic) pairs of states." Because of this finding, he concludes that "it appears that the contention of some that both states must be democratic before the war-inhibiting effect of democracy is felt is unsupported." On the contrary, Bremer asserts, "the presence of *a* democracy in a dyad significantly reduces its war propensity" (329).[14]

A review of all these results, plus all the results from the 1960s and 1970s discussed earlier, suggests that the nearly unanimous consensus in the literature on the democratic peace proposition that democracies, though unlikely to fight each other, are in general as conflict and war prone as undemocratic states rests on rather shaky empirical ground. Though the focus of this book is on the impact of joint democracy, the impact of having *one* democracy involved in a dispute or conflict is of more than marginal interest for two reasons. One has to do with the implication of the recent research on the democratic peace proposition for the future of international politics. Assume for the sake of the discussion of this point that within the near future all the major powers and the clear majority of all states in the world become democratic. In that case, according to the democratic peace proposition, the world will be a more peaceful place, regardless of whether democratic countries in general are more peaceful, because there will be an increasing proportion of pairs of states in the system that are jointly democratic.

But then assume that the current "third wave" of democratization referred to by Samuel Huntington (1991) is reversed, that Russia emerges as an autocratic state (probably enthusiastically opposed to liberal values), that China remains autocratic, and that, say, India becomes autocratic and increasingly powerful. Then the conflict and war proneness of "mixed dyads," one state democratic and the other not, will become a pressing issue. If mixed dyads are less war prone than jointly autocratic dyads, or even if they are no more war prone than jointly autocratic dyads, then the hypothetical setback for democracy under consideration here would not have such disastrous implications for international stability. But if mixed dyads are not just *as* war prone as jointly autocratic pairs of states (as would be implied by the oft-reported assertion that democratic states in general are just as war prone as autocratic states) but are actually more war prone, then the setback for democracy would have seriously destabilizing implications, which would call for increased attention in scholarly as well as policymaking circles on relationships between democratic and autocratic states.

Theoretically, the controversy regarding whether or not democracies in general are as war prone as autocracies, even though democracies are more peaceful in their relationships with each other, is of interest because it is so often cited as an anomaly that any theoretical explanation of peace *between* democracies must account for. Morgan and Schwebach (1992, 306), Bueno de Mesquita and Lalman (1992, 146), and Maoz and Russett (1993, 624) all assert that their theoretical approach to the democratic peace proposition is based on the (possibly erroneous, it appears) assumption, that though democratic states do not fight wars against each other, they are in general as war prone as autocratic states. Whether or not their theoretical arguments would be changed if that assumption were dropped in light of the evidence that it is unwarranted is a question of special interest because one theoretical approach, that is, Rummel's, is based on the opposite assumption, or actually hypothesis, that democratic states are less conflict prone, period, not just in their relationships with each other. In other words, if evidence continues to accumulate (as I would argue it has accumulated up to this point) that democracies are less conflict or war prone in *general,* as well as in their relationships with each other, general theoretical approaches that accommodate or generate hypotheses that democracy correlates with peace on both the monadic and dyadic levels of analysis would be deserving of more confidence.

The Most Recent Evidence on the Democratic Peace Proposition

The body of the most recent empirical evidence supporting the democratic peace proposition consists to an important extent of results reported by Zeev Maoz and Nasrin Abdolali (1989), who were the first to analyze systematically and statistically all pairs of states for each year from 1816 to 1976 with that proposition in mind. Their evidence regarding the democratic peace proposition consists of two basic findings. The evidence most pertinent to the validity of the democratic peace proposition focuses on the 332 pairs of states that were involved in wars against each other during that time period. Twenty percent of the initiators in those war dyads were democratic, and 23 percent of the targets in those dyads were also democratic. If democratic initiators were as likely to attack democratic targets as initiating states were to attack target states in general, then there would have been fifteen wars between democratic states (or, at least, fifteen democratic states fighting against each other in international wars, some of which might have been multilateral). In proportional terms, this means that by chance alone, 5 percent of the war dyads should have been democratic, but in fact 0 percent were. This difference is "significant," according to Maoz and Abdolali.

But Maoz and Abdolali (1989, 24) also acknowledge that "to provide a more powerful test of the dyadic hypothesis, we need to know something about whether the distribution of conflict dyads over regime types is different from what might be expected given the distribution of regime types in the population of states." In other words, the fact that 0 percent of the pairs of states in the international system from 1816 to 1976 that fought wars against each other were democratic is impressive only if the proportion of pairs of states in the system that were democratic was sufficiently high during that time period to make it likely, all else being equal, that they would fight wars against each other. Maoz and Abdolali calculate first the number of pairs of states per year that can be observed from 1816 to 1976 and come up with a total N of 271,904. Of all those dyad-years, 24,489, or 9 percent, were jointly democratic. If democratic pairs of states in a given year were as likely to fight an interstate war against each other as all pairs of states, .12 percent, or 29.8 of those jointly democratic dyad-years would have produced an international war. But none of them did, and Maoz and Abdolali again report this finding as statistically "significant."

There are reasons to debate this report. First, Maoz and Abdolali do not analyze a sample of dyad-years from which they are trying to generalize about a population. Instead, they analyze the available universe of dyad-years from 1816 to 1976. One might question whether they should utilize a significance test at all. They need to make no sample-based inferences about a population. They know that 0 percent of the jointly democratic dyad-years they observed were involved in an international war, whereas .1 percent of the other dyad-years were so involved.

This reader at least does not find it bothersome that Maoz and Abdolali (1989), as well as many others, have utilized significance tests even though they are analyzing the population of social entities on which they focus. Some time ago, Robert Winch and Donald Campbell (1969, 140) asked: "Is it legitimate to apply a test of significance where the researcher's data exploit the specified universe?" Their answer to the question was "If the problem is stated in the conventional way, the answer is clearly 'no.' But we elect to phrase the question differently. If we assume the [population] to be homogenous, what is the probability that dividing the population into two subsets on the basis of a variable of classification that makes no real difference would give a difference between subsample means as great as that observed? With this reasoning, there is every justification to run a test of significance."

If we apply that reasoning to the results reported by Maoz and Abdolali (1989), we can see that they have divided their population of observations into jointly democratic and not jointly democratic dyad-years. The question addressed by their test of significance might be put this way: What if, instead of dividing the population of dyad-years into subsamples according to whether or not they were jointly democratic, we divided those dyad-years into subsamples according to some kind of random process (or, in the words of Winch and Campbell, according to "a variable of classification that makes no difference")? What if, for example, we picked out of our population of 271,904 dyad-years a sample of 24,489 dyad-years randomly instead of by a process that identifies those dyad-years as jointly democratic? What is the probability that the randomly selected subsample would have 0 percent of dyad-years with international war occurring? A significance test will reveal that if Maoz and Abdolali had selected at random 24,489 marbles out of a jar of 271,904 marbles, .1 percent of which were black (representing dyad-years involved in an international war), the chances that *none* of the marbles would be black would be *very* small.

But so, too, is the difference between the 0 percent of the jointly democratic subsample of dyad-years that experienced a war and the .1 percent of the not jointly democratic dyad-years that experienced a war. Is it possible or likely that such a small absolute percentage difference can have any real *substantive* significance?

This objection, too, can be effectively dealt with. As Bueno de Mesquita (1984, 354) has pointed out, the proportion of smokers who get lung cancer is .00156, whereas the proportion of nonsmokers who get lung cancer is .000078. That, too, is an absolute difference of about .1 percent. Should we classify that difference as trivial or "insignificant" because it is so small? I think not, and I am likewise disinclined to write off the difference between the proportion of jointly democratic dyad-years that were involved in an international war, and the proportion of pairs of states in general that experienced an international war, as insignificant or uninteresting just because it is very small in absolute terms.

What makes one wonder about the substantive significance of the findings reported by Maoz and Abdolali (1989) and, as we shall see, essentially similar findings reported by several others, is the lack of independence in the observations they analyze, and therefore a directly related question about just how many *cases* they analyze. Maoz and Abdolali report their results as if they were based on 332 cases, independently observed, of wars between pairs of states. But in fact there were not 332 interstate wars between 1816 and 1976. They come up with the N of 332 by treating pairs of states involved in multilateral wars as separate (and, formally speaking, independent) observations. Furthermore, the observations of Britain and France, Britain and the U.S., and Britain with every other state in the world at each year they observe, are not independent. They are not really all different cases; they all involve Great Britain. Even less independent are the observations of Great Britain and the United States in 1816 and the succeeding observations of Great Britain and the United States in 1817, 1818, and so on for every year up to 1976, as well as analogous yearly observations of every other pair of states observed by Maoz and Abdolali. The nominal N, or number of cases, on which Maoz and Abdolali base their calculations of statistical significance is 271,904. The "effective N," or the number of cases to which their highly interdependent observations are equivalent, is arguably quite a bit lower, to an extent that is difficult or impossible to calculate precisely. Therefore, I would argue, it is impossible to specify exactly how unlikely it was that no pairs of democratic states would fight an interstate war against each other from 1816 to 1976.

A follow-up analysis by Zeev Maoz and Bruce Russett (1992) focuses only on the years from 1946 to 1986. The operational definition of "democracy" used here is more stringent, thus restricting the number of dyad-years and the number of conflicts involving democracies available for analysis and comparison. The results of greatest relevance to the democratic peace proposition as it applies to international war (as opposed to lower levels of international conflict) are as follows: There are a total of 264,819 dyad-years observed from 1946 to 1986, 3,878 of which were jointly democratic. Zero percent of the jointly democratic dyad-years experienced an interstate war, while 32/246,943, or .01 percent, of the not jointly democratic dyad-years were marked by an interstate war.

That one-hundredth of one percent difference can be augmented marginally by analyzing not all dyad-years but "politically relevant" dyad-years, which Maoz and Russett (1992, 249) define as dyads that are contiguous (directly, or indirectly via colonial or imperial territories) or that contain at least one major power. They observe 29,081 such politically relevant dyad-years from 1946 to 1986, 3,8778 of which were jointly democratic.[15] Zero percent of the jointly democratic, politically relevant dyad-years experienced an interstate war, whereas 32/25,203 or (the seemingly ubiquitous) .1 percent of the *not* jointly politically relevant dyad-years produced an international war in the years from 1946 to 1986.

This difference is statistically significant, if one assumes that it is based on (independent) observations of 29,081 "cases." But the number of cases observed and certainly the independence of the observations are both highly debatable. In defense of their findings, which are an important part of the empirical edifice in favor of the democratic peace proposition, it ought to be noted that in many of their analyses, Maoz and Russett focus on conflict escalation for pairs of states rather than simply whether or not the dispute in question ended in war. And the fact that the patterns in support of their hypotheses hold for the various steps up and down the escalation ladder, as it were, for a relatively large number of disputes does strengthen their case (as well as that for the democratic peace proposition). Nevertheless, doubts about the substantive significance of their findings might be reinforced by the fact that the number of wars involving jointly democratic dyads expected, statistically, just by chance (given the rate of wars among the general population of dyad-years) is 4.3. (See Maoz and Russett 1992, 255, table 3.) In other words, if there had been no democratic states in the world from 1946 to 1986, or if democracy had no pacifying impact, the data provided by Maoz and Russett suggest that there would have been four more international wars than actually occurred during the time. Perhaps that number is not so small as to seem totally insignificant substantively, but it must seem less significant if we remember that we are not talking here about four international wars, but four (possibly quite interdependent) observations of jointly democratic dyad-years involved in an interstate war, all of which might have occurred, for example, in the same multilateral interstate war.

Maoz and Russett (1992) go on to evaluate the possibility that the correlation between regime type and international conflict on the dyadic level of analysis is spurious, that is, brought about by other factors, such as contiguity, wealth, alliance ties, and political stability. They find, for example, "the notion that democracies do not fight one another *because* they are rich is flatly rejected" (Maoz and Russett 1992, 257). They reject each of the factors they analyze as possible confounding factors, except political stability. "Stable states are far less likely to fight one another than expected," they acknowledge, "regardless of their regime type." "This suggests that political stability," they conclude, "rather than or in addition to regime type, may account for the low rate of disputes between democracies."

But Maoz and Russett (1992, 248) also acknowledge that, as Ted Robert Gurr (1974) demonstrated, "democracies are far more stable than . . . autocracies." This suggests in turn that political stability is not a confounding factor, accounting for both regime type and conflict proneness, but a factor that intervenes between regime type and conflict proneness, a far different matter. In the second type of relationship, democracy can still be classified as a cause of peace, which exerts at least some of its impact indirectly because of its effect on stability. The second point to be made about the findings reported in this article is that the multivariate analyses focus not on interstate war but on "dispute involvement."

This potential obstacle to confidence about the relationship between regime type to war proneness is remedied somewhat in later work by Maoz and Russett, specifically in Russett with Maoz (1993), as well as Maoz and Russett (1993). In both of these pieces, they analyze the impact of regime type on conflict escalation, not just conflict involvement. They report that even with wealth, economic growth, alliance ties, contiguity, and capability ratios (between the initiators and the targets, a factor not included in the earlier analyses), joint democracy is still "significantly" related to a lower probability of conflict escalation.

As before, however, the significance tests are based on the assumption that the number of cases analyzed is equal to the number of dyad-years observed, an assumption that arguably exaggerates the amount of information actually available about the relationship between regime type and conflict proneness in such analyses. Furthermore, the index of the degree to which a pair of states is democratic utilized by Maoz and Russett in all their analyses of the democratic peace proposition is problematic. It consists of the sum of the democracy scores for each of a pair of states analyzed, divided by the difference of those scores plus one. This means that it reflects not only the extent to which a pair of states is democratic but also the extent to which they are *similar* in their degrees of democracy. A pair of states will attain a high score on this index *either* because they are relatively democratic *or* because they are relatively similar in regime type. This makes all of the results based on this index difficult to interpret (see Rummel 1994). I will assume for the sake of this discussion that this problem does not make the results reported by Maoz and Russett totally uninterpretable. I suspect that there is a positive correlation between the index used by Maoz and Russett and a simpler index that would reflect only the extent to which a pair of states is democratic, rather than the extent to which a pair of states is either democratic or similar in regime type and that the results obtained with the simpler index would be similar to a important extent to the results reported by Maoz and Russett.

The findings of Maoz and Russett are complemented nicely by two pieces authored by Stuart Bremer (1992, 1993). One of the ways that they are complementary to the efforts by Maoz and Russett is that they eliminate at least some of the interdependence in the observation of interstate wars. Maoz and Russett "include both disputes begun any time in [the observed] year and ongoing disputes that continued into this year from a previous one" (1993, 628). They also include all participants in multilateral wars. Bremer, in contrast, only includes dyad-years in which a war began, and he only includes the original belligerents, not "subsequent joiners" in interstate wars (Bremer 1992, 320). One of the reasons he can do this is that he focuses on a longer time period, from 1816 to 1965. He controls for variables not included by Maoz and Russett, such as "militarization" and the presence of a hegemon. Bremer (1992, 246) concludes the second of these articles by declaring: "Democracy has been subjected to some rather demanding tasks in this paper, and it has performed unusually well. We find that, even after controlling for a large number of factors . . . democracy's conflict reducing effect remains strong."

Bremer's analyses and findings are impressive, providing the single strongest source of support in the form of empirical evidence for confidence in the democratic peace proposition.[16] And yet it is fair to point out that even Bremer's findings are fragile in various respects. The rate of interstate war involvement for the jointly democratic dyads in his analyses is 0 percent.[17] The rate of war involvement for the dyad-years that were not jointly democratic is .05 percent. That is a small absolute difference. It is statistically significant, but the significance tests Bremer applies are, as usual, based on the assumption that the number of cases analyzed is equivalent to the 202,778 dyad-years observed. Many of those observations are highly interdependent in a way that makes one wonder how much confidence one should bestow upon the results of those significance tests. Clearly, there is considerably less "information" about the relationship between regime type and conflict proneness contained in 200,000 highly interdependent observations of dyad-years than there would be in 200,000 independent observations of different pairs of states in different years.

Nevertheless, what Bremer finds is that if democracy had no pacifying effect, or if no democratic states had existed from 1816 to 1975, there would have been nine more interstate wars in that time period than actually did occur. This is a significant number in substantive terms, but its small absolute size has at least two implications that will be considered in some detail in the pages that follow. The first implication is that it is important to determine how many of the alleged "exceptions" to the rule that democratic states never go to war against each other really are exceptions, because even if only a handful are, the difference between the number of wars between democratic states that might be expected by chance and the number that have actually occurred might disappear altogether. Second, it will be important to buttress evidence from aggregate data analyses regarding the democratic peace proposition with evidence based on detailed analyses of crucial cases because the difference in the incidence of wars between democratic states and the incidence of wars involving pairs of states that are not jointly democratic will always be microscopically small.

Findings reported by Erich Weede (1992) complement those reported by Maoz and Russett, as well as Bremer, in such a way that they deserve mention here. Weede analyzes the international system from 1962 to 1980. He adopts a strict definition of democracy that leads him to conclude that only twenty states qualify as democracies during that time. He eliminates a healthy portion of interdependence in observations found in the analyses reported by Maoz and Russett, as well as Bremer, because he does not utilize dyad-*years* as his unit of analysis. He first focuses on dyads, period, from 1962 to 1980. He finds that jointly democratic dyads were not "significantly" less likely to fight interstate wars from 1962 to 1980 than pairs of states including at least one undemocratic state, if he adopts the 1,000-battle-death threshold for interstate war established by the Correlates of War project (Small and Singer 1982) and if he focuses only on "politically relevant" dyads.[18] However, if he lowers the violence threshold to 100 deaths, he does find that the politically relevant jointly democratic pairs of states have been significantly less likely to fight "wars" against each other than other pairs of states.

This finding is of special interest because of the source of interdependence of observations Weede eliminates and because of the lower threshold of violence he utilizes. However, Weede's observations are not independent either. A rather large portion of the politically relevant jointly democratic dyads he includes in his analyses involve the United States, and all pairs of states involving the Soviet Union are also included. Accordingly, there must be some doubt whether the 11 percent of the not jointly democratic pairs of states from 1962 to 1980 that became involved in military conflict with each other is really "significantly" different from the 0 percent of doubly democratic dyads that became so involved.

As we have seen above, Immanuel Kant felt that international trade between democratic states would be a key factor bringing about peaceful relationships among them. It is a factor conspicuous by its absence from all of the empirical analyses we have discussed so far. Mark Brawley (1993) makes an interesting theoretical argument that "republics" find it easier to meet their international needs through trade than nonrepublican regimes. More to the point of our discussion here of empirical analyses of the relationship between the interval level measure of regime type and conflict proneness is an analysis by John Oneal, Frances Oneal, Zeev Maoz, and Bruce Russett (1993), which adds data on interdependence in terms of international trading ties to that utilized by Maoz and Russett in their analyses of the relationship between regime type and conflict proneness that we have discussed. They find not only that interdependence is significantly related to conflict escalation, that is, that militarized disputes between interdependent states are less likely to escalate, but also that introducing interdependence into an analysis of the relationship between regime type and conflict proneness eliminates that relationship. In other words, if interdependence is controlled for, they find no relationship between the extent to which a pair of states is democratic and the likelihood of conflict escalation.

Oneal et al. also find, however, that even when interdependence is controlled for, a relationship between a dichotomous measure of regime type and conflict escalation persists.[19] Furthermore, the disappearance of the relationship between regime type and conflict proneness when interdependence is controlled for probably does not suggest that the original relationship is spurious. A "theory" that the relationship is spurious would suggest that high levels of trade affect regime type, though it seems more likely that regime type affects levels of trade. In other words, it is probably the case that the disappearance of the relationship between regime type and conflict proneness when interdependence is controlled for suggests that interdependence is a factor that intervenes in the relationship between regime type and conflict proneness rather than a confounding variable that makes that relationship spurious.

Nevertheless, the analyses reported by Oneal et al. do suggest that interdependence has a more important impact on conflict escalation than regime type, and an impact of greater generalizability. Though it is apparently true that democratic states have avoided conflict escalation in recent decades at least in important part because they have traded a lot with each other, it is also true that lots of undemocratic states seem to have avoided conflict or conflict escalation because they have traded a lot with each other. Ultimately, one might conclude (though the authors do not) from this analysis that the democratic peace proposition is little more than a reflection of a fundamentally more important idea regarding the impact of international trade on international relationships.

But Oneal et al.'s analyses focus only on the years from 1950 to 1986. The Cold War confrontation of those years certainly had an impact on trading relationships and on conflict proneness of pairs of states in the international system. This suggests in turn that the relationship between interdependence and conflict proneness during the Cold War might be peculiar to that period and that the relationship during that period could have been spurious. In other words, pairs of states during that period might have been *un*likely to trade a lot with each other *and* prone to conflict escalation because they were involved in the Cold War confrontation. In addition, the relationship reported by Oneal et al. between interdependence and conflict may reflect the impact of conflict on trade, not trade on conflict, in spite of their efforts to deal with this problem.

In any case, though it is quite possible (as we will discuss in more detail in chapter 3) to support an argument to the effect that democratic states have never fought an international war against each other, it is not at all possible to argue persuasively that high levels of international trade have historically and consistently prevented pairs of states from engaging in international wars against each other. International trading ties among industrialized countries were very strong in 1913, right before World War I began. (See, for example, Rosecrance, Alexandroff, Koehler, Kroll, Laqueuer, and Stocker 1977, 432–33).[20] When Japan attacked the United States at Pearl Harbor in 1941, it was attacking its most important trading partner (Gaddis 1986, 112). Kenneth Waltz (1979, 138) points out that "the fiercest civil wars and the bloodiest international wars are fought within arenas populated by highly similar people whose affairs are closely knit."

John Gaddis similarly argues that each of the ten bloodiest interstate wars from 1816 to 1980 involved states directly adjoined to one another or actively involved in trade with each other. He also observes that "since 1945, there have been more civil wars than interstate wars; that fact alone should be sufficient to call into question the proposition that interdependence necessarily breeds peace" (Gaddis 1986, 112). In short, the impact of interdependence in the form of international trading ties on the relationship between regime type and conflict escalation reported by Oneal et al. is important and should certainly be kept in mind in interpretations of that relationship in the post–World War II period. However, their findings do not suggest that the relationship between regime type and conflict proneness is an uninteresting reflection of the impact of interdependence or international trading ties on conflict proneness, or that interdependence is in general more important to an understanding of international conflict than regime type in general or the democratic peace proposition in particular.

The Theoretical Underpinnings of the Democratic Peace Proposition

Much—perhaps too much—of the discussion in recent years of the theoretical underpinnings of the democratic peace proposition has focused on the differences between the structural and the cultural explanations. This distinction was emphasized almost simultaneously by Bueno de Mesquita and Lalman (1992) on the one hand and Morgan and Schwebach (1992) on the other. Bueno de Mesquita and Lalman (1992, 148) actually point to three different explanations, emphasizing in turn that democratic countries are "like-minded," about economic and political policies, that democratic political culture makes wars between democratic states less likely, and that political constraints on leaders in democracies make it more difficult for them to opt for force as a foreign policy option. The first two of these might be categorized together as the cultural explanation and the latter as the structural explanation of democratic peace. Morgan and Schwebach (1992, 307–8) discuss two arguments, the first of which specifies that "disputes between states do not escalate to war because the leaders *expect,* on the basis of common culture, to be able to work out their differences," and another that stresses that "greater decisional constraints on a state leader produce a lower probability that a dispute involving the state will escalate to war."

Bueno de Mesquita and Lalman (1992) dismiss the political culture argument on the grounds that democratic states have shown no disinclination to use force against nondemocratic states. On the surface, it seems that this evidence could be utilized as readily in criticism of the structural argument as the cultural argument. They resolve this problem, implicitly (since they do not acknowledge that it is a problem), by emphasizing the impact of structural constraints on bargaining between states. "Whenever democracies confront one another, it is common knowledge that each has unusually high confidence that the other is likely to be constrained to be averse to the use of force. And that common knowledge about the magnitude of the prior belief encourages states under all but the most unusual circumstances to negotiate with one another or to accept the status quo" (Bueno de Mesquita and Lalman 1992, 156–57). They attribute this knowledge about the opposition's aversion to the use of force to the fact that both democratic leaders will be aware of the political costs that the other will bear for using force, i.e., structural factors.[21] However, one might as logically attribute it to the fact that each leader, in conflicts between democracies, will be culturally biased against the use of force.

Bueno de Mesquita and Lalman (1992, 152–53) do provide some evidence that democratic states are more constrained in their use of violence against *each other* than in their relationships with undemocratic states. In particular they point out that their data contain "twenty-two cases [that] entail the use of force by a democracy against a nondemocracy when the non-democratic state did not itself initiate the use of force or retaliate with force." That evidence does suggest that any cultural tendency for democratic states to abhor violence is attenuated somehow when they interact with undemocratic states. (Supporters of the cultural argument maintain that this occurs because, in interaction with undemocratic states, democratic states must abandon their normative commitments to nonviolence in order to avoid being taken advantage of.)

But Bueno de Mesquita and Lalman also focus on the probability that states in disputes will negotiate or preserve the status quo as a function of their regime type. They find that if *either* state A *or* state B is democratic, that probability is higher. As they indicate, "the evidence supports the contention that democracies are *generally* [emphasis added] averse to the use of force" (Bueno de Mesquita and Lalman 1992, 157) What is needed to support the structural explanation of democratic peace that they prefer (which implies that it is the *interaction* of the regime types of both the original participants in a dispute) is evidence that democracies are averse to the use of force against *each other*. They do provide such evidence. But they also show that democracies are *generally* less likely to use force (that is, to negotiate or preserve the status quo) in their disputes with democracies *or* nondemocracies. At least part of the evidence they present, then, is equally supportive of both the cultural and the structural explanation of democratic peace.

Morgan and Schwebach (1992) and Morgan and Campbell (1991) are often interpreted as attempts to elaborate upon and provide more specific evidence regarding the democratic peace proposition. Their efforts would be more accurately characterized as aimed at debunking or discrediting the democratic peace proposition. As Morgan and Campbell (1991, 190) acknowledge: "The focus of our theoretical reformulation is on broadening the argument to include additional variables characterizing the domestic structure of states. One implication that we wish to stress at the outset and throughout the discussion is that many nondemocracies will also be affected by some types of decisional constraints." In other words, what Morgan and Campbell (1991), as well as Morgan and Schwebach (1992), attempt to establish is that it is the *level of decisional constraints* on national leaders and *not* regime type or democracy that has a pacifying impact.

Morgan and Campbell (1991) compare dispute participants categorized according to the extent that they face decisional constraints (operationally defined according to data on Executive Selection, Decisional Constraints, and Political Constraints generated by Gurr, 1974, 1978) to see if those participants with more constraints are less likely, in the years from 1816 to 1976, to become involved in war. They find that this is not the case, except for major powers.[22]

Morgan and Schwebach (1992) address directly the controversy regarding the cultural and structural interpretations of the democratic peace proposition. They analyze pairs of states involved in disputes and focus on the difference between constrained democracies and unconstrained democracies (again as operationalized by Gurr 1974, 1978) as a crucial test of the relative validity of the two explanations. That is, if structural constraints have a more potent pacifying effect than regime type, they reason, then constrained democracies should be more peaceful than nonconstrained democracies. They do acknowledge that their data show that "democracies, whether constrained or not, have not fought one another but constrained democracies and constrained non-democracies have in fact fought . . . 3 wars. This is consistent with the political culture argument."

However, they also analyze the impact of joint democracy on escalation to war and find that joint democracy has no impact on war involvement over and above regime type (or the structural constraints) on *either* party to a dispute. This is interpreted as evidence against the cultural version of the democratic peace proposition. "The cultural argument," according to Morgan and Schwebach (1992, 335) "is clear in the prediction that democracies will fight other states but not one another." This contradicts the argument by Bueno de Mesquita and Lalman (1992) that the cultural argument is weakened by the fact that democratic states show no reluctance to use force against nondemocratic states. In other words, whereas Bueno de Mesquita and Lalman (1992) argue that the cultural version of the democratic peace proposition is unable to account for the fact that democracies in general are as war prone as other kinds of states, even though they do not fight wars against each other, Morgan and Schwebach (1992) insist that the cultural model specifically stipulates that democratic states will not fight wars against each other, even though they do fight wars against other kinds of states!

My conclusion is that both Morgan and Schwebach (1992) as well as Bueno de Mesquita and Lalman (1992) are wrong. They argue, in the opposite directions, that the cultural and the structural interpretations of the democratic peace proposition are *different* in their implications about the impact of joint democracy and the war proneness of democracies in general or of mixed dyads. I would argue, to the contrary, that *both* the cultural and the structural versions of the democratic peace proposition in their most straightforward forms, imply that democracies in general, *and* in their relationships with each other, should be less war prone. The logic of the specific structural argument developed by Bueno de Mesquita and Lalman (1992), focusing on the impact of democracy on bargaining *between* states, does imply that joint democracy has an impact different from democracy in general. However, as we discussed above, they also provide empirical evidence that suggests that democratic states *in general,* when they are involved in disputes, are more likely to negotiate or preserve the status quo, regardless of the regime type of the other state involved in the dispute. And the theoretical arguments as well as the evidence presented by Morgan and Schwebach (1992) suggest that the logic of the structural interpretation of the democratic peace proposition is applicable to democracy in general, and this logic need not imply that it is *only* joint democracy that has a pacifying impact. (*That* argument they impute, unnecessarily I would contend, to the cultural interpretation of the democratic peace proposition.) In addition, it is fair to suggest that Morgan and Campbell (1991) and Morgan and Schwebach (1992) fail in their attempt to discredit the democratic peace proposition. To their credit, they are aware of and acknowledge this to be the case.[23]

Probably the most energetic attempts to evaluate the relative validity of the structural and cultural explanations of the democratic peace have been made by Russett with Maoz (1993) and Maoz and Russett (1993). They examine the relative explanatory potency of cultural norms, operationalized as the duration of a regime, or frequency of political executions, or levels of domestic conflict and violence, on the one hand, and structural constraints, operationalized according to a series of indicators based on data generated by Alexander Eckstein and Ted Robert Gurr (1975), as well as Ted Robert Gurr, Keith Jaggers, and Will Moore (1989), on the other. The indicators of structural constraints reflect the concentration of power within a regime, degree of executive control, centralization of power (federal or not), and the scope of government. Maoz and Russett focus particularly on regimes in which democratic norms are strong and political institutional constraints are low and vice versa (that is, regimes with weak democratic norms but strong institutional constraints), figuring reasonably enough that the two competing models make contradictory predictions in those cases, as they do not when both norms and constraints are strong or both are weak.

Their conclusion is that the cultural interpretation of the democratic peace proposition is superior in its predictive capacity to the institutional or structural interpretation, but their conclusion is not entirely persuasive. First, some of their analyses reveal that "the effects of *both* [emphasis added] norms and institutional constraints on conflict involvement and conflict escalation hold fairly consistent *even when we control for potentially confounding factors*" (Maoz and Russett 1993, 633). They conclude that the cultural explanation is stronger because of, first, the portion of a rather high number of separate analyses performed that show stronger results for the cultural variables. They have a lot of different comparisons to make because they utilize several operationalizations of both their independent and dependent variables. So, for example, at one point, Maoz and Russett (1993, 634) assert that "in the table as a whole, the normative constraints are significant in all but two of the 24 cells, whereas institutional constraints are significant in the correct (negative) direction in . . . 11 cells." Similarly, Russett with Maoz (1993, 92) observe that "in seventeen of the thirty separate tests, the probability of involvement when democratic norms are high and constraints are low is significantly below the probability of involvement when democratic norms are low and constraints are high." The second reason they conclude that the cultural model is superior is that "controlling for regime type eliminates many of the previously significant parameter estimates of political constraints, but not those for norms" (Maoz and Russett 1993, 634).

The limitations on the confidence warranted by these results stem in part from, once again, questions about the number of cases they analyze, stemming in turn from the lack of independence in their observations of dyad-years. In one table, Maoz and Russett (1993, 635) report that 2.89 percent of pairs of states with weak democratic norms but strong institutional constraints became involved in serious disputes, while only 2.11 percent of those pairs of states with strong democratic norms but weak structural constraints did so. This difference of .78 percent is reported as "significant" at the .01 level. But the significance test is based on 26,169 observations of dyad-years that are highly interdependent.[24]

Surely, also, the results reported by Maoz and Russett are affected by the relative quality of their measures of democratic norms, on the one hand, and of institutional constraints, on the other. If, for example, their measures of norms produce stronger coefficients, maybe that is because their measures of norms are more accurate than those of institutional constraints. Also, they choose to interpret the longevity of a regime as an index of the strength of cultural norms, when it might serve as logically as a measure of the strength of institutional constraints, *if* they focused on the *interaction* of the length of time that a regime has persisted and its regime type. As it is, because they look at regime persistence alone (without consideration of regime type), what they have created in effect is a measure that reflects the strength of democratic norms, *or* the strength of autocratic (monarchical, communist, fascist, or whatever) norms, depending on the type of regime in question.

Then, too, it is possible that the reason they find that controlling for regime type eliminates many "significant" relationships between institutional constraints and conflict but not between norms and conflict is not that the norm-based model is superior or that the correlation between constraints and conflict is spurious. Perhaps, instead, institutional constraints *intervene* in the relationship between regime type and conflict. Thus, controlling for regime type would curtail variation in institutional constraints, which in turn could eliminate the correlation between institutional constraints and conflict. This would not mean that the interpretation of the democratic peace proposition stressing the role of institutional constraints is any way inferior to that based on the effect of democratic norms.[25]

Two of the more important papers relevant to this controversy are authored by William Dixon (1993a, 1994). In the first of these papers, Dixon (1993a, 431) finds that "democracies are likely to be more amenable than others to efforts of third parties to resolve or ameliorate interstate disputes." In the second, he reports that those mediating efforts are more likely to be successful if the parties to a dispute are democratic, i.e., that disputes between democracies are more likely to be peacefully resolved. Dixon (1994) interprets his findings as supportive of the model stressing the impact of cultural norms, asserting that "the democracy-settlement hypothesis examined here rests on explanatory logic emphasizing norms of dispute resolution held by democratic leaders. Alternative explanations of democratic war involvement, particularly those focusing on decisional constraints, cannot easily account for the democracy-settlement results."

But is this really the case? The version of the institutional constraints model developed by Bueno de Mesquita and Lalman (1992), as we have seen above, specifically emphasizes the impact of those constraints on their *bargaining* behavior and the likelihood that those constraints will lead states to *negotiate* rather than escalate to violent conflict. That structural version of the democratic peace proposition is *quite* congruent with Dixon's (1994) results.

Probably the most convincing evidence in favor of the cultural defense of the democratic peace proposition is provided by Spencer Weart (1994a, 1994b). This work purports to look at all of history and finds that wars have never occurred between "well-established" democracies (and almost never between well-established oligarchic republics, for that matter). It is fascinating to see how consistently—in ancient Greece, in Italian city-states, among Swiss cantons, and elsewhere—regime type, the preservation of democracy, and so forth have been vital issues in relationships between states. Furthermore, the whole book is based on the idea that "close calls," i.e., conflicts which constituted wars between states that were *almost* democratic, are a particularly valuable source of evidence and insights into why it is that democratic states do not fight wars against each other, an idea echoed here in chapter 5.

Weart's conclusion is, in short, that it is political culture that best accounts for the lack of wars between democracies. Leaders tend to deal with foreign counterparts as they deal with political protagonists in domestic settings. If they resolve domestic political conflicts peacefully, they will be predisposed to resolve international conflicts without violence. Leaders with these proclivities are reliably found only in "well-established" democracies.

One might criticize this work as an energetic but haphazard fishing expedition for anecdotes that support the author's thesis. It is unfair to categorize it so because the author's scope is so comprehensive. In fact, perhaps it might be criticized on the grounds that the scope of the work cannot realistically be as comprehensive as the author claims it to be. At one point, for example, he asserts that "Taking the three Swiss conflicts together, the case may be weak but it is the best exception we have: the *only* full-scale combat [emphasis added] between well-established republics of the same kind" (Weart 1994b, chapter 6). And "only" in this context means in the *whole* of history. At another point he asserts that "history gives us barely five significant cases in the border zone." The five cases referenced here involve ancient Greece, the War of 1812 between the United States and Great Britain, Swiss cantons in 1847, the American Civil War, and the Boer War. So again, when Weart asserts that "history gives us," he means *all* of history. Weart is confronted here not only with the logical difficulty of proving the negative (this kind of thing has *not* happened *anywhere* else at *any* time) but also with the practical difficulty of familiarizing himself with so much history. Perhaps "republics" are sufficiently rare that these difficulties can be overcome. Weart, to his credit, certainly creates that impression. In any case, his argument is engaging and impressive and, to repeat, quite persuasive in favor of his thesis that it is political culture in democracies that makes them unlikely to fight against each other.

But wherever a democratic political culture is well ensconced, in well-established democracies, there too will democratic institutions be strong, exerting their constraints.

Then, too, as as David Forsythe (1992) points out, the United States has either threatened to use or has actually used forcible covert action against elected, arguably democratic governments in Iran (1953), Guatemala (1954), Indonesia (1955), Brazil (1960s), Chile (1973), and Nicaragua (1980s). Georg Sorenson (1992, 405) even goes so far as to argue that "as the events in Central America in the 1980s show, covert involvement with economic and military and 'expert' support for opposition forces can develop to a point where the distinction between such activities and open war becomes fairly academic." Patrick James and Glenn Mitchell (1994, 11) ask, obviously in a rhetorical tone: "If the shared cultural norms premise is correct, why would democratic states fight each other in ways short of open warfare but preclude war itself?"[26] Defenders of the cultural argument can argue that these targets of American covert activity were not really democratic and that they were not victims of full-scale military aggression. Bruce Russett (1993, 124) points out that "the normative restraints of democracy were sufficient to drive the operations underground amid circumstances when the administration might have otherwise undertaken an overt intervention." But was it the normative restraints that motivated the decision makers in question, or was it not the structural constraints in the form of anticipated political costs that inspired them to choose covert strategies rather than overt military force?

In short, the distinction between the cultural and the structural explanation of democratic peace does not seem either stark or crucial, nor does the available evidence seem to indicate that one is clearly superior to the other. As Morgan and Schwebach (1992, 318) conclude, "To a great extent, culture and structure go together. A nation imbued with a democratic culture will likely establish a correspondent political system and a state structured to constrain will likely foster a democratic culture." Even after having expended a lot of effort to evaluate the relative virtues of the structural/institutional and the cultural/normative models of the democratic peace, Russett with Maoz (1993, 92) correctly observe that "it would be a mistake to emphasize too strongly the subtlety or persuasiveness of the distinction between [the] cultural/normative and structural/institutional" models.

More fundamental, perhaps, is the difference between the democratic peace proposition and both realism and neorealism. In their ideal-typical forms, at least, realism and neorealism assert that differences in regime types do not have systematic important impacts on international politics or foreign policies. Russett (1993), Morgan and Schwebach (1992), and many others stress how fundamental the tension is between realism and neorealism and the idea that democratic states have foreign policies that are strikingly different from those of autocratic states, as well as the notion that universal democracy would revolutionize international politics. And Bueno de Mesquita and Lalman (1992) devote their entire book to evaluating the relative utility of two international interaction games, the realpolitik variant based on realist or neorealist assumptions and a domestic variant based on the assumption that domestic political factors, such as regime type, play a key role in determining the outcomes of interactions between states.

It is this last work in particular that has convinced me that the democratic peace proposition constitutes not so much a fundamental repudiation of realism or neorealism as an important modification in the predominant paradigm in international politics.[27] In spite of the emphasis that Bueno de Mesquita and Lalman (1992) put on the distinction between the realpolitik version and the domestic variant of their international interaction game and the consistent efforts by Bueno de Mesquita to portray his expected utility approach as quite different from realism or neorealism (in, for example, *The War Trap* [1981] or in "The Contribution of Expected-Utility Theory to the Study of International Conflict"), it is still quite possible to argue that the similarities between Bueno de Mesquita's approach and the interaction game in *War and Reason* (1992), and realism or neorealism, are more important than the differences between them.

As Robert Keohane (1983) points out, the three assumptions that constitute the "hard core" of the realist research paradigm are (1) states are the most important actors, (2) global politics can be analyzed as if states are unitary rational actors, and (3) states calculate their interests in terms of power, as an end in itself or as a necessary means to other ends. Even a casual perusal of Bueno de Mesquita's work since *The War Trap* appeared in 1981 will reveal that it is certainly based on a state-centric assumption, and the assumption that states can be treated as unitary rational actors. And although Bueno de Mesquita justifiably argues that his approach focuses on other considerations, power calculations certainly play an essential part in it, utilizing as it does a comparison of military-industrial capabilities of the principal belligerents in disputes, for example, as an indicator of the probability of success for the actors involved.

On a superficial level, Bueno de Mesquita's expected utility theory, or the strategic interaction game in Bueno de Mesquita and Lalman (1992), seems to pertain primarily to the national, or at most the "minimally dyadic" (Midlarsky 1989), level of analysis. Upon examination, though, Bueno de Mesquita's approach and the strategic interaction game might best be conceived as focusing on a conflict system, i.e., not only the initiator and the target in disputes or international interactions but also those allies and other third parties that might, or might not, become involved. The latter states are brought into Bueno de Mesquita's model, or interaction game, by way of the proposition that the initiator and the target make estimates regarding which states might enter into a dispute or interaction sequence, on which side, and with what impact.

As Keohane (1983, 509) points out, the distribution of power takes on particular importance in neorealistic theory. In this way, too, Bueno de Mesquita's approach to international politics has a neorealistic flavor, since it focuses not only on the ratio of power between the original disputants but also on the distribution of power in the entire conflict system. Keohane (1983, 523) also asserts that at least in its strongest version, neorealism tends to assume "full fungibility of power." Bueno de Mesquita, as well as Bueno de Mesquita and Lalman (1992), treat power as operationized by the same six basic indicators generated by the Correlates of War project (Singer 1988), as crucially important to the outcomes of disputes or interactions, regardless of which states or issues are involved across most of the last two centuries. In short, Bueno de Mesquita's approach is based on an assumption about the fungibility of military power, in the manner of a realist or neorealist, that reaches impressive proportions.

Finally, if we analyze the differences between the realpolitik variant of the interaction game presented in *War and Reason* and the domestic variant, we see that they share six basic assumptions (Bueno de Mesquita and Lalman 1992, 40–41). The *only* difference between the two variants on the level of basic assumptions is reflected in the seventh basic assumption. The realpolitik version of the game is based on the assumption that an initiator attempts to maximize its expected utility "within the international context, without regard for the wishes or objectives of domestic political constituencies." But in the domestic variant, the seventh basic assumption is that an initiator will attempt to maximize its expected utility within the context of a domestic political process, "determined by internal political rules, procedures, norms, and considerations."

In light of the extensive realistic and neorealistic aspects of Bueno de Mesquita's expected utility approach, then, it is not surprising that Keohane (1983, 512) categorizes *The War Trap* as among "some of the finest work" of the realist genre. It is also not surprising that Alexander Wendt (1987, 351) designates Bueno de Mesquita's "Towards a Scientific Understanding of International Conflict" (1985) as the definitive "discussion of the philosophy of science underlying neorealism."

Now, Bueno de Mesquita and Lalman (1992) have developed a strategic interaction game from which can be derived the proposition that democratic states are unlikely to fight international wars against each other. As we have seen, that version of the game shares six out of the seven basic assumptions with a realpolitik, or realist, version, from which that proposition cannot be derived. But a theoretical framework that modifies only the seventh out of seven basic assumptions can hardly be considered a fundamental repudiation of the theoretical approach with which it shares six fundamental assumptions and much else.

There are other reasons to conclude that the democratic peace proposition is not so inherently incompatible with realism or neorealism. Perhaps the most important of these reasons is that the basic realistic argument that foreign policymakers will make decisions that are in the "national interest" has always implied a quite "unrealistic" tendency of national leaders and foreign policymakers to be altruistic, self-abnegating, and self-sacrificial. Would it not be more realistic or plausible or at least consistent with the fundamental notion that political actors will behave in self-interested ways to assume instead, for example, that "political elites wish to attain and stay in office" and that "political elites in government will fight war if it will extend or protect their terms in office" (Domke 1988, 105)? Or, as the democratic peace proposition would imply, to assume that political elites will avoid a war if doing so will extend or protect their terms in office?

Kurt Gaubatz (1993, 20) makes much the same point when he asserts that "unless our view of popular passions is so lofty that we always see in the public voice some best approximation of the national interest, we will have to be concerned about the temptation for elites to knowingly sacrifice their conception of the common good for their own political gain." He also makes clear that this temptation can arise not from "venality or short-sightedness" but from "rational utility maximization, from reason."

The democratic peace proposition, in this light, can be seen as quite compatible with the metatheoretical notion from realism and neorealism that political actors will behave in ways calculated to serve their interests best. But, unlike the most pristine versions of realism and neorealism, at any rate, the theoretical underpinnings of the democratic peace proposition can be formulated in such a way as to recognize that what is in the national interest and what is in the interests of the current leaders in the regime of the moment may not always be identical. Accordingly, this version of the theoretical base for the democratic peace proposition would assert that leaders in democracies might avoid wars against other democratic states not necessarily because of normative convictions about how political conflicts ought to be resolved, nor because they are unable to overcome political, structural obstacles in the way of such policies, but because they feel that fighting such wars might be harmful to their chances of staying in power.

This is not to say that democratic regimes might not also avoid wars for normative reasons or because of structural impediments to decision making in democracies or because of the impact of joint democracy on bargaining behavior. The point here is only that *another* reason that democratic states might avoid wars against other democratic states (or possibly be more often inclined to avoid wars in general) would involve the impact of such wars on their own political fortunes, in addition to the national interest.

The point is made more intriguing in the light of recent research reported by Bruce Bueno de Mesquita, Randolph Siverson, and Gary Woller (1992) about the impact of international wars on regime changes. They calculate the impact of interstate wars fought between 1816 and 1975 on the probability that the co-belligerent states will experience violent changes in political regimes in the aftermath of those wars. They find clear evidence to indicate that "regimes that initiate wars and do not prevail are at the highest risk of being replaced" (Bueno de Mesquita, Siverson, and Woller 1992, 643). "War," they point out, "is . . . a powerful force shaped by, and giving shape to, domestic political affairs and for making *or breaking* the political fortunes of national governments" (639).

The implications of these findings for the democratic peace proposition are particularly striking in light of the possibility that "the true effects of war on regime change are probably stronger than the observed effects reported here" and that "the true effects include instances of wars that did not happen because of the anticipation of domestic political punishment" (Bueno de Mesquita, Siverson, and Woller 1992, 639). They are reinforced by related research by Bueno de Mesquita and Siverson (1993), who report that war can increase the likelihood that a political leader will lose his or her grip on power, particularly in democracies.[28] The striking aspects of the implications of these findings for the democratic peace proposition are highlighted when they are combined with the findings of David Lake (1992, 24), who, focusing on interstate wars from 1816 to 1988, finds evidence to support his idea that "democracies, constrained by their societies from earning rents, will devote greater absolute resources to security, [and] enjoy greater societal support for their policies . . . democracies will be more likely to win wars."[29]

There is a Sherlock Holmesian "the dog that didn't bark" problem facing any attempt to evaluate the validity of the idea in question here. That proposition suggests, first, that the fate of regimes is affected by international wars, whether those regimes win or lose those wars. The evidence in favor of that idea is persuasive. But the second half of the proposition is that democracies avoid wars against each other in part because they anticipate that democratic governments will be particularly difficult to defeat, and that they imperil the tenure of their regimes by getting involved in wars against other democratic regimes. Since there have never been (arguably) wars between democratic regimes, there are no examples to point to in support of the idea that fighting wars against democratic regimes is perilous to the continued existence of democratic regimes. However, there is evidence in Lake (1992) that democratic states are particularly difficult to defeat and that defeat in war does imperil the continued existence of political regimes that suffer those defeats. Thus, the proposition that democratic regimes avoid wars against each other in part because they are aware or intuit that such wars would be particularly difficult to win and that defeat imperils the continuation of their governments in power is congruent with existing evidence, even though no examples of democratic governments losing wars to democratic governments and then losing their hold on power actually exist.[30]

Conclusion

This review of the philosophical and historical roots of the proposition that democratic states will not fight wars against each other, of the empirical evidence relevant to it, and of its theoretical base supports the conclusion that the proposition is worthy of continued serious consideration. In the chapters to follow, I will focus on three issues that are particularly pressing in light of the current status of evidence and theory regarding the democratic peace proposition.

The first of these has to do with global trends in regime transitions. The implications of the democratic peace proposition for the future of global politics depend on those trends, which deserve, I believe, more attention than they have traditionally received from analysts of international politics. Global trends in regime transitions, and competing explanations for those trends, will be analyzed in chapter 2.

The second issue involves the question of whether or not democratic states have never, or only rarely, fought international wars against each other. Since wars between states are so rare statistically (99 percent of the pairs of states in the international system in most years do not fight wars against each other), the existence of even a few wars between democratic states would wipe out entirely the statistical and therefore arguably the substantive significance of the difference in the historical rates of warfare between pairs of democratic states, on the one hand, and pairs of states in general, on the other. Therefore, it is important to deal directly with the issue of whether or not, and according to what criteria for "democracy" (and "war"), there have been even a small number of wars between democratic states. This issue is the main topic of chapter 3.

The third issue, to be the topics of chapters 4 and 5, is also a function in part of the statistical rarity of interstate wars. There have been by this time a number of impressive analyses of aggregate level data regarding the alleged differences in the propensity to war of democratic states and undemocratic states. But a need exists to supplement the kind of evidence that can be produced by aggregate data analyses with the complementary type of evidence that can be produced by the intensive analysis of a few crucial cases.

That case studies can be complementary to aggregate data analyses of large numbers of cases is an assertion that commands wide assent. Nevertheless, it seems to me that case studies informed by the findings of aggregate data analyses are relatively rare, and the integration of the findings of large-N analyses with those of case studies faces a number of epistemological questions and difficulties. Those questions and difficulties will be addressed in chapter 4.

Then, in chapter 5, two cases, namely the Spanish-American War and the Fashoda Crisis, will be subjected to a "pseudo-experimental" analysis with two basic purposes in mind. One will be to provide an example of the integration of the findings of large-N studies with the intensive analyses of specific cases. The second will be to generate insights into the differences in relationships between pairs of states that are jointly democratic and those that are not and, even more important, to generate evidence that is relevant to an evaluation of the democratic peace proposition.

Finally, chapter 6 reviews the main points of the previous chapters and concludes with speculation about the future viability of the democratic peace proposition.

Notes

1. There is also the complicating problem, which deserves mention here, that a "dovish" public can, under some circumstances, make a country more rather than less war prone (Bueno de Mesquita and Lalman 1990).

2. At another point, Doyle (1983a, 225) asserts specifically that "Liberal states are as aggressive and war prone as any other form of government or society in their relations with nonliberal states."

3. Fukuyama (1992, 59) is aware that his enthusiasm for Hegel is unusual, acknowledging that "Hegel has never had a good reputation in the Anglo-Saxon world, where he has been accused of being a reactionary apologist for the Prussian monarchy, a forerunner of twentieth century totalitarianism, and worst of all from an English perspective, a difficult to read metaphysician." But Fukuyama's interpretation of Hegel is not without support. Torbjorn Knutsen (1992, 198) for example, asserts that Hegel "saw in the French Revolution the irresistible rise of progressive values, and he saw in the Napoleonic Wars the triumphant dissemination of those values throughout the world."

4. Let me say in a preemptive note that I make this argument in spite of the fact that Hegel is widely regarded as a rather unsavory character (as Fukuyama [1992, 349], to repeat, is aware) whose glorification of the state provided some inspiration, perhaps, to both the Kaiser and Adolf Hitler, who were hardly advocates of liberalism. I am also aware of the serious tension between the ideas and philosophies of Kant and Hegel; Johnson (1991, 814) points out that Hegel "turned his back decisively on Immanuel Kant's notion of perpetual peace." Kenneth Waltz (1962) argues quite persuasively that even Kant himself felt that perpetual peace was not a practical or realizable goal.

5. It can also be argued, however, that many "liberals" such as Rummel (1979) and even Bueno de Mesquita and Lalman (1992) *also* "focus on democratic pressures against aggression from ordinary citizens."

6. At one point in this discussion, Babst (1972, 57) asserts that "studies have shown that a country's chances of having a freely elected government improve as levels of literacy and subsequent industrialization increase. These two factors are increasing rapidly in the Soviet Union, which suggests that eventually the Russians also may have freely elected government" (Babst 1972, 57). I will resist the temptation to infer that Babst's transition from references to the "Soviet Union" to a statement about the "Russians" constitutes a subtle allusion to the eventual demise of the USSR.

7. On the other hand, Babst's articles in both the *Wisconsin Sociologist* and *Industrial Research* are cited, though much less prominently than in Small and Singer (1976) by Rummel in the fourth volume of *Understanding Conflict and War* (1979). One might reasonably surmise that Babst's articles were called to his attention by Small and Singer (1976), except that, interestingly enough, Rummel (1979) does not cite Small and Singer (1976).

8. However, Rummel (1994, chapter 2) points out that the significance tests on which this conclusion is based were miscalculated.

9. Waltz does state this view, specifically for the purpose of vigorously refuting it, which is not the impression one would get from this passage in *Contending Theories*.

10. Kant's ideas on ethics, metaphysics, and epistemology are brought up repeatedly in *Understanding Conflict and War,* but his essay on "Perpetual Peace" is virtually never mentioned, even though it is cited in volume 5.

11. Another possible starting point would be the work of Michael Doyle (1983a, 1983b, 1986), already discussed above; he did much to "popularize" the democratic peace proposition, at a very high level and to a very select audience. The idea was also discussed in some detail in Russett and Starr (1981), which is particularly good in its discussion of various factors that might but apparently do not make the correlation between democracy and peace spurious. Interestingly, the only sources that Russett and Starr (1981, 440) cite in support of the proposition that democratic countries are unlikely to fight each other are Small and Singer (1976) and Wallensteen (1973).

12. Russett (1993, 139) also asserts that "virtually all . . . agree that democracies are not in general markedly less likely to go to war than other states." But Russett also acknowledges that Bremer (1992) reports that democracies are less likely to originate wars with all kinds of states.

13. It is also reported by Maoz and Abdolali (1989, 24–25) that "in the general MID [Militarized Interstate Dispute] population as well as the war subset, dyads involving at least one democratic state are underrepresented . . . whereas dyads with only anocratic or autocratic states are generally overrepresented." Such evidence would support the proposition that democratic states *in general* are less conflict prone, but my reading of the table to which Maoz and Abdolali refer in this passage does not support their conclusion.

14. Bremer (1992, 329) also acknowledges that when he uses a Gurr-based index of democracy, rather than a Chan-based index, "we do not find a significant difference in the probability of war between dyads containing one or no democratic states." However, the significance level in question is .06, missing the arguably unsacred .05 level by what is arguably an insignificant amount.

15. It is interesting to note here, I believe, that though only 11 percent of the not jointly democratic dyad-years were politically relevant during this time period, 22 percent of the jointly democratic dyad-years were politically relevant. This makes the absence of warfare among the latter set of dyad-years twice as impressive, everything else being equal.

16. Perhaps it is appropriate to point out that another source of confidence in the validity of that proposition is the fact that not too many years ago, Bruce Bueno de Mesquita, Stuart Bremer, and Zeev Maoz were all quite skeptical about its validity, but in each case their own empirical and theoretical analyses led them to change their minds.

17. Actually, Bremer's data contain one or two wars between democracies, depending on which index of democracy he utilizes. But these can be ignored for the moment. Whether or not they really are exceptions to the rule that democratic states do not fight wars against each other is a question we will take up in detail in chapter 3.

18. Dyads are politically relevant in Weede's terminology if they are contiguous, if they include the United States or the Soviet Union, or if they have experienced territorial conflict in the previous sixty years.

19. This brings to mind the possibility that interdependence eliminates the relationship between regime type and conflict proneness because of the problematic nature of

the index of democracy that Maoz and Russett apply to pairs of states. However, John Oneal has shown me the results of analyses in which that index is simplified so that it reflects only the extent to which a pair of states is democratic, and not the extent to which the regimes are similar, and the initial results at least suggest that the major findings of this paper regarding the impact of controls for interdependence on the relationship between regime type and conflict proneness are unchanged.

20. "Certainly economic interdependence did little to prevent Germany, France, Britain, Russia,and Austria-Hungary from going to war in 1914" (Gaddis 1986, 112).

21. These arguments, as is the case with most arguments I have come across in the recent literature, can be found in at least a nascent form in Wright (1942, 1965, 842). "Consequently, in the game of power diplomacy, democracies pitted against autocracies are at a disadvantage. They cannot make effective threats unless they really mean war; they can seldom convince either themselves or the potential enemy that they really do mean war; and they are always vulnerable to the dissension of internal opposition, capable of stimulation by the potential enemy, whatever decision is made."

22. Here again, as usual, the significance tests calculated by Morgan and Campbell (1991) are based on the assumption that their roughly two thousand observations of dispute participants constitute two thousand "cases," or independent observations, when in fact, many of the disputes observed are multilateral, and the same states are involved in several different disputes.

23. Morgan and Campbell (1991) conclude that "unfortunately, there is no obvious interpretation to provide for the results presented in this article." Morgan and Schwebach (1992, 319) admit that "primarily because of data limitations our results are not as clear as we had hoped."

24. Russett with Maoz (1993, 146) acknowledge that "use of the dyad-year involves a statistical problem in that a particular dyad's conflict status is not independent from one year to the next." They also state that "in partial compensation for this effect we report two-tailed statistical tests." But interdependence in these observations is not limited to those involving conflict. Their observations of regime types are, if anything, even more interdependent from one year to the next. And two-tailed tests constitute a rather limited step in the direction of dealing with this problem.

25. The elimination of the correlation between institutional constraints and conflict proneness by controlling for regime type also reflects a stronger correlation between institutional constraints and regime type than between normative constraints and regime type, which in turn is a function in part of the fact that "one of the variables used to produce the institutional constraints index was instrumental in producing the democracy-autocracy index" (Maoz and Russett 1993, 637).

26. They go on to assert that "the covert attack, the instigation of rebellion, the use of political propaganda, the interference in democratic elections, etc., are not tolerant or conciliatory acts. Covert attacks provide a serious challenge to the cultural premise of democratic peace" (James and Mitchell 1994, 11).

27. Sorenson (1992, 412) asserts that "the distance between Kant's idealism and neorealism is often overdrawn."

28. These findings in turn are reinforced by experimental studies that indicate that "democracies do not fight each other because their leaders have very few political incen-

tives to do so" (Mintz and Geva 1993, 484). See also Geva, DeRouen, and Mintz (1993).

29. Specifically, Lake (1992, 637) finds that "of the 26 wars fought since 1816 between democracies and autocracies, the former have won 21 (81%) and lost 5 (19%)." It is interesting to compare Lake's reasoning in his explanation for this result with the argument by Quincy Wright (1942, 842) from some fifty years ago. "Democracies are likely to be more prosperous in times of peace because their economy is likely to aim at welfare rather than at military invulnerability, and in wars of attrition their superior economies give them advantage."

30. A counterargument might assert that the superior performance of democracies in interstate wars could engender such confidence in those states that they would be more likely to initiate wars, even against other democratic states. But I am not arguing here that leaders of democratic states have been consciously aware of the superiority of democratic states in war and that they base decisions for war or peace in part on that awareness. Rather I am arguing that it is possible that states will be more wary of engaging in wars with states that have successful records in past wars and that therefore the disproportionately successful records of democratic states in interstate wars might play a role in deterring attacks from states in general, as well as from their democratic counterparts.

Chapter 2

Global Trends in Regime Transitions

If regime type does have an important impact on relationships between states, then trends in regime types in the global political system have an obviously important bearing on international politics. As I have argued in chapter 1, the importance and the implications of the alleged pacifying impact of democracy on international relationships are dependent to a crucial extent, for example, on the distribution of regime types in the international system. In other words, the proportion of democratic and undemocratic regimes in the world may have profound implications for prospects for peace. In recognition of the potentially crucial impact that it has on international conflict, the distribution of regime types in the global political system, trends in that distribution, and forces that may play a role in those trends, will serve as the focus of this chapter.

Recent Trends in Regime Transitions

Nineteen eighty-nine was a watershed year in the global political system, marked most dramatically by the rapid transformation of most of the political regimes in Eastern Europe, accompanied by the continued reform efforts of Mikhail Gorbachev in the Soviet Union. In a quieter, less noted process, Latin America experienced a transformation throughout the 1980s that moved it also in the democratic direction. "Since 1979, the politics of Latin America have been transformed by the longest and deepest wave of democratization in the region's history" (Remmer 1990, 315).

In the mid-1970s, the redemocratization of Portugal, Greece, and Spain made Western Europe entirely "democratic" for the first time in history. And the democratization process that, by the beginning of the 1990s, had influenced Eastern Europe, Latin America, and Western Europe ultimately left visible traces in virtually every other region in the globe. Perhaps the most dramatic of these appeared in the People's Republic of China, where the process was brought to a sharp halt in Tiananmen Square in June of 1989. But elsewhere in Asia in the 1980s, a trend toward democracy was quite visible (even when and where it was repulsed on occasion) in Taiwan, South Korea, the Philippines, as well as Nepal, Mongolia, Burma, and Bangladesh.

Sub-Saharan Africa seemed for some time impervious to any global trend toward democracy. But by 1990, this region too was swept up in that trend. President Felix Houphouet-Boigny in the Ivory Coast, President Matheiu Kerekou in Benin, President Omar Bongo in Gabon, President Kenneth Kaunda in Zambia, President Mobuto Sese Seko in Zaire, and President Hassan Mwinyi in Tanzania, dictators all, had each, by 1990, made possibly important concessions, moving their countries away from one-party dictatorial rule toward multiparty, more democratic systems.[1] In the fall of 1990, Richard Fatton could declare that "the process of redemocratizing African politics is . . . becoming the hegemonic issue in African studies, not only because of a theoretical and moral search for an alternative to the existing authoritarian predicament, but also because there are indications that peasants, workers, and intellectuals of Africa are no longer prepared to put up with being the victims of despotic regimes" (Fatton 1990, 455–56). Similarly, according to J. Leo Cefkin (1992, 22), "there are solid reasons to judge 1991 as a true watershed in Africa's affairs. One-party regimes are falling. Multi-party democracy is the order of the day."

The Middle East may well be the region of the world most resistant to any global trend toward democracy, but in the 1980s Turkey and Pakistan moved in a democratic direction, (Pakistan has since moved back, as well as forth), King Hussein of Jordan allowed multiparty elections to a parliament, and North and South Yemen united into a new country that showed some signs of heading in a pluralist direction. In what was at the time the most promising development for democracy in the Middle East, Algeria instituted some reforms reminiscent of those in socialist countries of Eastern Europe.

But, ultimately, scheduled elections in Algeria were called off when it looked like fundamentalist Islamic elements would probably win them. This is a setback for the democratic trend in the Middle East, perhaps even a devastating one. Nevertheless, writers such as Robin Wright (1992, 141) insist that "in a series of interviews over the past year, Islamists throughout Central Asia and in north Africa have talked convincingly about crafting their own models of an Islamic democracy." She feels that there have been encouraging signs of moderation in Iran and further that in the Middle East generally there is a "preference for ballots over bullets" stemming from a realization that "the costs of extremism in the 1980s proved too high" (132).[2] Samuel Huntington, though cognizant of powerful antidemocratic forces in the Middle East, points out that most of the undemocratic countries of the world entering into that range of development, as indicated by GNP per capita, in which most of the transitions to democracy have occurred in recent decades are now in the Middle East and North Africa. Accordingly, he concludes that "the wave of democratization that . . . swept about the world from region to region in the 1970s and the 1980s could become a dominant feature of Middle Eastern and North African politics in the 1990s" (Huntington 1991, 313–15). So, ultimately, and perhaps not in the very distant future, the global democratizing trend will take root, too, in the Middle East (Ray 1995a).

George Modelski and Gardner Perry (1991) analyze the proportion of the globe's population living in democracies since 1450 and conclude that there has been a slow, gradual substitution of democratic regimes for monarchical and dictatorial forms of government over that time period. Commenting more specifically on the last three hundred years, Modelski (1989, 16) notes that around 1700 no more than 1 percent of the world's population lived in democratic communities, a proportion that rose to 2 or 3 percent by 1800, to 10 percent by 1900, and to at least 30 percent in recent times. Even more recently, Modelski (1990, 22) acknowledges that by the late 1980s, the proportion of the world's population living in democracies has increased to about 40 percent. "From the Dutch Republic onward," Modelski argues, "there has been a progressive growth . . . of an increasingly weighty community of democracies."

Similarly, Ted Robert Gurr (1974, 1501) reports in his review of regime transitions from 1800 to 1971 that "marked increases were found between the 19th- and mid-20th century polities in the extent of 'democratic' authority characteristics such as institutional constraints on chief executives and the openness of the process by which they attained office." Huntington (1991, 21) observes that "in the fifteen years following . . . 1974, democratic regimes replaced authoritarian ones in approximately 30 countries." In its 1992 survey, Freedom House reported that in 1991 "there were 91 democracies and another 35 countries in some form of democratic transition—a staggering 126 out of 183 nations evaluated—compared to forty-four democracies in 1972 and 56 in 1980" (McColm 1992, 47). And, of course, Francis Fukuyama (1989) claims in his well-known (or infamous, depending on your point of view) essay that the global process of democratization has reached the point of no return.[3]

Admittedly, the "end of history" looks further away in the middle of the 1990s than it did when the Cold War ended. "The period of rapid democratic gains occasioned by the collapse of Soviet communism appears to have ended" (Karatnycky 1993, 16). In fact, according to Freedom House, an organization that monitors political and civil rights on a global basis every year, "As 1993 drew to a close, freedom around the world was in retreat while violence, repression and state control were on the increase in a growing number of countries" (Karatnycky 1994, 4). In short, the "third wave" toward democratization of the globe identified by Samuel Huntington (1991) seems at present to be receding.

In this chapter, I will discuss attempts to account for regime transitions toward as well as away from democracy and ultimately focus on the impact of events in the former Soviet Union and its relationship with other "world leaders" such as the United States, Japan, and China on such transitions. One major point of that discussion will emphasize the possibly underappreciated role of emulation and international diffusion processes in regime transitions. I will conclude with an attempt to evaluate empirically the impact of system level forces on the average level of democracy in the international system and the relative strength of international system-level forces and state-specific factors on regime transitions.

Systemic Level Impacts versus
State Level Forces on Regime Transitions

Area or comparative politics specialists have an understandable tendency to analyze regime transitions in isolation, one country at a time, or, at most, to focus on one region. Even some analysts who are inclined to generalize about transition processes tend to emphasize the impact of factors all or most of which are internal to the states being analyzed. For example, Guillermo O'Donnell and Philippe Schmitter (1986, 18) conclude a volume devoted to the analysis of *Transitions from Authoritarian Rule* (O'Donnell, Schmitter, and Whitehead 1986) by asserting that "the reasons for launching a transition can be found predominantly in domestic, internal factors."[4] Similarly, Tatu Vanhanen (1990, 50) argues that "the relative distribution of economic, intellectual and other power resources among various sectors of the population is a fundamental factor that accounts for the variation of democratization." Dietrich Rueshemeyer, Evelyne Stephens, and John Stephens (1992) argue that working class mobilization buttressed by middle-class support is a key to democratization. Charles Gillespie (1987), most of the articles in the volume edited by Guillermo O'Donnell, Philippe Schmitter, and Laurence Whitehead (1986), Enrique Baloyra (1987), virtually all of the chapters in Larry Diamond, Juan Linz, and Seymour Martin Lipset (1989), all the works reviewed by Jorge Nef (1988), and most of those discussed in the review essay by Herbert Kitschelt (1992) focus almost exclusively on internal structures and processes in their accounts of recent regime transitions.[5]

Daniel Levine (1988) argues that most analysts have shunned global and regional elements in their work on regime transitions and emphasize the play of forces within national societies because they have become disenchanted with models such as world-system analysis and dependency theory that emphasize exogenous factors. In an important analysis of "Democratization in the Late Twentieth Century" (the subtitle of the book), Samuel Huntington (1991, 37) presents a lengthy list of variables that are alleged to lead to democracy and democratization:

1. A high overall level of economic wealth
2. Relatively equal distribution of income and/or wealth
3. A market economy
4. Economic development and social modernization
5. A feudal aristocracy at some point in the history of society
6. The absence of feudalism in the society
7. A strong bourgeoisie
8. A strong middle class
9. High levels of literacy and education
10. An instrumental rather than a consummatory culture
11. Protestantism
12. Social pluralism and strong intermediate groups
13. The development of political contestation before the expansion of political participation
14. Democratic authority structures within social groups
15. Low levels of civil violence
16. Low levels of political polarization and extremism
17. Political leaders committed to democracy
18. Experience as a British colony
19. Traditions of toleration and compromise
20. Occupation by a prodemocratic foreign power
21. Influence by a prodemocratic foreign power
22. Elite desire to emulate democratic nations
23. Traditions of respect for law and individual rights
24. Communal (ethnic, racial, religious) homogeneity
25. Communal (ethnic, racial, religious) heterogeneity
26. Consensus on political and social values
27. Absence of consensus on political and social values

What is striking about that list from the point of view of this chapter is that all but four of the almost thirty factors are internal to the states whose regime transitions are being analyzed. And three of those (experience as a British colony, occupation by a prodemocratic foreign power, and influence by a prodemocratic foreign power) could be subsumed under a single rubric. (The fourth, the elite desire to emulate democratic nations, is a factor that can at least be induced by the international environment, and a factor to which we will pay special attention in this chapter.)

In contrast, Huntington (1991, 45–46) himself posits that the most recent (currently curtailed third) wave of democratization in the global system was a result of (1) legitimacy problems of authoritarian systems on the global level, (2) global economic growth, (3) changes in the policies of the Catholic Church,

(4) changes in the policies of the European Community, the U.S., and the Soviet Union, and (5) snowballing or demonstration effects from the earlier democratizers of this time period. All of these factors are basically external to the states being analyzed; Huntington's apparent belief is that it is the *environment* of the states that is foremost among those factors that must be analyzed to understand regime transitions.[6] Harvey Starr (1991) has already provided some empirical evidence that Huntington's hunch about the impact on recent regime transitions of snowballing or demonstration effects (and indirectly the legitimacy problems of authoritarian regimes that could be both a cause and a consequence of the snowballing) can be supported by reproducible empirical evidence. Starr's evidence applies to the years from 1974 to 1989.

The Importance of Competition and Emulation

Evidence in favor of snowballing or demonstration effects suggests that there is tendency for states in the international system to imitate one another in political as well as economic practices. This imitative tendency may stem in important part from the anarchic nature of the international system. "Competitive systems," Kenneth Waltz (1986, 66) points out, "are regulated . . . by the 'rationality' of the more successful competitors. . . . Either their competitors emulate them or they fall by the wayside. . . . Competition spurs actors to accommodate their ways to the . . . most acceptable and successful practices."[7]

However, the argument I would like to make about the global trend to democracy does not attribute it exclusively to bloodthirsty power politics competition in the manner of realists or neorealists. One reason is that the trend involves so many small, nonmajor powers of a type to which neorealism, in particular, is not readily applicable, even though one might argue that those smaller states face competitive pressures from states in their own regions that create dynamics analogous to those among great powers. But explanations of state behavior that stress the importance of competition and emulation need not rest entirely on realist or neorealist theoretical bases. Such explanations are supported by a wide variety of theoretical approaches and their advocates. For example, Francis Fukuyama (1992) is quite critical of realism in general and downright contemptuous of Waltz's neorealistic approach in particular (see, for example, p. 381), but he argues that "the possibility of war is a great force for the rationalization of societies and for the creation of uniform social structures across cultures. Any state that hopes to maintain its political autonomy is forced to adopt the technology of its enemies and rivals. More than that, however, the threat of war forces states to restructure their social systems along lines most conducive to producing and deploying technology" (73).[8]

But Fukuyama's argument also puts too much stress, perhaps, on the possibility of outright military conflict and less on the impact of more economically oriented competition (and emulation) than current global conditions warrant. States in the global political system tend to imitate the more successful innovators among themselves for reasons similar to those explaining the diffusion of innovations among states within the United States, for example (Walker 1969; Downs 1976; Berry and Berry 1990). Like states within the federal American system, nation-states in the global system see themselves as facing fundamentally similar problems and striving after similar goals, such as political autonomy, territorial integrity, and economic well-being. It is only natural, or rational, that political leaders in the great majority of those states would watch and see who among them best achieves these goals and how. Then, too, precedents and momentum count in virtually any political arena. Success breeds success, failures accumulate and snowball, bandwagoning flourishes. Finally, if James Rosenau's (1990, 327) thesis about the emergence of "turbulence" in the current international system is valid, the analytic skills of leaders and citizens are much improved. One effect of this improvement might well be a "trend toward performance [as opposed to traditional] criteria for legitimacy,"[9] a trend that increases pressures on the world's governments to emulate successful methods and avoid failures based on contrasting methods and policies.

Competition, Emulation, and the Role of the Soviet Union

The importance of competition and emulation among the states of the world to an explanation of regime transitions among those states means that the rise and the fall of the Soviet Union, so to speak, over the last sixty years or so is a factor of particular importance to an understanding of trends in transitions over that time period. The Soviet Union began to build an image as a prototype or model for other countries to emulate in the 1930s. The Western industrialized countries were in the throes of the Great Depression while the Soviet Union, according to the image it managed to project, was undergoing a period of dynamic economic change and progress under the beneficent guiding hand of Joseph Stalin.[10] This state of affairs was reflected in an article published in 1932 in the influential American quarterly *Foreign Affairs,* written by British political scientist Harold Laski (1932).[11] Laski noted that the capitalist world in the 1930s was in the grip of a depression of unprecedented intensity, with millions unemployed, and that pessimism was universal. In contrast, in the Soviet Union, the "Five Year Plan [gives] it an integrated and orderly purpose such as no capitalist country [can] rival. . . . The whole temper of Russia [is] optimistic. The authority of its government [is] unchallenged." Laski acknowledged that the Russian government was "in a rigorous sense, a dictatorship" but argued that nevertheless the "mood of the Russian experiment [is] one of exhilaration." He concluded that "there is an uncomfortable sense in the world that what is happening in Russia may be a prelude to a renaissance of the human spirit. There is no such prophetic confidence in capitalist society" (95, 96, 106).

Hitler's surprise attack in 1941 dealt a stunning blow to the Soviet Union, but it recovered in such a way as to establish for itself a reputation as a first-rate military power by the end of World War II. This reputation was solidified when the Soviets developed an atomic bomb by 1949, sooner than most in the West had assumed likely. The emergence of the Soviet economy in the 1950s as the world's second largest gave it natural prominence as a possible model for emulation by all those countries hoping to duplicate its rapid industrializing effort. Then the launching of two sputnik satellites in the fall of 1957 made the Soviet Union and socialism appear more than ever before (and, as it turns out, since) to be the irresistible wave of the future.

The Soviets were neither slow nor shy about taking advantage of the coup represented by the sputniks. They proclaimed that their technological virtuosity reflected the overall superiority of their system that would soon be demonstrated on a much broader front. Khrushchev spoke to the Supreme Soviet in November 1957 and pointed out that the per capita income of the Soviet Union had increased thirteen times since 1913, whereas it had less than doubled in the United States during that time. Within the next fifteen years, Khrushchev estimated, Soviet production would surpass American production of basic items (*Bulletin of Atomic Scientists* 1957, 360). About a year later, Khrushchev's confidence soared. He declared that "within a period of, say, five years following 1965, the level of U.S. production per capita should be equaled and overtaken. Thus by that time, perhaps even sooner, the U.S.S.R. will have captured first place in the world both in absolute volume of production and per capita production, which will ensure the world's highest standard of living." By 1961, the prediction regarding imminent Soviet superiority in per capita production vis-à-vis the United States had been incorporated into official Communist party proclamations (Brzezinski 1989, 35, 53).

The Impact of Soviet Success

The launching of the sputniks made an obvious impression on the outside world. One news story published in the United States a couple of weeks after the launching of the first sputnik reported that "a leading Western ambassador" had cabled a report to his government that "on October 4 [the day sputnik's launching was announced], the balance of political and diplomatic power shifted from Washington to Moscow" (*Newsweek* 1957, 29). A few weeks later, Robert Wallace (1957, 109) speculated in *Life* that the Russians were developing an enormous pool of technicians who would be exported into developing countries. "Sent into Africa, India, and Indonesia," Wallace predicted, "they may develop these areas according to the Communist scheme while the U.S., still talking bravely about free enterprise . . . declines." In January 1958 another story in *Newsweek* explained: "Success . . . speaks for itself, and the Soviet Union's obvious success in raising itself from backward agrarianism to become the world's No. 2 industrial nation and the No. 1 military power, all in 40 years, speaks in almost deafening tones to nations that are also backward but highly ambitious. From Syria to Indonesia, from the Cameroons to Ceylon, Communism seems a short cut to greatness" (*Newsweek* 1958, 69).

Journalists were by no means the only observers who were impressed by the stellar accomplishments of the Soviets. Hans Morgenthau (1958, 133–34), for example, a few months after the launching of the sputniks, acknowledged:

> The prestige which the United States has enjoyed among the uncommitted nations derives primarily not from the qualities of political freedom and equality of opportunity . . . but rather from its standard of living and its technological achievements. . . . The demonstration of American technological inferiority has greatly diminished the prestige of the United States among the uncommitted nations, since that prestige was built upon the assumption of American technological superiority. And in the measure that American prestige has fallen the prestige of the Soviet Union, by virtue of its accomplishments in one spectacular field of technology, has risen.[12]

The Impact on Theories of Development

In the decade or so after the sputniks, Western academics developed theories of political development that, in retrospect at least, can be viewed as rationalizations for dictatorship. They may even have been, in small part at least, self-fulfilling prophecies. Writing in 1959, Robert Heilbroner in *The Future of History* displays the attitudes and opinions of many American academics of the era. He points out that up to that time the United States had been generally considered the paragon of economic progress in the world but that "this is no longer true" (1959, 87). He refers repeatedly to the "worldwide retreat from capitalism." He argues "in their situations of genuine frustration, one lesson will not be lost upon underdeveloped nations. This is the fact that two peasant countries in the twentieth century have succeeded in making the convulsive total social effort which alone seems capable of breaking through the thousand barriers of scarcity, ineptitude, indifference, inertia. These are the Soviet Union and . . . China" (86). This leads him to conclude that "there is little doubt . . . of the overwhelming power of popular aspirations in the underdeveloped nations, or of the likelihood that those aspirations, in the frustrating conditions of underdevelopment, will lead toward economic collectivism and political dictatorship" (188). Similar reasoning led both Alexander Gerschenkron (1962) and Barrington Moore (1966) to develop arguments to the effect that latecomers to the industrialization process needed to deal with problems much different from those faced by early industrializers and that this required governmental structures that were different from the bourgeois democratic forms of the early industrializers.[13]

Perhaps the most influential argument that "democracy is not relevant to the problems of Third World Countries" was developed by Samuel Huntington in *Political Order in Changing Societies* (1968, 1). The very first assertion in that book is: "The most important political distinction among countries concerns not their form of government but their degree of government. . . . Communist totalitarian states and Western liberal states both belong generally in the category of effective rather than debile political systems." This serves to introduce a theme that pervades the book. "The Lockean American is so fundamentally anti-government," according to Huntington, "that he identifies government with restrictions on government. . . . In many modernizing societies this formula is irrelevant. . . . The problem is not to hold elections but to create organizations" (Huntington 1968, 7).

There is in many of the arguments by Western scholars such as Huntington during this time a hint that it is ethnocentric to prefer or prescribe democratic forms of political systems in Third World countries and that achieving an understanding of the forces that push Third World regimes in antidemocratic directions is a sign of admirable broadmindedness and cosmopolitanism. Robert Packenham (1973, 189) expressed this notion quite explicitly in *Liberal America and the Third World:*

> The chances for liberal democracy in most Third World countries in the foreseeable future are not very great; and the chances that the United States can be effective in advancing the cause of democracy through positive actions are even smaller. The attempt to promote liberal constitutionalism is often both unrealistic from the point of view of feasibility and ethnocentric from the point of view of desirability. The ethnocentricity inheres partly in the American tendency to define democracy mainly or exclusively in political terms, whereas many people in the Third World define democracy in economic or social terms as well, often giving greater weight to the latter.

This attitude became quite common, probably even predominant, among American scholars and Western academic writers in the field of economic and political development. Even as recently as 1980, Kenneth Bollen (1980, 370) observed that "increasingly, many researchers view political democracy as a luxury that can be ill-afforded in Less Developed Countries (LDCs), facing more pressing problems of socioeconomic development, income inequality, and rapid population growth."

In the 1960s and into the 1970s, the Soviet Union proclaimed itself as the regime most worthy of emulation by developing countries, and its claim seemed validated by its general economic performance as well as the launching of the sputniks. At the same time, many (or most?) Western scholars of development acknowledged that democracy was probably not appropriate for the problems facing most Third World countries.[14] Some autocratic regimes in the Third World that emerged during this time period were tolerated and/or supported by the United States government because it feared that leftist authoritarian regimes were the most likely alternative. Others emulated the Soviet Union and/or the Chinese systems to a greater or lesser degree. Almost all of the modernizing dictatorships, of the left or the right, were influenced by and derived support from various sectors of their societies evoked by the notion that the Soviet Union had demonstrated that an autocratic regime is both necessary and desirable for the task of facing up to the type and number of problems confronting developing nations in the twentieth century. As Huntington (1968, 137–38) explained:

> Today, in much of Asia, Africa, and Latin America, political systems face simultaneously the needs to centralize authority, to differentiate structure, and to broaden participation. It is not surprising that the system which seems most relevant to the simultaneous achievement of these goals is a one-party system. If Versailles set the standard for one century and Westminster for another, the Kremlin may well be the most relevant model for many modernizing countries in this century. . . . The primary need these countries face is the accumulation and concentration of power, not its dispersion, and it is in Moscow and Peking and not in Washington that the lesson is to be learned.[15]

The Demise of the Soviet Union and Its Impact on Regime Transitions

The world looks rather different in the 1990s. By the 1980s, the Soviet economy had not surpassed the U.S. economy in either total or per capita production. The Soviet GNP was still, by the estimate of the Central Intelligence Agency (1989, 274, 309) only about half that of the United States, and that estimate may have been overly generous, perhaps wildly so. (A study by the International Monetary Fund, the World Bank, and several other institutions released in December of 1990 estimated that the GNP per capita of the Soviet Union in 1989 was $1,780, while that of Mexico was $2,165. The study's estimate of the GNP per capita of the United States was $20,903. See Ullman, 1990). Furthermore, Mikhail Gorbachev argued repeatedly and persuasively (and his arguments were beamed around the world nightly on the powerful shortwave radio service based in Moscow) that Stalin had imposed on the Soviet Union a political and economic system that had to be drastically reformed if that country was not to be relegated to a position of permanent inferiority and irrelevance.

This point was dramatically reinforced by the fact that during the period when the Soviets had projected that they would surpass the U.S. economically, instead they were surpassed by democratic and non-Western Japan, which as recently as 1965 had an economy only 25 percent as large as that of the Soviet Union. "One can easily surmise that it must have been a shock for Soviet leaders to go from brave (and at the time credible) talk about 'burying' the United States economically in the 1950s, to the point in the 1980s, where they have not only failed to narrow the gap between themselves and the United States, but have been surpassed by the Japanese in terms of GNP" (Ray 1992, 530).

The Soviet Union also ceased to seem worthy of emulation in the eyes of many because of its failures in its attempts to achieve economic equity. In 1989, for example, it was reported by the *New York Times* that "Soviet authorities, who once denied that poverty existed in their country and pronounced it an evil of capitalism, now say that tens of millions of Soviet citizens—at least 20 percent of the population, live in poverty" (Fein 1989, 1). Added to this were stories about corruption enriching bureaucrats in the Communist party in the Soviet Union, as well as East Germany and Romania, and the revelations about the lavish lifestyles of dictators such as Ceausescu.

Huntington (1968, 342) explained that Leninism was a theory of political development. It provides guidelines for political mobilization, political institutionalization, and the foundations of political order: "The modernizers of the seventeenth century canonized the king, those of the twentieth century the party. But the party is a far more flexible and broad-gauged institution for modernization than the absolute monarchy. It is capable not only of centralizing power but also of expanding it. This is what makes the Leninist theory of political development relevant to the modernizing countries of Asia, Africa, and Latin America." Or so it seemed in the 1960s and the 1970s. But now the Soviet Union has fallen apart entirely and Leninism seems to have failed, in the long run, at the crucial political tasks of political integration and concentration of power in the central government. This may well constitute another blow to authoritarianism (added to its failures in the area of economic development and equity) as a model to be emulated.

The Impact of "Western" Success

But it would almost certainly be a mistake to attribute influence only to Soviet problems and to overlook the role that the positive attraction of Western democratic societies has played in the democratizing trend. In 1988, for example, every country in the world with a GNP per capita over $10,000 a year, and a life expectancy of seventy-five or over (a pair of indicators that arguably reflect a desirable combination of economic dynamism and a high level of physical well-being) was democratic (World Bank 1990, 179).[16]

For decades the performance of Western democratic societies in terms of GNP and/or GNP per capita has been discounted on many grounds. The relevance of that indicator to the quality of people's lives has been disputed. (However, as we have just seen, their performance in terms of what many consider to be the most comprehensive indicator of quality of life, i.e., life expectancy, has been almost as impressive in relative terms.) Others, especially dependency theorists and world-system analysts, have argued that democratic (capitalist) societies achieved this success only at great cost to most of the rest of the world and thus in a way not open to developing countries in this century. Another important argument has been that although there is great wealth in democratic (capitalist) societies, it is very unequally distributed.

The credibility of the prescription offered by most dependency theorists and world-system analysis, that is, socialism, has been severely damaged by the recent experiences of the Soviet Union, Eastern Europe, and many socialist countries in the developing world, such as North Korea, Vietnam, Mozambique, Tanzania, Angola, Ethiopia, Nicaragua, and Cuba. The credibility of the description of the success of Western democratic (capitalist) countries as the result of exploitative options no longer available in the contemporary era is an issue on which the jury is still out. The idea that democracy (or capitalism) should be avoided because of the great inequalities they lead to is at least quite disputable. Thomas Dye and Harmon Ziegler (1988) argue that controlling for GNP per capita, capitalist and socialist societies are quite similar to each other in the levels of inequality they exhibit. The strongest correlate with economic inequality is GNP per capita, and the correlation is strongly negative. In other words, since democratic countries have such high per capita GNPs, their distributions of wealth are generally less unequal than those in socialist countries.[17] They also suggest that wealth was more inequitably distributed in the Soviet Union (when it existed) than in the United States.

Admittedly, to support that assertion, Dye and Ziegler rely on a source published some time ago (Ward 1978), and the data in that source pertain to the early 1970s. Furthermore, more recent data on the distribution of incomes suggest that, for example, the ratio of the income of the richest 20 percent to that of the poorest 20 percent is 4 to 1 in the Soviet Union, and 12 to 1 in the United States (Durning 1990, 138). However, possession of money was apparently necessary but not sufficient for the purpose of achieving access to goods and services in the former Soviet Union. Communist party membership, or some functionally equivalent basis of political power, was also apparently necessary if one was to avoid long lines and empty store shelves. Therefore, it is possible that even if money income was distributed more equally in the Soviet Union, access to goods and services, and therefore wealth (the focus of the data in Ward 1978), was more evenly distributed in the United States. Better, even if inadequate, access to health services even for relatively disadvantaged groups in the United States, for example, might have accounted for the fact that "in 1985, a male infant born in the Soviet Union had an expected life span of 63 years . . . two less than a black baby boy [in the United States]" (Heise 1989, 36). In any case, the point here is that by the 1980s, the idea that socialism was a sure path to economic equity—thanks to stories of inequity from the Soviet Union and to data that made it possible to argue that democratic-capitalist societies had in fact achieved in some instances important gains in efforts to ameliorate gross economic inequalities—deprived advocates of autocracy of yet another basis for their arguments.

Although I suspect that democracy's increased appeal and the corresponding decrease in the strength of antidemocratic ideas by the 1980s were fundamentally rooted in the relative economic performances (in terms of growth as well as equity) of the major democratic and autocratic states of that era, it is possible, perhaps, to overemphasize the role of the "bottom line" in these matters. Francis Fukuyama (1989, 6), while fulsomely declaring the superiority of Western liberalism in both the economic and political spheres, also complains about "the *Wall Street Journal* school of deterministic materialism that discounts the importance of ideology and culture and sees man as essentially a rational, profit-maximizing individual." The cultural influence of the West in particular may be an important cause of both changes in the Communist bloc and the global democratizing trend.

Bruce Russett (1985, 228–30) argues that the pervasive cultural influence of the United States, for example, is a neglected dimension of the American power base. The near-global acceptance of American culture, he feels, provides a basis for "cultural hegemony." In important part because of this hegemony, Americans have had substantial control over essential outcomes without the need to exert overt power. "Other's values [have been] already conditioned to be compatible with American wishes in ways that benefit Americans." One of the values that Russett explicitly mentions is "antiauthoritarianism." He concludes by noting that "the internalization of Western . . . norms . . . by the rulers and middle classes of the Third World forms a constant theme in *dependencia* writing" and by pointing to the "mushroom expansion of American television, film, and printed matter in the world."

An aspect of American culture that Russett does not mention explicitly is music. But Timothy Ryback (1990, 26–27) reports that in 1958, a NATO journal "advanced the theory that jazz, rock, and other modern dance music could be employed in the war against Communism." The Soviet Union and its Eastern European allies took that threat seriously. The East Germans were quite concerned about the implications of the induction of Elvis Presley in the U.S. Army and his placement in West Germany in 1958. In the same year, "Bulgaria launched an ambitious campaign to eradicate rock and roll from all public establishments" (26–27).

The battle by the Communist regimes against rock music was ultimately futile. In February 1984, for example, a punk band in Hungary was arrested and put on trial for alleged attacks on the public order. The members of the band were convicted and jailed. But by 1987, Mikhail Gorbachev and his wife met Yoko Ono in Moscow; "Gorbachev invoked the memory of [John] Lennon as a fighter for world peace . . . his wife . . . revealed that she and Misha were admirers of the former Beatle" (Ryback 1990, 3). James Markham (1989, 5) notes that in 1988 when Paul McCartney of the Beatles was a guest on a talk show on the British Broadcasting Corporation, "more than a thousand Russians" telephoned in the hope that they could talk to him. Ryback (1990, 3–4) argues that rock music provided the "sound track of the Gorbachev revolution."[18] With the benefit of hindsight, it might now be plausibly argued that the revolution evoked in part by rock music turned out ultimately to be more profound even than Gorbachev's.

The impact of television, and particularly of American television, may have been even more profound. Rosenau (1990, 350), for example, suggests that "it may be more than mere coincidence that public unrest in Eastern Europe became increasingly manifest after 1981, when the first of some 700,000 VCRs were smuggled into or otherwise acquired in Poland and large numbers of sets also started coming into Hungary, Czechoslovakia, and Bulgaria." Television's impact has not been limited to Communist countries. George Quester (1990, 196) observes that "a number of people in Papua New Guinea . . . are now more familiar with Ted Turner's CNN and the American news it offers than they are with any news of their own region." He also points out: "Many Americans are relatively unaware of the extent of the success of their entertainment business in selling television programs abroad. Most of us realize that all of the world has heard of Hollywood and that almost all of the world now has television. Yet the news that 'Dallas' is the most popular program not just in West Germany but also in Algeria, with similar programs for decades capturing an hour of the evening in most homes in Rumania or Yugoslavia, usually comes as a surprise" (42).[19]

The impact of American television and television programming has almost certainly been enhanced by the rapid spread of television technology around the globe. "Between 1965 and 1985 the number of television transmitters at least doubled in every region of the world, and the number of receiving sets at least tripled; at the global level, the increase was sevenfold for transmitters and more than threefold for receivers" (Rosenau 1990, 338). This spread has been especially impressive in the Third World. Ninety percent of adults in Beijing regularly watch television, and 500 million Chinese are part of the television audience. More than half of India's population had access to television by 1986, which was double the proportion in the early 1980s. Television has permeated Latin America also. "Access to television has become sufficiently global in scope that it must be regarded as a change of parametric proportions" (Rosenau 1990, 343).

Taken all together, American and Western television, music, movies, books, and radio broadcasts have arguably saturated the world in the last decade or two. "The implications of the American entertainment conquest extend well beyond economics. As the age of the military superpower ends, the U.S., with no planning or premeditation by its government, is emerging as the driving cultural force around the world, and will probably remain so through the next century" (Bernstein 1990, 2).

As Russett (1985) argues, this penetration by American and Western culture has probably augmented "antiauthoritarianism" around the world by a process roughly analogous to osmosis. But there are other more explicitly definable processes through which it may have done its part to strengthen the global democratizing trend. In many cases, authoritarian governments that have tried to deny access to American and Western culture (Communist governments mostly but also, for example, some Islamic fundamentalist regimes) have been weakened by those attempts because of the antagonism they foster in people determined to enjoy it. Also, American and other Western cultural vehicles in the main portray American and other Western industrialized societies in a favorable light, even if unrealistically. It is by now trite to say it, but as in most cliches, there is an element of validity in the notion that an implicit message in many of these vehicles is that you, too, can enjoy big houses, TV sets, two cars, and blue jeans if only your country will adopt political (and economic) systems similar to those in the Western industrialized countries.

Unfortunately, however (from a democrat's point of view), the demise of the Soviet Union and the recent economic fate of Russia (as well as other successor republics) may already be having a negative impact on the global trend toward democracy in the middle of the 1990s. The Russian GNP has contracted disastrously (an average of 14 percent in each of the last three years; see the *Economist* May 7, 1994, 118), and its experiment with democracy as well as market-oriented economic policies have brought mostly economic dislocations and suffering, at least so far. (The Castro regime in Cuba reportedly points out the condition of Russia and Eastern European economies repeatedly in an attempt to stifle any reform movements there in the direction of democracy or market liberalism.)

The impact of these dire economic problems in Russia and the rest of the post-Communist world around it threatens to be especially pervasive because of the way it contrasts with recent developments in the People's Republic of China. The Chinese regime has implemented market-oriented economic reforms, but it firmly rejected democracy at Tiananmen Square in June of 1989. A former member of the Chinese Communist Party suggests that the Chinese leadership moved in that direction because it was impressed by the performance of Hong Kong, Singapore, South Korea, and Taiwan, neighboring countries that delayed any movements toward democracy until they had achieved a rather high level of economic development (Binyan 1989, 22). Even Francis Fukuyama observed recently that the "'soft authoritarianism'" of countries like Singapore "is the one potential competitor to Western liberal democracy, and its strength is growing daily" (Branegan 1993, 36). Singapore's influence is already apparent in China. "Singapore . . . has . . . found an ardent fan in mainland China . . . where officials are studying the city-state for ideas on how they can throw off Marxist economics but keep dictatorial political control" (Branegan 1993, 36). In 1992, the *New York Times* reported in a story headlined "China Sees Singapore as Model for Progress" that Deng Xiaoping was of the opinion that "Singapore's social order is rather good. Its leaders exercise strict management. We should learn from their experience" (Kristoff 1992, 4).

The Soviet Union and then Russia have implemented reforms in the direction of democracy and have experienced mostly economic disaster. China, emulating the Asian Tigers (Hong Kong, Singapore, South Korea, and Taiwan), firmly rejected democratic reforms in 1989 and in the early 1990s enjoyed the most rapidly growing GNP in the world (*Economist* May 7, 1994, 118). There are "lessons" there that are likely to be "learned" in widespread areas of the globe, according to the notions about regime transition I advocate in this chapter.

Do System Level Forces Leave Visible Traces?

The foregoing thesis regarding the systemic origins of global trends toward or away from democracy is overwhelmingly persuasive (at least to its author). Possibly, though, it need not depend entirely on impeccable logic and rhetorical flourish for its plausibility. Arguably, if systemic level forces *on balance* do have an important impact on the constituent units of the system, they will leave visible traces on the extent to which the average regime in the system is democratic and on the *collective* profiles of the individual regimes if they are observed over time. This argument is congruent with and to some extent evoked by ideas from "world-system" analysis. Albert Bergeson (1992, 34), for example, in a recent discussion of "communism's collapse" asserts that "if these revolutions and state changes are occurring across the state socialist world, then either these states are experiencing the same problems at the same time, which suggests a tremendously high degree of synchrony in historical development, *or there is something more world-systemic affecting this fraction of the semi-peripheral zone in general*" (emphasis added). Bergeson clearly feels that the latter argument is more valid.

Consider, for example, the possibility that the balance of system level forces exerts a powerful effect on economic growth rates of states in the "periphery" of the global system. "If that is true, it has certain implications for the development of states making up the world economy. The more powerful [system] forces are . . . the more homogenous should be variations in economic growth rates in the states in the peripheral areas. . . . Conversely, if attributes of the separate countries exert a more powerful impact, the variation in growth rates in those [countries] should be correspondingly disparate" (Ray 1982a, 369).

Fortunately, analysts of voting behavior have devoted their attention to a roughly analogous problem of estimating the relative impacts of, for example, national, state, and county level forces on voting turnout, or the distribution of votes between Democrats and Republicans. Donald Stokes (1965, 1967) was the originator of this line of research. More recently, Claggett, Flanagan, and Zingale (1984) have developed the procedures for "partitioning variance" that we will adopt and adapt to the task of estimating the relative impact of system level and national level forces on regime transitions in the global system.

Those analyses will focus on the question of where, on a continuum running from one ideal-typical system to its extreme opposite, the "real world" falls with respect to those forces that bring about regime transitions. In the first ideal-typical system, shown in table 1, all of the variations in regime type, it can be inferred, are brought about by factors peculiar to each of the constituent states. In table 2, all changes are exactly the same in every state in the system, suggesting quite strongly that the changes have common origins. The suggestion would be even stronger, of course, in systems with a larger number of constituent units.

Table 1

An Ideal-Typical System in Which

State-Specific Forces Account for All Regime Transitions

States	1950	1960	1970	State Means
A	3	7	5	5
B	7	5	3	5
C	5	3	7	5
System Mean	5	5	5	5 (Grand Mean)

The numbers in the matrix represent imaginary scores for each state for each year on a scale of democracy with values from -10 (autocratic) to +10 (democratic). All of the variation in democracy within each state is apparently the result of forces specific to each state (even if it might result from the interaction of system level forces and state level factors) and each time period. There is no variation, within the whole time period, across states (i.e., the mean score for each state in the whole time period is 5), and there is no variation in the average democracy score over time.

Table 2

An Ideal-Typical System in Which

System Level Forces Account for All Regime Transitions

States	1950	1960	1970	State Means
A	3	7	5	5
B	3	7	5	5
C	3	7	5	5
System Mean	3	7	5	5 (Grand Mean)

The numbers in the matrix represent imaginary scores for each state for each year on a scale of democracy with values from -10 (autocratic) to +10 (democratic). All of the variation in democracy within each state is apparently the result of system level forces. There is no variation across space between states. All the changes are exactly the same in every state at every observation point.

The arguments here regarding forces bringing about regime changes in the international system imply that system level forces should leave visible traces in the system-wide profile of regime changes. If, for example, the rise and fall of the Soviet Union as a "role model," so to speak, and the relative success of democratic rivals in general, and Japan in particular, were important factors effecting regime transitions within the entire system, then some important portion of the variation in regime types within the system, when the data are subjected to a partitioning of variance as previous analysts of voting data have performed, should be attributable to system level, as opposed to national level forces. In other words, if data on regime types were organized in a fashion analogous to that depicted in tables 1 and 2, a partitioning of the variance could demonstrate where on the continuum with end points idealized in those tables the "real world" global system falls.

The Research Design

In order to investigate empirically the relative strengths of nation-specific factors and the balance of global or systemic level forces on regime transitions, I will utilize Polity II, a data set generated by Ted Robert Gurr, Keith Jaggers, and Will Moore (1989).[20] Polity II provides annual data from 1800 to 1986 on political regime characteristics for 132 contemporary countries, "including virtually all of those whose present population approaches or exceeds one million" (Gurr, Jaggers, and Moore 1989, 2). It also contains data on 20 additional countries that existed in the time period from 1800 to 1986 but that by 1986 had either broken up or been absorbed by others.

The analyses to follow focus on two of the variables for which data are provided in Polity II. One is labeled "Institutionalized Democracy." It focuses on the competitiveness of political participation, competitiveness of executive recruitment, openness of executive recruitment, and constraints on the chief executive. Each state is assigned a score for each year on each of those dimensions. The result is that the most democratic states receive a score of +10 and the least democratic receive a score of 0.

The index of democracy to be used in the analyses here modifies the institutionalized democracy scores from Polity II by subtracting from them the Polity II scores for institutionalized autocracy. This indicator, too, ranges from 0 to +10, with the most autocratic states receiving scores of +10. It focuses on four dimensions, that is, the competitiveness of participation, the regulation of participation, the competitiveness of executive recruitment, and constraints on the chief executive.

It might seem redundant to use indicators of democracy and autocracy, since one is for the most part, on a conceptual level, the mirror image or the complement of the other. But Gurr, Jaggers, and Moore (1989, 37–38) note that they "prefer to leave open for empirical investigation the question of how Autocracy [and] Democracy . . . have covaried over time," making it clear that in their minds the two concepts are at least partially independent. They also observe that "many polities have mixed authority traits, and thus have middling scores on both Autocracy and Democracy scales."

Thus, the index of democracy relied on here is based on the notion that it might be important to distinguish, for example, between those states that have middling democracy scores along with middling autocracy scores (on the Polity II scales), on the one hand, and the states that have middling democracy scores along with very low (or very high) autocracy scores, on the other. In short, the democracy scale here equals the Polity II democracy scores minus the Polity II autocracy scores. It ranges from -10 to +10, with the most autocratic regimes receiving a score of -10 and the most democratic states a score of +10.[21]

Regime transitions are relatively rare events. In addition, typically, regimes change only over rather long periods of time. The interest here is not only in the relative impact of the balance of general, systemic level forces and particular nation-specific factors on regime transitions in the contemporary era but also in the extent to which the relative importance of those two categories of regime-transforming forces might have changed over time (much the way that students of voting behavior have been interested in possible changes in the relative potency of local and national forces on voting turnout or the distribution of votes between the two main political parties over time). Then, too, I am interested in the most visible result of the balance of system level forces on regime transitions, which is reflected in the mean level of democracy or autocracy in the entire international system, and how that balance and the resulting mean level of democracy in the system might have changed over time.

The time period of greatest interest to me is that from 1945 to 1985, the last year (with the exception of 1986) for which Polity II data are available. Working backwards from that most recent time period has led to a focus on the forty-year time periods from 1825 to 1865, from 1865 to 1905, and from 1905 to 1945. The relative infrequency of changes in regime scores revealed by an inspection of those scores led me to conclude that important changes brought about by system level forces were most likely to become visible only over relatively long periods of time. (In other words, my impression is that the system level mean democracy score changes so little from year to year that annual observations are unnecessary and might even have a tendency to obscure important changes that become visible only over longer periods of time.) For that reason, I have calculated democracy scores for each state in Polity II every tenth year during these four forty-year time periods. For example, in the time period since 1945, I have calculated for each state a democracy score for the years 1945, 1955, 1965, 1975, and 1985. This means, obviously, that it is possible to calculate the average democracy score in the entire global system for each of those years.

The method used here to partition the variance in these scores is that suggested by William Claggett, William Flanigan, and Nancy Zingale (1984) in their study of the "Nationalization of the American Electorate." They partitioned the variance in election returns in an attempt to evaluate the relative strengths of national, regional, and local forces on levels of party support in the United States from 1842 to 1970. Here we will focus on a somewhat simpler task in the sense that in this initial analysis we will evaluate the impacts of only two categories of forces acting on regime transitions over time, that is, the global systemic level forces and nation-specific factors. (We will also take into account differences in democracy scores across space in the forty-year periods we analyze.)

Substituting terms appropriate for the analyses here for the terms utilized by Clagget, Flanigan, and Zingale in their study of election returns, we can stipulate that we will partition the total variation in democracy scores in the sets of states observed every ten years according to the following formula: The Total Sum of Squares (SS) = Between Year (SS) + Between State (SS) + State-Year Interaction (SS). More formally, this can be expressed as shown below:

$$\sum_{i=1}^{I} \sum_{j=1}^{J} (x_{ij} - \overline{X}_{..})^2 = \sum_{j=1}^{J} (\overline{X}_{.j} - \overline{X}_{..})^2 + \sum_{i=1}^{I} (\overline{X}_{i.} - \overline{X}_{..})^2 + \sum_{i=1}^{I} \sum_{j=1}^{J} (x_{ij} - \overline{X}_{.j} - \overline{X}_{i.} + \overline{X}_{..})^2$$

where

i = a state in the international system at observation point j

j = a decennial observation point

I = the set of states observed at each decennial observation point

J = the set of decennial observation points during a forty-year time period

x_{ij} = the democracy score of state i at observation point j

$\overline{X}_{..}$ = the mean democracy score of the set of states I over the set of decennial observation points J

$\overline{X}_{.j}$ = the mean democracy score of all the states in the system at decennial observation point j

$\overline{X}_{i.}$ = the mean democracy score of state i during the forty-year observation period

The first term in that equation represents the total variation of the democracy scores around the grand mean of the set of data covering each forty-year period being analyzed. The next term will reflect the strength of system level forces on changes in the extent of democracy in political regimes. It will be a function of the degree to which all the states in the system experience similar changes during the same ten-year periods. This term is calculated by subtracting the grand mean (the mean for all observations during a given forty-year observation period) from the mean democracy score for all the states in the system at each decennial observation point, squaring that difference, and weighting those squared differences by the number of states in the system at each of those observation points. In the extreme, the sum of all those weighted squared differences, that is, the between-year sum of squares, will equal the total sum of squares, as in the ideal-typical system depicted in table 2.

The third term in the equation will reflect the differences among states across space during each of the forty-year observation periods. This term is less relevant to our focus on regime transitions over time. Still, one might reason, as do Claggett, Flanigan, and Zingale (1984), that if the subunits converge or become more similar over time, this is an indication of the strength of system level forces. This term is calculated by subtracting the grand mean for the forty-year period being analyzed from the mean democracy score for each state during that forty-year time period, squaring those differences, and weighting those squared differences by the number of observations of each state during the forty-year time period (which is five in our case). The sum of all those weighted, squared differences is the between state sum of squares.

The fourth term will reflect the strength of factors peculiar to each state at each observation point. In other words, it will reflect the extent to which the states in the system experience dissimilar changes in regime characteristics between the decennial observation points during the forty-year periods being analyzed. This term is calculated by subtracting from each democracy score for each state the mean democracy score for the system at that point in time, subtracting also the mean democracy score for that state during the entire time period being observed, and adding to the result the grand mean for the time period.[22] The resulting differences are squared, then summed at each observation point. In the extreme, that sum will equal the total sum of squares, the ideal-typical situation depicted in table 1.

Analyzing the Data

Our first analysis of the impact of system level forces on regime transitions, or democratization in the global system, is presented in figure 1. It shows the mean democracy score in the system every ten years from 1825 to 1985. There was a rather dramatic increase in the average democracy score in the global system throughout the nineteenth century, punctuated by an increase in the post–World War I period up to the highest average score during the entire period from 1825 to 1985, in 1925. A system-oriented approach to regime transitions and democratization might suggest that those decades of increases in the average democracy score in the global system were primarily the result of the

American Revolution, the French Revolution, and the preeminence of the democratizing Great Britain during the nineteenth century, and, finally, victory by the democratic states over their autocratic opponents in World War I.

FIGURE 1

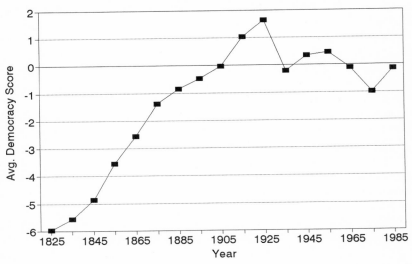

Average Democracy Score (Polity II)
International System, 1825-1985

But then the Great Depression occurred. The wealthy democratic countries went into an economic tailspin. The first to recover was Germany under the Nazis. Hitler staged a "far more effective attack on unemployment than in any other industrial country. By 1935, Germany unemployment was minimal" (Galbraith 1975, 275). And the autocratic Soviet Union embarked upon its first five-year plan, creating, along with the concurrent economic catastrophe in the democratic countries, the impression that its autocratic form of government was the wave of the future. The result, a system-oriented approach would suggest, was a rather sharp drop in the average level of democracy in the global system from 1925 to 1935, because of the system-wide economic problems associated with the Depression, as well as the apparent economic successes in large, powerful autocratic states.

The rise from 1935 to 1945 is to some extent, perhaps, an artifact resulting from our choice of observation points. One might be skeptical about the increase, depicted in figure 1, in the average democracy score in the system from 1935 to 1940. Nevertheless, as the democratic states, especially the United States, were successful in World War II, one should not be surprised by the increase in the average level of democracy after that war, until 1955.

The decrease in the average democracy score after 1955 reflects a dramatic increase in the number of independent states in the world as a result of the decolonization that occurred in those years. Most of these new states did not adopt democratic political systems. "There are so many convincing explanations for this . . . that it is difficult to decide which one is most important" (Ray 1992, 302). But almost certainly one factor involved the Soviet launching of Sputnik in 1957 (at about the same time that the U.S. went into a recession). The extent to which the Soviets managed again to create the impression that their autocratic regime was the wave of the future was reinforced, perhaps, when the U.S. got caught in the quagmire of the Vietnam War. The result (if regime transitions are affected by system level forces of this kind) was another distinct drop in the extent to which political regimes in the world were democratic, from 1955 until 1975.

Then, finally, starting around 1975, it became clear that the Soviet boasts of the Sputnik era that the USSR would soon surpass the United States economically were unfounded. The subsequent wave of democratization in the global system got its start, as reflected in the increase in the average democracy score in figure 1 from 1975 to 1985. If Polity II democracy scores were available for the years since 1985, we can safely assume that they would show that this increase continued for another five years, at least. More recently, as we have already discussed, this third wave has apparently subsided.

Two other recent analyses of democratization at the level of the global system generate results that are quite similar to those shown in figure 1. One is by Nils Petter Gleditsch (1993), who calculates the percentage of democratic dyads, or pairs of states, in the global system from 1816 to 1986. He counts as "democratic" for this analysis any state receiving a score of 6 on the Polity II democracy scale. Gleditsch's focus on pairs of states results, perhaps, in more accentuated decreases and increases before and after 1925, but basically his measure of democratization on the global level produces results similar to the measure used here.

Samuel Huntington (1991, 16) argues that there have been three waves of democratization in the global system since the beginning of the nineteenth century, without ever stipulating very precisely, however, the definition of "democracy" upon which he bases that assertion. He stipulates that those three waves occurred, respectively, from 1828 to 1926, from 1943 to 1962, and from 1974 to the present. All three waves appear quite clearly in figure 1. The two reverse waves, in Huntington's view, took place from 1922 to 1942, and from 1958 to 1975. Those, too, show up clearly in the system-wide averages in the democracy scores depicted in figure 1.

Partitioning the Variance in Regime Changes

In short, our first review in figure 1 of the systemwide averages in the democracy scores based on data from Polity II provides results that confirm an impression, or broad hypothesis that we developed earlier in this chapter, that regime transitions in the global system are to an important extent a function of global, or system-wide, forces to which those who study specific nations or regions are, perhaps, insufficiently sensitive. Let us now take a more detailed look at these data, decomposing or partitioning the variance in democracy scores from 1825 to 1985 in order to assess more precisely the relative impact of global forces on the one hand and nation-specific forces on the other.

Figure 2 shows the results of partitioning the variance in democracy scores in the global system from 1825 to 1865. This is, interestingly, the forty-year time period, of the four we analyze from 1825 to 1985, during which the single largest net change in democracy scores occurred. The average net change in all the forty-year periods was +1.46. The net change from 1825 to 1865 was more than twice that, or +3.41. Because this was a relatively dramatic change in the system level average, one might reasonably surmise that system level forces on regime changes might have been relatively strong during that time period. But figure 2 does not confirm this notion. The portion of the variation in democracy scores attributable to system level forces (because it is shared in common by all or many states on average over time) is only 8.5 percent. Nation-specific forces, in contrast, accounted for 27.8 percent of the variance in democracy scores for that time period. The largest portion of variance, 63.9 percent, is accounted for by between-state or across-space differences in democracy scores. This reflects the unsurprising fact that the states were quite different in their levels of democracy at the beginning of the time period and stayed that way throughout the forty years from 1825 to 1865. (In other words, although across-space variation is large, it is less central than the other two types of forces to an understanding of regime transitions over time.)

It might also seem reasonable to assume that as we look at increasingly more contemporary forty-year observation periods, the effects of system level forces on regime transitions would become increasingly important, because of the impact of modern transportation and communication systems.[23] That reasonable assumption is not borne out. The partitioning of the variance in the democracy scores for the 1865 to 1905, the 1905 to 1945, and the 1945 to 1985 time periods (the results of which are shown in figures 3, 4, and 5) reveal that the proportion of the variance in democracy scores attributable to system level forces during those time periods decreases from 2.7 percent in the forty years after 1865, to 1.4 percent in the forty years after 1905, down to an almost en-

FIGURE 2

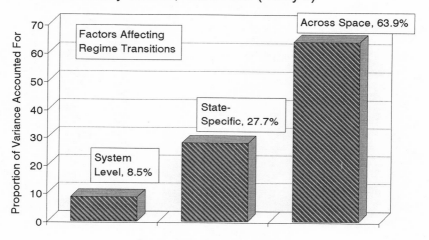

Partitioning of Variance
Democracy Scores, 1825-1865 (Polity II)

Factors Affecting Regime Transitions

Across Space, 63.9%

State-Specific, 27.7%

System Level, 8.5%

Proportion of Variance Accounted For

Categories of Forces Analyzed

tirely invisible .6 percent in the more recent 40 years from 1945 to 1985. In contrast, the portion of the variance accounted for by dissimilar changes in democracy scores brought about (it is reasonable to infer) by nation-specific factors remains markedly constant over the 160-year time period we analyze here. That proportion is at a low point of 17.8 percent in the 1865–1905 time period, but it is 27.7 percent, 29.3 percent, and 28.5 percent in the 1825–1865, the 1905–1945, and the 1945–1985 time periods respectively. (The relationship over time between the relative strengths of all the categories of forces we analyze is summarized in figure 6.) In short, the global system in the last 160 years has been a lot more similar to the ideal-typical system shown in table 1 in which nation-specific forces account for all regime transitions than it has been to the ideal-typical system shown in table 2 in which system level forces account for all regime transitions. The actual "real world" system, though, has been quite different from both of those ideal-typical systems because there has always been, instead of equal average scores for all states as in both ideal-typical systems, a lot of diversity in the average democracy scores for all the states in the global system during each of the five forty-year periods analyzed.

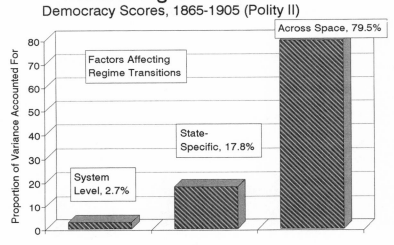

FIGURE 3

Partitioning of Variance
Democracy Scores, 1865-1905 (Polity II)

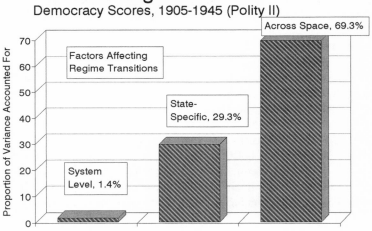

FIGURE 4

Partitioning of Variance
Democracy Scores, 1905-1945 (Polity II)

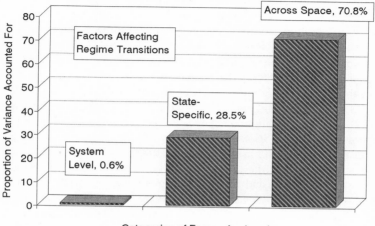

FIGURE 5

Partitioning of Variance
Democracy Scores, 1945-1985 (Polity II)

Across Space, 70.8%

Factors Affecting
Regime Transitions

State-
Specific, 28.5%

System
Level, 0.6%

Proportion of Variance Accounted For

Categories of Forces Analyzed

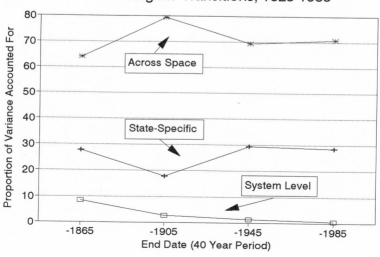

FIGURE 6

Relative Impacts Over Time
Regime Transitions, 1825-1985

Across Space

State-Specific

System Level

Proportion of Variance Accounted For

End Date (40 Year Period)

Modified Analyses

If it is true that regime transitions in the global system tend to be affected by general system level forces, the impact of those forces, at least as it might be expected to be reflected in variation in Polity II democracy scores, does not show up in our analyses here. This is especially surprising, perhaps, because the systemwide average in democracy scores varies in a way that my admittedly intuitive or impressionistic analysis of at least some of those forces would lead one to expect. Why is that the case?

One reaction to empirical analyses not supportive of expectations is "If the data do not support my theory, I will wait for better data to come along." Partitioning the variance in democracy scores in the Polity II data set has certainly provided an extended and intensive opportunity to become familiar with that data. All data sets contain anomalies and could be improved. Polity II is no exception. The United States, for example, is assigned the same democracy score in Polity II in 1845 as it receives in 1985, that is, a +10. An index of democracy that assigns the same score to the United States at a time when slavery was still in force and women were not allowed to vote (to cite only two of the possibly more striking examples) as it receives in 1985 is obviously insensitive to rather profound variation in "democracy" on the conceptual level. In addition, from this example one might infer that there is in Polity II some kind of implicit or tacit adjustment over time of the democracy scale, so that what counts as "most democratic" in 1845 would no longer be considered deserving of that score one hundred years later. Such a sliding or moving scale might eliminate the kind of systemwide variation or trend in democracy scores that would otherwise show up as a function of system level forces in the partitioning of variance.

However, for the most part, my impression is that the annual democracy scores in Polity II are reasonable, especially if we keep in mind that the partitioning of variance technique is sensitive only to quite broad trends and patterns over the rather large number of observations we deal with in these analyses. That impression is reinforced in an important way by what certainly appears to me a high level of face validity in the systemwide averages of the democracy scores. Finally, I am certainly not aware of any other data set that reports annual evaluations of regime characteristics except in very broad categorical terms (such as in Chan 1984). In sum, I doubt that modifications or improvements upon the Polity II data set would change the findings reported here very much.

Assuming, then, that the fault lies not in data of poor quality, the more defensible conclusion is that the impact of system level forces on regime transitions is simply not as pervasive as I had assumed. A plausible fall-back position is that system level forces (or the *balance* of system level forces, a distinction to which I will return) affect regime transitions at times and places more discriminatingly defined than have been analyzed up to this point. Perhaps, for example, the effect of system level forces might be visible if the focus were restricted to developing countries in the post–World War II era.

The results of an analysis evoked by that idea are shown in figure 7. Variance in democracy scores for less developed countries from 1945 to 1985 is partitioned.[24] The refinement in the scope of the partitioning analysis changes the estimate of the relative impact of system level forces not at all. For the whole system, the estimate is that system level forces account for .6 percent of the variance in regime transitions from 1945 to 1985; for the Third World, or LDCs, it is .7 percent. LDCs constitute a more homogenous set of countries, and this reduces the impact of across-space forces from 70.8 percent to 53.6 percent. But this means that the apparent impact of over-time, nation-specific forces is even greater among LDCs only (that is, they account for 45.7 percent of the variance in democracy scores) than it is for the whole system during that time period. The analogous figure for the entire system is 28.5 percent.

FIGURE 7

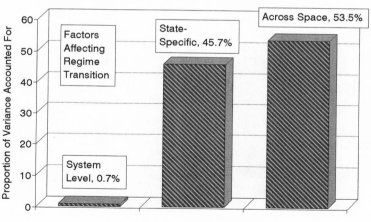

Partitioning of Variance
Democracy Scores, 1945-1985 (LDCs only)

Perhaps, then, the impact of system level forces is restricted to the most recent twenty years, culminating with the dramatic revolutions in the Soviet Union and Eastern Europe? This question cannot be addressed with Polity II data, as they stop in 1986. But Freedom House has been generating annual estimates of political "freedom" for every country in the world since 1973, up to 1993. In order to ascertain the relative impact of system level, nation-specific, and across-space forces on democracy scores in the most recent twenty years, I have partitioned variance in political freedom scores as reported by Freedom House in the years 1973, 1978, 1983, 1988, and 1993.[25] The Freedom House scores do reflect a global trend toward democracy for the twenty-year period from 1973 to 1993, but the change in the global average score is not profound. It goes from -1.07 in 1973 to a +1.33 in 1993. And, as figure 8 indicates, system-wide forces apparently account for only 2.3 percent of the variance in democracy, or "freedom" scores during that time period.

FIGURE 8

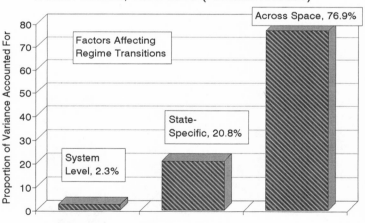

Partitioning of Variance
Demo. Scores, 1973-1993 (Freedom House)

Categories of Forces Analyzed

Conclusion

The partitioning of variance technique has potential applications beyond the analysis of regime transitions on the global level (or of patterns in elections returns in the United States). To repeat, such analyses of growth rates in Third World countries could reveal the relative impact of system level and nation-specific forces on economic processes there. Similar analyses of growth rates, inflation rates, or prices might have interesting implications for the analysis of interdependence among the more wealthy, industrialized countries. Partitioning variance in defense budgets among, say, the major powers, or military expenditures within regional subsystems might offer new insights into the dynamics of arms races or conflict relationships. In general, the relative impact of environmental, system level forces, on the one hand, and nation-specific, internal factors, on the other, is a controversial, even central issue in several areas of enquiry (Russett 1983; Bueno de Mesquita and Lalman, 1988), and the partitioning of variance technique offers one useful way of addressing it.

Here, it has been used to analyze the global process involving transitions in all the regimes that were part of the international political system over the last 170 years. One—I believe invalid—critique of analyses of this sort in previous, more preliminary, reports asserts that they exclude or ignore this or that factor that is crucial to an understanding of regime transitions. *No* explanatory factor is included explicitly in the analyses reported here; the only data analyzed pertain to regime transitions. *All* conceivable explanatory factors have been taken into account implicitly, because the categories of causal factors to which variations in regime scores can logically be attributed are mutually exclusive and exhaustive.

A more valid criticism points out that system level forces might have had a profound impact on regime transitions, despite the results reported here. Critiques of earlier drafts of this work, combined with Whitehead's (1986) essay have helped to make this point clear to me. Whitehead evaluates the efforts of the United States and European countries to encourage transitions to democracy. If those efforts were successful, they would constitute a global level force accounting for a trend toward democracy of the type that is of interest here. But if, say, the Soviet Union over the same time period engaged in *equally* successful efforts to encourage transitions away from democracy to one-party dictatorships, then the transitions brought about by the efforts of the United States and European countries would not be attributed to system level forces by the kind of analysis I have done here. In the extreme, if global level forces are perfectly counterbalancing, the analysis technique used here would attribute all variation to state-specific forces even if the global level forces in question (in the form of democratizing efforts by some major powers, and efforts in the opposite direction by other major powers) accounted for every transition that took place, because the *net,* or *general* impact of system level forces would under those circumstances be nonexistent.

Alternatively, one could argue that system level forces might affect, in the terminology of world-system analysis, different categories of states in different ways. Perhaps, for example, states in the periphery are pushed in the autocratic direction by world-systemic processes, while semiperipheral states are pulled in the democratic direction. Bollen (1983) argues that semiperipheral status makes states more likely to be autocratic, while Bergeson (1992) asserts that semiperipheral status is a key to understanding transitions to democracy in the immediate post–Cold War era. If either of those assertions is valid, and the trends among states in the periphery and among states in the semiperiphery counterbalance each other, then a decomposition of the variance in regime scores would not attribute any of those transitions to *general* system level forces.[26]

I do not see such results as a shortcoming of the technique I have used here because in this work I have been particularly interested in the impact of the *balance* (or the net impact) of system level forces that accounts for global trends to (or away from) democracy, as it is such trends that will have the most important impact on the future of global politics if the democratic peace proposition is valid. System level forces that counterbalance each other in such a way that they do not have an impact on global trends to (or away from) democracy are, at least for this effort, of less interest.

Furthermore, it is important to understand that the decomposition of variance technique used here is not blind to the impact of counterbalancing system level forces. If the impact of world-system processes, for example, is different for states in the periphery and in the semiperiphery, this means that those processes *interact* with peripheral and semiperipheral status. The decomposition of variance technique I have used here does reveal the impact of the interaction of system level forces and attributes of individual states (such as peripheral or semiperipheral status), contrary to the impression of some readers of earlier versions of this work; that impact is categorized as a 'state-specific' effect.

Clagget et al. (1984) evaluate the impact of regional level forces (e.g., in the south) on voting patterns in the United States. Analyzing the impact of forces specific to states in the periphery or the semiperiphery would involve quite straightforward modifications of the analyses of regional level forces by Clagget et al. Analogous analyses of regime transitions in the global political system could reveal the impact of important regional level forces on changes in regimes in Latin America, Africa, the Middle East, and Asia. Related techniques might also reveal the impacts of system level forces not confined to specific geographic areas or preconceived categories of states (Archer and Shelley 1988; Shelley 1989).[27]

But the major conclusion compelled by the analyses reported here is inescapable. Whether the focus is upon the entire world from 1825 to 1985, less developed countries from 1945 to 1985, or the entire global system from 1973 to 1993, the impact of state-specific factors (possibly interacting with system level forces in a way that reduces the more general impact of those forces) on regime transitions or democratization has been greater than the net impact of general, system level forces. The net impact of such system level forces has not often, in the past 170 years, produced widespread, uniform, and simultaneous changes in the levels of democracy in the political regimes of the world. Despite the fact that the average level of democracy in the regimes of the world from the early nineteenth century to the present does seem to reflect in an intuitively plausible manner the impact of important system level forces, dissimilar changes toward or away from democracy have been substantially more common than transitions in tandem with that system level average.

Notes

1. President Daniel Arap Moi in Kenya also came under considerable pressure to hold elections. They were in fact held, but they were of questionable fairness.

2. Wright (1992, 132) also notes that "Islamists have not failed to recognize that pluralism and interdependence are the catchwords of the 1990s."

3. Max Singer and Aaron Wildavsky (1993) make a similar claim and elaborate on the implications of widespread democracy on international politics.

4. O'Donnell and Schmitter (1986, 17–18) also acknowledge that "the most frequent context within which a transition from authoritarian rule has begun in recent decades has been military defeat in an international conflict." But this is not the type of factor that might account for a global, homogenizing trend in regime transitions, short of an attempt by a state or coalition to conquer most of the states in the world.

5. There are exceptions, of course. An important one is Karen Remmer (1992–93), who stresses the impact of such external, international factors as the oil shocks of the 1970s, the related expansion of international lending, the subsequent debt crisis, and global political change on the process of democratization in Latin America.

6. My hunch is that Huntington feels that way in part because he straddles to a rather unusual degree the subfield division between comparative government and international politics.

7. Waltz (1990, 7) applies this general theoretical point to a case of special interest here when he says that "the changes taking place in the Soviet Union follow in good part from external causes. Gorbachev's expressed wish to see the Soviet Union enter the twenty-first century with dignity suggests this. One expects great powers to resist falling to lower international rankings. Brezhnev's successors, notably Andropov and Gorbachev, realized that the Soviet Union could no long support a first-rate military establishment on the basis of a third rate economy." (This argument is repeated in Waltz 1993, 50.) Daniel Deudney and John Ikenberry (1991/92, 97) make a similar argument.

This explanation now faces the not inconsiderable problem that Gorbachev's policies were a prelude to the dissolution of the Soviet Union instead of its revival. However, it is still possible to argue that the hope for revival, inspired by its more successful competitors, was an important motive for perestroika and glasnost, and that their unintended result was the dissolution of the country.

8. Fukuyama (1992, 75) also argues, in a manner very similar to Waltz, that "perhaps the most recent example of defensive modernization was the initial phase of Mikhail Gorbachev's own *perestroika*. It is quite clear from his speeches and those of other senior Soviet officials that one of the chief reasons that they initially considered undertaking a fundamental reform of the Soviet economy was their realization that an unreformed Soviet Union was going to have serious problems remaining competitive, economically and militarily, into the twenty-first century."

9. Rosenau (1990, 429) also agues that "just as people are increasingly inclined to demand that the claims of collectivities be grounded in persuasive evidence and proof, so they are more and more likely to insist that the legitimacy of leaders and their policies be grounded in appropriate and successful performances."

10. The image Stalin managed to project in the West is nicely reflected, perhaps, in the attitudes of several leading cultural figures of the time. According to H. G. Wells, during those years, Stalin was "candid, fair, and honest . . . no one is afraid of him and everybody trusts him." Ernest Hemingway reflected the attitudes of many in the intellectual and cultural elite of the Western world when he supported the Socialist Eugene Debs for president in the 1932 election. "By 1935, he had become a willing exponent of the Communist party line on most issues. . . . Hemingway's view, throughout the decade, seems to have been that the CP was the only legitimate and trustworthy conductor of the anti-fascist crusade, and that criticism of it, or participation in activities outside of its control was treachery" (Johnson 1988, 156). And George Bernard Shaw, upon concluding a visit to the Soviet Union in 1931, exemplified the ideas of many in the West and elsewhere that the Soviet Union and its socialist system represented the wave of the future in an address to the Soviet people when he said: "When you carry your experiment to its final triumph, and I know that you will, we in the West, we who are still playing at socialism, will have to follow in your footsteps whether we like it or no" (de Jonge 1986, 281). Favorable attitudes toward Stalin and the Communist revolution at this time were not restricted to novelists and writers. The American ambassador to the Soviet Union, Joseph E. Davies, asserted in the 1930s that Stalin was working hard for the "liberalization of the constitution" and intended eventually to institute "actual secret and universal suffrage" (Johnson 1983, 276).

11. Laski, admittedly, was not exactly a disinterested observer. Nobody ever is, of course. According to Paul Johnson (1988, 280), "Laski . . . had been converted to Marxism in 1931, and usually followed the CP line until 1939." But Laski, Marxist though he may have been, was not uncritical of the Soviet Union during this period, as even Johnson (also a far from disinterested observer from the opposite end of the ideological spectrum) acknowledges. And his Marxist sympathies were in themselves a reflection of the tenor of times that I am trying to portray here.

12. As John Mueller (1990, 146) points out, "The impact of the space race can hardly be overstated. For the better part of a decade the Soviets scored triumph after

triumph as the United States struggled desperately to get into the game. . . . These developments made some Americans feel like losers. The Communists seemed to be on the march everywhere, winning hearts and minds left and right in the third world, and outclassing the West in important areas of technology."

13. See also Apter (1965). This idea was eventually reinforced by dependency theorists, who typically concluded that highly centralized governments of the socialist type were necessary to deal with those problems (Gunder Frank 1968; Cardoso and Faletto, 1978; Fagen, 1978), and by theorists such as O'Donnell (1973), who argued that the economic difficulties faced by Latin American states in particular made "bureaucratic-authoritarian" regimes a more or less natural outcome.

14. Interesting evidence that such theoretical speculation can have practical consequences surfaced in an article by Lucian Pye (1990, 17), who acknowledges that "theorists in both the Chinese Academy of Social Sciences and some of China's leading universities . . . came to the support of the official orthodoxy in 1988 by trying to develop what they call the theory of 'neo' or 'new' authoritarianism and which they thought might legitimize China's economic reforms under conditions of political restriction . . . they even sought to support their analysis by citing U.S. scholars who in the 1950s and 1960s suggested that dictatorial systems had some advantages in modernizing." Pye goes on to specify that the scholars the Chinese referred to were Samuel Huntington and members of the Social Science Research Council Committee on Comparative Politics.

15. Although the tone of these comments on Huntington's thesis is certainly implicitly critical, it is only fair to point out that in this passage, Huntington alludes to the importance of successful examples and emulation in the process of regime transition in a manner entirely congruent with the major argument here.

16. This continued to be true in 1990, although the GNP per capita threshold would have to be raised to $12,000 to exclude the only partially democratic colony soon to be absorbed into China, Hong Kong (World Bank 1992, 219).

17. Specifically, they assert that "inequality diminishes with increases in personal freedom ($r = -.52$), and increases in political participation ($r = -.48$)" (Dye and Ziegler 1988, 54).

18. Ryback (1990, 5, 233) goes on to explain: "Today, rock music blasts from apartments in Moscow and Leningrad, it thunders in sports stadiums of Poland and Hungary, it rattles the ancient windows of Prague, and shakes apartment blocks of East Berlin. With 50 percent of the Soviet-bloc population under the age of thirty and with official polls confirming that listening or dancing to music is the primary leisure activity of young people, rock and roll is unquestionably the single most pervasive form of mass culture in the Soviet bloc. . . . In a very real sense, the triumph of rock and roll in Eastern Europe and the Soviet Union has been the realization of a democratic process."

The impact of rock music in the Communist world has not been limited to the Soviet Union and Eastern Europe. (The impact of the revolution that rock music allegedly helped bring about is reflected in the fact that the phrases "Soviet Union" and "Eastern Europe" are already beginning to sound quaint.) Its influence in China is often remarked on, and its impact in Mongolia may be indicative of its potentially powerful political implications even in the more remote areas of the world. "The democracy movement here overthrew the Communist Party leaders in March with street demonstrations, hunger strikes—

and rock and roll. Street protests invariably get the most attention, but many Mongolians say rock songs were among the most effective weapons the dissidents used to gain popular support. One song, 'The Ring of the Bell,' became the anthem of the opposition, and the dissident rock band that sings it has become the hottest group in Mongolia" (Kristoff 1990, 1).

19. It might also be significant that "in the mid-1980s, 'The Cosby Show' was the most-watched program in the homes of whites in South Africa" (Quester 1990, 195).

20. I am indebted to Will Moore for sending Polity II to me. There is a valuable discussion of this data set in Gurr, Jaggers, and Moore (1990).

21. Gurr, Jaggers and Moore (1989, 38) give scores of 99 to states experiencing an "interruption/interregnum/transition." To decrease substantially the number of such "missing data" scores, I have replaced many of these 99's with interpolated scores. I interpolated only if scores were assigned in Polity II to the states in question within five years before and after the year in question. Otherwise, the state was coded as "not in the system that year."

States that were "not in the system that year" had to be assigned some score, as the partitioning of variance technique I used cannot deal with matrices containing empty cells. So, states that were not in the system during any of the decennial observations points within the forty-year periods I analyze were assigned the mean democracy score for the states that were in the system during that year.

One review of an earlier version of this work argued that assigning states not in the system in a given year the system mean would reduce the systemic variance and so obscure the impact of system level forces. But the impact of system level forces is reflected in the variation of the system level means, and assigning that system mean to states not in the system during that year changes those means not at all. The same reviewer suggested that I should restrict my analyses to states that are in the system for the entire time periods that I analyze. That is one of many reasonable ways in which the analyses I will report might be modified (which I mean with admittedly not quite 100 percent determination to eventually get around to). Analyses might also be restricted to states that meet more demanding thresholds in terms of population or size of economy; alternatively, the states might be weighted by the size of the population or economy.

22. The addition of the grand mean, rather than its subtraction, may seem counterintuitive, but the grand mean has, in effect, already been subtracted from each score twice when the mean score for all states at each observation point and the mean score for each state during the whole forty-year time period have been subtracted. Adding the grand mean has the effect of subtracting the grand mean only once, rather than twice, from each score at each observation point.

23. For example, Samuel Huntington (1991, 101) asserts that "demonstration effects were much more important in the third wave than in the first waves of democratization, or, very probably, in any other political waves in the twentieth century. The reason is the tremendous expansion in global communications and transportation that occurred in the decades after World War II and particularly the blanketing of the world by television and communication satellites in the 1970s."

24. I excluded from these analyses all the OECD countries (except Greece, Spain, and Portugal), as well as the Communist countries of China, the Soviet Union, and the

allies of the Soviets in the Warsaw Pact, that is, Bulgaria, Czechoslovakia, Hungary, Poland, and Romania. I included Greece, Spain, and Portugal because they were less developed than the average OECD country and because they were, according to Huntington (1991, 21–22), to cite just one example, the site of the origin to an important extent of the global wave of democratization from 1973 until the early 1990s.

25. The procedures for generating these data in the most recent year can be found in *Freedom Review,* February 1993, 11–16. A more comprehensive discussion of the process can be found in Gastil (1990). Freedom House supplied to me that data from the annual reports on which this analysis is based, for which I am grateful.

In order to enhance the comparability of the Freedom House index scores with the Polity II index, I transformed the Freedom House index, which runs from +2 for the "most free," to +14 for the "least free" into a scale that runs from -10 for the least democratic to a +10 for the most democratic. This is, admittedly, an artificial way to force comparability. Nevertheless, the Polity II index produces an average score of -.14 for 1985, whereas the worldwide average for the transformed Freedom House scores for 1983 is a quite similar -.82.

One reviewer of an earlier version of this work thought that perhaps the observations of the system spaced ten years apart were obscuring the impact of system level forces. My impression is that, on the contrary, such forces are likely to have a larger, cumulative effect over long periods of time and that their impact is likely to be more visible the further apart those observations are, within limits. But to evaluate at least partially the contrary expectations of the reviewer, I partitioned the variance in Freedom House "freedom scores" for annual observations of the period from 1983 to 1993. Even in that decade containing the end of the Cold War and the demise of many authoritarian regimes, the partitioning of variance reveals that the balance of general system level forces accounts for only .2 percent of the variance in the freedom scores.

26. Another argument with a logical structure that is similar from the point of view of the decomposition of variance technique would assert that the global Great Depression in the 1930s might have helped to discredit *existing* regimes everywhere, whether democratic or autocratic, leading to transitions in different directions (away from democracy in democratic countries, and toward democracy in autocratic countries), even though the changes did have common, system level origins. Analogously, in the area of voting behavior, Katz (1973) argues about the partitioning of variance in elections returns in the United States that Stokes (1965, 1967) underestimates the effect of national (i.e., systemic) forces on voting patterns because of his assumption that all districts (predominantly black as well as predominantly white districts, for example) would react to all national level forces in the same manner.

27. These techniques identify empirically groups of social entities whose characteristics of interest covary over time, without requiring the analyst to identify or define those groups a priori.

Chapter 3

"Wars" between Democracies

The subject of the allegedly peaceful nature of relationships among democratic states lends itself to categorical assertions. In their seminal article on this topic, Melvin Small and J. David Singer (1976, 51) cite the statement by Dean Babst in the "influential American business journal *Industrial Research*" to the effect that "no wars have been fought [since 1789] between independent nations with elective governments." Rummel (1979), Doyle (1983, 1986), Maoz and Abdolali (1989), Levy (1988), and Maoz and Russett (1992, 1993),[1] to cite only some of the additional examples, make quite categorical claims that democratic (or "liberal" or "libertarian") states *never* fight interstate wars against each other.

However, even many of those who are most enthusiastically in support of the declaration that democratic states never fight wars against each other are aware that several analysts either acknowledge reluctantly or proclaim quite militantly that there are exceptions to this rule. Jack Levy (1988, 662), for example, comments that there are "marginal deviations from a robust finding." Even a cursory review (and I have tried to be more thorough than cursory) of the writings of those who have considered and discussed this issue will uncover a list of references to reputedly "marginal" exceptions to the "rule" regarding the absence of war between democracies that achieves a rather disconcerting length. That list would contain (at least) the following "exceptions." (Brief explanatory comments are provided for some cases whose potential relevance might seem especially dubious.)

Alleged Exceptions to the Rule That Democratic States Never Fight Wars against Each Other

1. Athens versus Syracuse, 415–413 B.C. (Modelski 1990, 34–35; Russett and Antholis, 1992)
2. United Provinces versus England, 1780–1783 (Cole 1990, 19; Modelski 1988, 16)
3. English versus the French during the French Revolutionary Wars, 1792–1802 (Cole 1990, 19)
4. War of 1812 (Cole 1990, 19; Modelski 1989, 16; Rummel 1979, 279; Russett 1990b, 123)

5. Belgium versus Holland, 1830 (Mueller 1991, 59)
6. Swiss Civil War, 1847 (Mueller 1991, 59)
7. Rome (Papal States) versus France, 1849 (Rummel 1984, 11; Small and Singer 1976, 67; Russett 1990b, 123)
8. American Civil War ("While the war fought in North America from 1861 to 1865 is known as the American Civil War it would not have been so named if the breakaway Confederacy had won. As it began as a war between two sovereign states, each of which had all the paraphernalia of government from president to judiciary and army, I prefer to classify it as an international war." [Blainey 1988, xi]; see also Coulter 1950; Parish 1975; Mueller 1991, 59; and Bueno de Mesquita and Lalman 1992, chapter 5)
9. Spanish-American War, 1898 (Cole 1990, 19; Modelski 1990, 29; Lake 1992, 33)
10. Second Philippines, 1899 ("One can make a very good case . . . that the Philippines Republic destroyed by the democratic United States in 1899 was an anti-colonial liberal democratic state." [Bello 1986, 46])
11. Boer War, 1899–1902 (Russett 1990b, 123)
12. World War I ("Imperial Germany is a difficult case. The Reichstag was not only elected by universal male suffrage, but by and large, the state ruled under law, respecting the civic equality and rights of its citizens." [Doyle 1983, 216])
13. World War II ("With knowledge of subsequent events it is uncomfortable to refer to any part of Hitler's Germany as democratic, but we cannot escape the fact that Hitler and the National Socialistic Party were elected to the German Parliament in 1933." [Bueno de Mesquita and Lalman 1992, 150])
14. Finland versus Great Britain and numerous other democratic allies, World War II (Rummel 1984, 11; Lake 1992, 33; Chan 1984, 645)
15. Israel versus Lebanon, 1948 (Russett 1990a, 2; 1990b, 123)
16. India versus Pakistan, 1948 (Wilkenfeld, Brecher, and Moses 1988, 122)
17. Israel versus Lebanon, 1967 (Doyle 1983, 213)
18. Turkey versus Cyprus, 1974 (Chan 1984, 646)
19. Peru versus Ecuador, 1981 (Doyle 1983, 213; Ray 1982, 176)
20. Various conflicts in the post-Communist world (Serbia versus Croatia, Serbia versus Bosnia-Herzegovina, Armenia versus Azerbaijan, etc.)

Can all these "exceptions" be explained away so as to preserve the validity of the statement that "democracies never fight wars against each other?" Of course they can, rather easily, in fact. If one adopts a sufficiently restrictive definition of "democracy" (or "international war," for that matter), then none of the alleged "exceptions" in the list above would count as real exceptions. If, for example, one defines "democracy" as a form of government based on *universal* suffrage (including children), then it is safe to conclude that none of the conflicts listed could be categorized as wars between "democracies." In this admittedly trivial hypothetical example, there never has been a "true" democracy.

One can just as easily discredit the assertion that "democracies never fight wars against each other" by adopting a definition of "democracy" (or "war" or "independent state") that is quite broad. If one defines as a "democracy" any government that has the support of the majority of its citizens or is merely elected, a quite lengthy list of wars between democracies can be generated, partly because a lot of autocratic, even tyrannical, governments have *apparently* had the support of a majority and because lots of one-party states have elections where people have no choices among candidates.

Because the validity of the assertion that democracies never fight wars against each other depends on the definition of "democracy" (as well as "international war" and "independent state") and definitions are arbitrary, perhaps the controversy about the validity of the proposition regarding nonwarring democracies is ultimately meaningless. Different people can choose whatever definitions they want in order to defend or to subvert, according to their personal preferences, the proposition about nonwarring democracies. Because choices among arbitrary definitions cannot be criticized in terms of logic or evidence, the debate boils down to meaningless exchanges of equally arbitrary opinions.

A counterargument might begin with the observation that though definitions are ultimately arbitrary, they can be evaluated according to their utility in efforts to understand the world, as well as the extent to which they conform to generally accepted meanings of and understandings about the concept in question. "Democracy" is an emotionally charged term with many dimensions, and it is difficult to define conceptually, as well as operationally. But it is not so difficult as to make any controversy involving it doomed to totally unresolvable disputes. There is a kind of "core meaning" to the term, the content of which is agreed upon by a rapidly increasing community of scholars, as well as a rapidly increasing number of people outside that community. Alex Inkeles (1990, 5) notes, for example, that though there are many different definitions utilized in research on democracy (its effects or its causes), "it seems clear that indicators most commonly selected to measure democratic systems generally form a notably coherent syndrome, achieving high reliability as measurement scales. . . . In the real world they are so intimately linked as to be almost perfect substitutes for each other. When measured separately they correlate at .90 and above."[2] In short, confusion and disagreement about what "democracy" means are not so rampant that it is impossible to devise a definition for evaluating the validity of the assertion about nonwarring democracies in a convincing way.

The Ideal Definition of Democracy

Let us admit, in a rather unorthodox way, that the definition we are looking for will be sufficiently restrictive that no states categorized as democratic will have fought wars against each other, but sufficiently inclusive that the number of states that qualify (now and historically) as democratic is large enough so that the absence of war between "democratic" states is statistically and substantively significant. I will also acknowledge that I think that it is important to come up with such a definition of democracy that excludes all pairs of states that have warred against each other but includes a sufficiently large number of states to make the assertion about nonwarring democracies empirically interesting for reasons that might be described disparagingly as "public relations." People in general, undergraduate students, graduate students, policymakers, and scholars will be impressed to a rather strictly limited extent by assertions to the effect that democracies are, say, 80 percent less likely to get involved in wars against each other than other kinds of states. All those categories of people will be much more interested in a claim that democratic states *never* fight wars against each other.

Admitting that the intent here is to devise a definition of democracy that excludes all states that have warred against each other but includes enough states that the absence of war among them is interesting might seem to undermine the legitimacy of the effort. Perhaps that legitimacy can be restored somewhat by rephrasing the argument. What we are engaged in here (as is everybody engaged in research in social sciences) is a battle for the attention of the general public, students, policymakers, and other researchers. Even a rudimentary familiarity with the sociology of knowledge will suggest that those theoretical ideas that receive attention from all of those groups, and thus become most influential and important, tend to be striking in the breadth of their impact and in their basic simplicity. Attempting to devise a definition of democracy that can serve as the basis for a convincing effort to evaluate the validity of the assertion that democracies never fight wars against each other is not merely a "PR" stunt. It is a strategically important step, grounded in the sociology of knowledge, toward securing a place for the idea in the ongoing intellectual battles regarding foreign policy and international politics.

It is also a goal defensible in terms of the purest of "pure" science and basic research. If there is a category of states that is large enough so that, everything else being equal, they would by now have fought a significant number of interstate wars against each other, which have not in fact fought even one war, that is a pattern of profound theoretical significance (and quite possibly, policy relevance). The predominant realist, or neorealistic paradigm, in the field of international politics suggests that the type of political regime a state has affects its foreign policy only to a limited extent, if at all. As Stuart Bremer (1992, 338) points out in the course of presenting his evidence regarding the pacific impact of democracy, "Realists generally dismiss domestic factors as unimportant, yet these results suggest that they have greater impact on the likelihood of war than other things they consider far more important." Similarly, Russett (1990, 127) asserts that "realism has no explanation for the fact that certain kind of states—namely democratic ones—do not fight or prepare to fight one another." This challenge to realism (or neorealism), to repeat a point from chapter 1, may call for an important modification rather than a total rejection of realism. But it is likely to be more effective if it can be argued persuasively that the absence of war between states is absolute, or at least marred only by superficial or easily explicable exceptions. Furthermore, all the arguments and evidence presented so far are based on thresholds on the continuum from autocracy to democracy established for the purpose of defining a category of states as "democratic." This is inescapable, given the nature of the argument. Yet it is not clear to me that any of the thresholds utilized so far, or the definitions of democracy on which they rest, are very well-suited to the task of convincing the unconvinced or disinterested observers of this debate.

A definition of "democracy" that will best serve as a basis for a persuasive evaluation of the validity of the assertion that democracies never fight wars against each other should, first, be based on the realization that democracy is a continuous concept. Any attempt to dichotomize it is bound to lump together "countries into the same category when in reality they have very different degrees of political democracy" (Bollen 1990, 13–14). This means, for one thing, that implicitly at least it is important for those who attempt to defend the assertion that democracies never fight wars against one another to acknowledge that in reality the assertion they are defending, in more precise terms is "States that have achieved a certain level of democracy (on a continuous scale of that concept) have never fought wars against each other." In other words, among the cognoscenti at least, it is important to acknowledge that, conceptually, the purpose of the definition being described here in the abstract will be to designate that point on a continuous scale of democracy above which states will be categorized as "democratic" for the purpose of evaluating the assertion that democracies never fight wars against each other. A clear implication of this point is that the definition of democracy that specifies such a threshold will be different in purpose and content than a more comprehensive definition whose aim is to describe the continuum from autocracy to democracy upon which states fall.

The ideal definition of this threshold (as well as the broader definition of the continuum) will also be theoretically grounded, even if not formally derived from a theory. Perhaps, ideally, the definition would be derived precisely, but in fact even the most formal of theories are not usually so exact in their implications as to allow the precise derivation of definitions, or operationalizations. Bueno de Mesquita and Lalman (1992), for example, provide no really formal definition of democracy of their own and utilize the definition and operationalization provided by Michael Doyle (1986)—even though, it might be added, they have quite a few critical things to say about it. Still, the threshold to be specified here (as well as the broader conceptual definition on which it will be based) will, ideally, be informed by, if you will, those theoretical ideas about democracy that are most pertinent to the alleged lack of warfare between democratic states.

The Most Crucial Theoretical Considerations

As we discussed in chapter 1, several analysts, such as Bueno de Mesquita and Lalman (1992), Maoz and Russett, (1993), Morgan and Schwebach (1992) and Starr (1992), have noted that theoretical explanations of the absence of war between democracies tend to fall into two categories. One category emphasizes the impact of norms regarding appropriate methods for conflict resolution that develop (hypothetically speaking) within democratic societies; these are commonly referred to as *cultural* arguments. The other category stresses the impact of *structural* constraints on policymakers in democracies, such as perceived potential opposition to any decision to use force or go to war.

Certainly one of the most elaborate theoretical explanations for the absence of war between democracies is found in Rummel (1979), an explanation integrated into a five-volume effort. Rummel explains that "in open systems . . . initiating a war or military action is usually precluded by the restraint of public opinion and opposition of interest groups" (1979, 278). Rummel explains further that "between libertarian states there is a fundamental sympathy of their peoples toward each other's system, a compatibility of basic values" (1979, 278). Thus, Rummel might well be interpreted to stress the impact of both political structures and cultural norms.

Bueno de Mesquita and Lalman (1992) provide an elaborate game theoretical explanation of the absence of war between democracies that, in a fashion similar to Rummel, emphasizes the impact of political constraints on decision makers in democracies, emphasizing in particular the impact that the perceptions of those constraints have on democratic elites when they bargain with each other. Bueno de Mesquita and Lalman discount the impact of a cultural abhorrence of violence on the grounds that democracies have demonstrated repeatedly their willingness to use force against nondemocracies. Nevertheless, it is clear that the political constraints that Bueno de Mesquita and Lalman do emphasize have their roots in cultural attitudes within the general public and elite groups about how disputes ought to be settled in general and between democratic states in particular.

In his impressive effort to demonstrate the impact of political culture in relationships between democracies, Spencer Weart (1994, chapter 9) argues that "the recourse to coercion, instead of peacefully tolerating political differences, consistently distinguishes well-established republics from any combination of authoritarian and anocratic government. Not by coincidence, this also reliably distinguishes those regimes that will make war on one another." Thus, Weart, in his attempt to distinguish between states that are democratic enough not to fight wars with each other from those that are merely somewhat democratic, focuses on tolerance toward political enemies. The threshold to be developed here will also focus on such tolerance but will be somewhat more precise and operational because a reliance on tolerance alone would leave a lot of room for controversy. (I am personally uncertain whether one can argue that *any* regime totally avoids coercion of *all* political opponents.)

In short, the conclusion here is that, theoretically speaking, one should anticipate that the characteristics of democracy that should be most important in reducing the incidence of violence between democracies will involve political constraints on decision makers that will increase the costs to them of selecting violence as an option in efforts to resolve conflicts with other democracies. Logically, these costs can be the result of political structures that allow opposition groups most easily and effectively to retaliate against leaders who choose war. Further, such opposition groups are likely to be more passionate in their opposition to violence, and leaders more receptive to such opposition, if democratic cultural values regarding the peaceful resolution of conflict (e.g., "ballots instead of bullets") are highly developed. Also important is the extent to which the constraints on decision-makers are *perceived* by elites in states with whom democracies become involved in conflict. These are considerations to keep in mind when specifying the threshold that might most clearly (and convincingly) differentiate between states that may have achieved democracy to some degree but still fight wars against one another and states that are sufficiently democratic that they will not fight wars against each other. Also, a threshold defined in terms of attributes and characteristics selected with these considerations in mind is likely to seem intuitively more appealing on the grounds that it "naturally" divides countries into "democratic" and "autocratic" (or "insufficiently democratic") categories.

The Necessity for Simplicity

Another, perhaps even more crucial characteristic of a threshold of "democracy" that will serve as a basis for theoretically informed, intuitively ap-

pealing and therefore more convincing evaluation of the proposition that democratic states never fight wars against each other is that it be simple, precise, and
easily operationalized. My feelings on this point are inspired by impressions
formed in the review of the efforts by several researchers to defend the idea that
"democracies never (or only rarely) fight wars against each other." Too often
the credibility of those efforts has been undermined by reliance on definitions
and/or measurements of democracy that are far too complex or so vague that
they look suspiciously like they were rigged to provide escape clauses, so to
speak, when difficult cases that seem to be exceptions to the rule that democracies never fight wars against each other come up. Then, too, there has been a
lack of awareness, perhaps, regarding the difference between providing a broad
definition of "democracy" that provides a basis for placing states in an operational manner on a continuum from autocracy to democracy and the related but
different task of specifying the threshold on that continuum that divides states
into democratic and undemocratic (or, more precisely, sufficiently democratic
and insufficiently democratic) categories for the purpose of evaluating the democratic peace proposition.

For example, one of the most determined, and exhaustive efforts to defend
the proposition that democracies never fight wars against each other is made by
R. J. Rummel in his five-volume work *Understanding Conflict and War*. He
never defines, and hardly ever mentions, "democracy." He refers instead to
"libertarian" systems, which he says are "open system[s] with virtually com-
plete group autonomy, customary law, and present goals. Laws are limited to a
few . . . customary principles and rights, with the judiciary limited to matching
these principles to concrete cases" (Rummel 1976, 307). From his discussion,
we can conclude that for Rummel a truly libertarian system is one in which the
government focuses on two major purposes only, namely, law (and contract)
enforcement and national security. Rummel recognizes that this is an ideal-
type, which few if any existing states approach. For example, "the United States,"
according to Rummel, "comprises more a libertarian system, but increasingly
is oriented in the totalitarian direction as the modern welfare state and the political elites . . . intervene in the activities of all groups" (Rummel 1976, 307). If
the United States is "increasingly totalitarian," how many truly libertarian states
are there in the world? In general, the definition of "libertarian" in the five
volumes of *Understanding Conflict and War* is too broad and vague to serve as
a sound basis for efforts to convince those who are skeptical of the assertion
that "democracies never fight wars against each other." (It also is so stringent
that it looks suspiciously like a definition designed to delimit a category of
states so small that it would be very unlikely for two states within it to become
involved in wars against each other even if they were no less than normally
inclined to do so.)

In later efforts to defend his thesis, Rummel does become more specific in his effort to categorize regimes. In a couple of journal articles, he stipulates that libertarian political systems have "free and open elections for top leaders, competitive party systems, freedom of speech and the press, freedom of groups to oppose government, individual rights, and limited government, and so forth" (Rummel 1985, 426). For the purpose of operationalizing this concept, he utilizes Raymond Gastil's annual ratings of states for Freedom House (Rummel, 1983).

Gastil's data generation efforts on behalf of Freedom House have been persistent, conscientious, and widely relied upon.[3] I suspect that the data he (and Freedom House) have generated are worthy of respect and that analyses based on these data should be taken seriously. But the fact remains that Gastil's procedures are quite complex (typically he ranks states on civil liberties and political rights on seven-point scales, referring to lengthy checklists for both liberties and rights) and the ratings system that Gastil developed might be described as rather militantly idiosyncratic and impressionistic. Gastil has himself described his rating system as "loose [and] intuitive." He seems quite proud, in fact, of the extent to which his data are not reproducible by independent investigators, pointing out that "with little or no staff support, the author has carried out most of the research ratings. . . . By working alone the author has not had to integrate the judgments of a variety of people. The hunches and impressions that are so important in a survey of this kind would be almost impossible to keep on the same wave length if one had an Asianist, Africanist, and Latin Americanist to satisfy before the ratings were finalized for each year" (Gastil 1990, 26). Gastil's dedication to his task is admirable, but again, his ratings do not provide a very promising basis for resolving disputes about whether there has ever been a war between "democratic" states. Skeptics, or even sympathetic but prudent observers, naturally want to know, when informed about the nonwarring democracies proposition which states are categorized as democracies and why. Assertions to the effect that democracies are states that, say, score at least a 2 on Gastil's (rather intensely personal, almost idiosyncratic) annual ratings for Freedom House would rightly be greeted with serious doubts about their validity as a basis for resolving disputes about controversial cases.

Many important efforts to establish the validity of the idea that democracies do not fight wars against each other have been based on data generated by Ted Gurr and various coworkers, most specifically, the Polity II data set (Gurr, Jaggers, and Moore 1989). This is an impressive data set, based on extensive and detailed analyses of the history of some 155 countries from 1800 to 1986. The original Polity I data set was generated by a single coder, Erika B. K. Gurr, "who worked with increasingly refined versions of category definitions and coding guidelines" (Gurr, Jaggers, and Moore 1990, 105). The Polity II data set is an extension of the Polity I set, and it was generated by Mark Lichbach and Keith Jaggers, then students of Gurr. These coders ranked each regime according to such characteristics as "Competitiveness of Political Participation,"[4] and "Constraints on the Chief Executive." Regimes are coded into five categories on the first of these characteristics, into seven categories on the second. Gurr, Jaggers and Moore (1990, 106) acknowledge that "no intercoder reliability tests have been carried out" on this quite detailed and complex scheme. Researchers such as Maoz and Russett (1992), for example, take the numbers generated by this coding scheme and develop indices that themselves are rather complex.[5]

The point here is not, despite what might be appearances to the contrary, that the Freedom House or the Polity II data sets are seriously flawed or that no work based on those data should be taken seriously. In fact, I believe that the data generated by Gastil, as well as Gurr and his associates, are of relatively high quality and certainly capable of supporting research that deserves to be taken seriously. In other words, I doubt that removing the shortcomings that do exist, say, by making the Gastil or the Gurr scales totally operational and subjecting them to exhaustive tests of intercoder reliability, all of which produced very high scores, would alter the results of research based on them very much.

My criticism of the Gastil and Gurr indexes, and work based on them, is rather that they will not serve as satisfactory bases for moving toward a resolution of the controversy about whether or not democratic states have *ever* fought wars against each other. The methods used to generate the data are so complex that any attempt to draw a line, say, at 30 on the Maoz and Russett (1992) scale, and stipulate that all the states above that line will be considered "democratic" for the purpose of evaluating the validity of the assertion will not only seem arbitrary (as all decisions about definitions are to an inescapable degree) but contrived and artificial.[6] That complex character of the coding decisions, along with the unavoidably arbitrary nature of the definitions in question, will make it impossible to convince observers, much less skeptics, of the possible validity of the assertion regarding nonwarring democracies. Furthermore, refusal to be convinced on the basis of numerical democracy scores—whose exact meaning, through the haze of various mathematical manipulations—would be justified.

Other attempts to evaluate or defend the validity of the assertion about nonwarring democracies are unconvincing not so much because the categorization of countries by regime type are too complex (and/or too idiosyncratic) but because the definitions on which the categorizations are based are too general or vague. Michael Doyle (1983, 1986) compiles a list of "republican" governments that meet four criteria: (1) they have market or private property economics, (2) they have polities that are externally sovereign, (3) they have citizens with juridical rights, and (4) they have representative governments. One problem with this definition involves the fact that in the contemporary era *all* economies have market or private property aspects but government-controlled and "socialistic" characteristics as well. Then, too, are there any societies whose citizens do not have juridical rights, at least on paper? Doyle (1983, 212) also stipulates that the "legislative branch have an *effective* [emphasis added] role in public policy." How does one ascertain whether the legislative branch is "effective?" (One might ask with only a hint of the facetious whether or not the U.S. Congress in the contemporary era is "effective.") Finally, Doyle (1983, 213) declares that "even though liberal states have become involved in numerous wars with nonliberal states, constitutionally secure liberal states have yet to engage in war with one another." States on the verge of war are by definition in tense situations. Any seemingly democratic states that get into war with one another can easily be categorized as *not* constitutionally secure because of the tension induced by the impending war. There may be some theoretical merit to this distinction involving constitutional security (and in fact the definition I advocate below will be based in part on a similar idea regarding the importance of "stability"), but in "sociology of knowledge" terms it looks suspiciously like an escape clause.

Small and Singer (1976), in one of the earlier systematic attempts to evaluate the legitimacy of the assertion that democracies do not fight wars against each other define a "bourgeois democracy" as a nation that (1) holds periodic elections in which opposition parties are as free to run as government parties, (2) allows at least 10 percent of the adult population to vote, and (3) has a parliament that either controls or enjoys parity with the executive branch of the government. The first of those criteria is not free of problems. Are third parties in the U.S., for example, "as free" to run as the Democrats or Republicans? Even more problematic, it seems to me, is the third criterion. Again, in the United States, does the Congress control or enjoy parity with the executive branch of government?

Steve Chan (1984, 630), in his categorizing effort, also stipulates that a state have at least a "partially effective" legislature to check the executive's power. In addition, Chan suggests that in the modern era, states that are democratic must have "partially competitive" nominating process for legislative elections. Whether or not legislatures are "partially effective" or nominating processes are "partially competitive" are not likely to be decisions that would be easy to make in a noncontroversial, operational fashion. (In the pre-Gorbachev days, for example, were not the legislative bodies in the Soviet Union at least *partially* effective?)

Conceptual Definitions and Operational Indicators of Democracy

In an intelligent essay on this definitional problem, Kenneth Bollen (1990, 9) makes the good point that "the starting point in evaluating the validity of political democracy measures is the theoretical definition of the concept."

Webster's Ninth New Collegiate Dictionary (1987, 338) defines democracy as "government by the people, esp. rule of the majority." Certainly one of the more authoritative and cited definitional discussions about democracy is in Robert Dahl's *Polyarchy* (1971, 1). He begins that book by declaring that the "key characteristic of a democracy is the continuing responsiveness of the government to the preferences of its citizens, considered as political equals." Bollen (1990, 9) himself defines "political democracy as the extent to which the political power of elites is minimized and that of the nonelites is maximized."

The problem with each of these conceptual definitions is that on a more specific, operational level they are applicable (I am tempted to say equally applicable) to political systems ranging from tyrannical dictatorships of the proletariat to ideal-typical anarchies (as well as, to be sure, Western, industrialized "democracies"). And it is crucial that the conceptual definition of "democracy" should focus on *procedural* aspects of the phenomenon rather than on the outcomes that a political system may or may not produce. To define democracy as synonymous with "responsiveness to the people" or "maximization of the power of the nonelite" or, say, economic equity is to confuse political process with political, social, or economic outcomes. With that kind of definition, "there is no way to analyze how variation in the political dimension relates to variation on the others" (Diamond, Linz, Lipset 1989, xvi). Even more troublesome is the tendency for definitions of "democracy" that equate it with desirable political, social, or economic outcomes to serve as a rationale (or rationalization) for *any* political process, no matter how blatantly "undemocratic" procedurally, which might (even if only theoretically) achieve that outcome. And even more directly to the point at hand, such definitions serve as the bases for endless, unresolvable arguments about which political systems (and when) are "really" democratic.

With that thought, as well as theoretical arguments about the relationship between regime type and international conflict in mind, I will argue that it is most useful to conceive of democracy, on the theoretical and conceptual level, as a form of government in which the identities of the leaders of the executive branch and the members of the national legislature are determined in fair, competitive elections.[7] In moving to a more operational level, I would first stipulate that for elections to be "competitive," at least two different, formally independent political parties must offer candidates for elections.[8]

I recognize that defining democracy as dependent on "fair" elections leaves the definition vulnerable to the Marxist-Leninist position that competitive elections in a system dominated by capitalists are inherently "unfair," because the ruling (economic) classes control the media. Stipulating that fair elections are the heart of democracy will also open the door to a nearly endless list of characteristics, many of which are impossible to evaluate or ascertain in a straightforward, operational way, which are allegedly necessary if the elections are to be truly "fair." For example, in his discussion of democracy, Dahl (1971, 2–3) insists that there are at least eight "institutional guarantees" necessary to democracy, and many of those guarantees have more than one dimension. Though lengthy lists of characteristics are probably justifiable for attempts to define the continuum from autocracy to democracy and to place states precisely on that continuum, they are inadequate or inappropriate for attempts to define a threshold of "democracy" on which to base evaluations of the claim that democracies do not fight wars against each other.

For that purpose, a small number of characteristics, easily identified in an operational way, must suffice. Ideally, those characteristics will subsume other important ones and/or indirectly indicate their presence in a reliable and intuitively appealing fashion. With these thoughts in mind, I will stipulate that elections are "fair" (having already stipulated that they are "competitive" if at least two formally independent political parties participate) if (1) at least half the adult population is eligible to vote in those elections, and (2) if the possibility for the leaders of the government to be defeated in an election and replaced has been demonstrated by historical precedent.

The stipulation that elections will be categorized as fair only if at least 50 percent of the population is eligible to vote is motivated at least in part, I would admit, by strategic considerations. Every percentage figure from as low as 10 to as high as 100 could be defended. Furthermore, I would acknowledge that on the most austere logical level, it is difficult to construct a better argument for 50 percent than for 37.8 percent or 67.89 percent. But in terms of a strategy of inquiry (and for the sake of appealing to disinterested observers) I would argue that there is some benefit to a 50 percent cutoff point because it is a figure halfway between (roughly) the most extreme positions on this issue; it is the "50 percent solution" in more than name only. Adoption of a significantly higher suffrage threshold would exclude all pre-twentieth-century states from the category "democratic" because female suffrage is with only minor exceptions a twentieth-century phenomenon. States with at least universal male suffrage will not be excluded (at least not automatically) on the grounds that several pre-female-suffrage states had substantial democratic characteristics, and they should not all be treated as totally lacking in interest for students of the behavior of democratic states. Insisting on at least 50 percent suffrage, on the other hand, is consonant with the democratic practice of basing political decisions on the preferences of the majority, or the proportion of the population equal to 50 percent plus one.

In addition, I think one can argue persuasively that any society that deprives over half the population of the vote displays a tendency to categorize human beings as subhuman, or at least undeserving of citizenship to a degree that is inconsistent with democratic values that, some argue, play an important role in inhibiting wars between democratic states. Then, too, such a society places heavy restrictions on the ability of groups potentially opposed to war as an option to make that opposition effective, another mechanism pointed to by some as important to an understanding of the democratic peace phenomenon.

The emphasis on peaceful, constitutional transfers of power as a crucial indicator of democracy is inspired in part by Karl Popper's (1963, 124) argument that "we may distinguish two main types of government. The first type consists of governments of which we can get rid without bloodshed—for example, by way of general election. The second type consists of government that the ruled cannot get rid of except by way of successful revolution." I recognize that, at least logically, political systems might have their leaders selected in processes based on fair competitive elections and still be "undemocratic," that is, fail to exhibit many characteristics that are considered essential (by various observers) to democracy. Political regimes might, for example, possess all the characteristics that I have chosen to be defining and not have a free press, or freedom of religion, or civil rights for minorities, or trade unions, and so forth. But most of the extensive list of attributes that are allegedly crucial to the existence of democracy are deemed so because they are necessary for elections to be "fair." Elections cannot really be fair if the government controls the media or can arrest and imprison the opposition with impunity. Thus, to be democratic, this argument contends, systems must have a free press, civil rights, and so forth.

The focus of the threshold of democracy specified here on peaceful constitutional transfers of power addresses such concerns indirectly. It brings in through a kind of conceptual back door most and possibly all of the characteristics that are alleged in other definitions or operational indices to be necessary for democracy. The assumption on which this definition is based (and it cannot be an *entirely* safe assumption) is that there will not be constitutional transfers of power between political opponents in systems without some access by the opposition to the media, civil liberties, and so forth. The advantage of the focus on peaceful transfers of power is that it removes the necessity to deal with sticky questions about whether the press is *really* "free" and to what extent and about whether the civil liberties in the constitution are respected in practice rather than just on paper, and so forth. Such questions are not likely ever to be resolved on the basis of operational indicators. It is virtually impossible, in principle, in fact, to determine whether the government controls the media by invisible means or whether rumors circulated by opponents of the government about political prisoners are true. In contrast, whether or not there has been a transfer of power between political opponents based on election results can be ascertained with relatively little controversy. And such transfers indicate that at least the *minimum* conditions necessary for "fair" elections are present in a given political system.

Using peaceful transfers of power as a criterion in this fashion is perhaps most vulnerable to criticism on the grounds that it will exclude from the "democratic" category some regimes that are genuinely democratic, in that they reflect accurately the will of the people, who might simply be continuously satisfied with the same ruling party, faction, or coalition. To require people living under such regimes to become dissatisfied to the point that they vote the party that they prefer out of office at least once might understandably be considered perverse. Also, this criterion will categorize as "undemocratic" some regimes almost universally considered "democratic" perhaps for considerable periods of time, until there is a transfer of power from one party to another. Examples would be the United States until Jefferson was elected president in 1800, India until the Congress party was defeated (in 1979), and Japan until recently, when the Liberal Democratic party was, at long last, removed from power.

My first response to these objections would be that in practice it is unlikely that one party in any political system will be able to avoid indefinitely the accumulation of grievances that will deprive it of the support of the majority of voters.[9] More important, I would argue that it is impossible to know if the ruling elites who brought an ostensibly democratic regime into being are willing to allow the identity of the political leaders of a system to be determined in fair, competitive elections (i.e., if it is genuinely democratic) until they have allowed themselves to be removed from positions of power in an electoral process. Until that occurs, nobody knows for sure if they are *that* tolerant of their political opponents (to borrow to some extent from Spencer Weart's [1994a] choice of a threshold), and most important, elites in countries with which the country in question interacts cannot be expected to *perceive* that the country is democratic.

The Theoretical Relevance of Peaceful Transfers of Power

This last point converges nicely, I would argue, with the most important reason for categorizing countries (in part) according to whether or not they have experienced peaceful, constitutional transfers of power between opposing, formally independent political parties. The threshold based on such transfers of power resonates with, and so takes advantage of, several important strands of theoretical work regarding nonwarring democracies. Rummel (1979, 1983, 1985) emphasizes the impact of the freedom that groups opposed to any possible war have to organize in a democracy as a key factor accounting for the absence of war between democracies. Transfers of power from one party to another should be a reliable indicator of the effectiveness of opposition groups in general within any society, as well as the extent to which ruling elites might be expected to heed such opposition. (If they never have lost an election, leaders of a ruling party might understandably be confident that they never will.)[10]

Bueno de Mesquita and Lalman (1992) emphasize the impact of democratic regimes on bargaining between states; such regimes make it obvious, in their view, that a state is "dovish," which in turn exerts a powerful impact on the probability of peaceful outcomes in disputes, *if* both regimes perceive each other as "dovish." Bueno de Mesquita and Lalman, in fact, may exaggerate the extent to which states are readily identifiable as "democratic" (and therefore "dovish"): "In general," they assert at one point, "leaders cannot know the political costs that their opponents anticipate from using force. . . . However, it is common knowledge whether a given state is a liberal democracy" (Bueno de Mesquita and Lalman 1992, 156). This may underestimate the subtlety of the concept and the effectiveness of attempts made by states to make it appear that they are democratic. In any case, constitutional, peaceful transfers of power between opposing political parties within a political system are an easy-to-detect indicator of "democracy." Leaders of other states can be fairly sure, for example, that the government of a state is not just staging elections primarily for the purpose of impressing outsiders (or insiders, for that matter) if its leaders relinquish power when the results go against them.

Commitment to democratic values within a system is important to those writers who have emphasized the impact of "culture" on relationships between democratic states (Doyle 1986; Maoz and Russett 1992, 1993; Russett 1990, 1993; Weart 1994a, 1994b). A system in which the rulers are willing to give up the most important positions in the government in deference to election results is a system in which one can infer with some confidence that respect for democratic values runs relatively deep. If those values do have a pacifying impact on relationships between democratic states, then it is appropriate to focus on constitutional transfers of power to evaluate claims regarding that pacifying impact.

Similarly, if somewhat less directly, peaceful transfers of power should be a reliable indicator of respect for and the strength of laws, rules, and institutions that allegedly constrain leaders within democracies, according to the structural explanation of peace between democracies (Morgan and Schwebach 1992, 307–8). And Maoz and Russett (1992, 1993), among others, stress the importance of *stability* within democratic systems, if democracy is to have its allegedly pacifying impact. (Recall Doyle's [1983, 213] emphasis on the absence of war between "constitutionally secure" liberal states.) Regimes in which peaceful transfers of power between contending political groups have taken place cannot be, virtually by definition, brand new and/or only tentatively established. They must have been in existence long enough for the terms of the first set of elected leaders to have expired. Then, too, a willingness by political leaders to step down and give control of the government to opponents reflects, usually, confidence that the system will endure and provide opportunities for defeated parties to return to power. In short, if *stability* is an important aspect of truly democratic systems that are, in theory, the least likely to fight each other in wars, constitutional transfers of power that are a key feature of the definition and indicators of democracy proposed here should serve as a reliable and valid indicator of that kind of stability.

In sum, in our following evaluation of alleged deviant cases, we will consider a state to be democratic if the identities of the leaders of its executive branch and the membership in the national legislature are determined in competitive, fair elections. We shall categorize electoral systems as competitive and fair as long as they involve at least two formally independent political parties, confer suffrage on at least half the adult population, and produce at least one peaceful, constitutional transfer of power between opposing political parties, groups, factions, or coalitions.

Defining Wars and Independent States

Disagreements about or ambiguities in definitions of democracy are not the sole cause of controversies regarding the alleged historical absence of warfare between democracies. Controversies also arise about the categorization of conflicts as international or interstate wars. The controversies focus on thresholds of violence that disputes must cross to be classified as "wars" rather than "incidents," "crises," "border clashes," and so forth, and on differences between international wars, on the one hand, and civil wars, on the other.

According to Melvin Small and J. David Singer (1982), *international* wars are wars between different political entities, one of which might *not* qualify as an independent *state*. (Criteria for statehood will be discussed below.) Interstate wars involve independent, sovereign states on *both* sides of a military conflict. The criteria for statehood, in the Correlates of War project, change through time. At all times, political entities must have populations of at least 500,000 to qualify as states. Up to World War I, Small and Singer (1982) count as independent states only those entities in which both France and England (designated "legitimizers") had established diplomatic missions. After World War I, to be designated as independent states, political entities must meet the population threshold, be members of the League of Nations or United Nations, and have received diplomatic missions from *any* two major powers.[11]

These may sound like tedious details unlikely to have a crucial bearing on any topic of real significance, but as we shall see they do come into play in the controversy regarding nonwarring democracies. Rules that determine which entities are independent states, for example, determine in turn which wars are classified as international (or interstate) conflicts, and which are categorized as civil wars. "Democratic" states, of course, have had civil wars, which some insist are really international wars between democratic states. In other cases, democratic states have attacked nonstate entities that some insist are "really" independent (as well as democratic) states.

There are also those who are uncomfortable with the stipulation that military conflict must involve 1,000 battle deaths (deaths of combatants, rather than civilians), to constitute a "war," a convention established by the Correlates of War project and almost universally accepted by those engaged in quantitative research on international war. The convention is, of course, arbitrary. But lower thresholds would risk categorizing as "wars" extremely minor incidents of no real consequence. In addition, a significantly lower threshold would impose severe demands on data generators for *specific* battle death counts. If, say, 100 battle deaths were the threshold, there would be a host of minor incidents around that dividing line about which haphazard guesses would have to suffice. A threshold of 1,000 battle deaths assures that no phantom wars get counted. In addition, it turns out empirically that most of the military conflicts in question fall quite clearly above or below the more substantial threshold of 1,000, making it possible to avoid large number of coding decisions based almost entirely on guesswork.

In our attempt to evaluate the validity of the claim that democratic states never fight wars against each other, we will accept Correlates of War definitions of "independent states" (and therefore the project's distinctions between civil and international conflicts) and of "wars." We will also recognize that if a war escapes classification as an international war between democratic states only because of what seems to be a quirk or odd and probably unintended result of those definitions, relatively disinterested observers are unlikely to be persuaded that there are really *no* exceptions to the rule that democratic states never fight wars against each other.

"Wars" between Democratic States?

Ancient Greece

Whether or not there were wars between democracies in ancient Greece is not one of the more pressing questions in this controversy, since "democracies" then were in nascent form, lacking many of the modern characteristics that might well be crucial to their foreign policies vis-à-vis each other. Nevertheless, it is possible that Greek city-states did have political systems in which political leaders were selected in competitive elections in which at least half the population was eligible to vote and in which peaceful, constitutional transfers of power took place. Especially if this is the case, and if the causal connection between regime type and international conflict on which we focus here is universal, then the connection ought to be visible, too, in ancient Greece.

It is not, apparently. Bruce Russett and William Antholis (1992) analyze ancient Greece thoroughly in an attempt to evaluate the validity of the hypothesis regarding nonwarring democracies, and they "accept the war of Athens— with her democratic allies—against Syracuse as cases when democracies really did fight each other." They find further that "Athens fought five other wars against clear democracies" (425).

The wars that "democratic" Athens fought are unambiguous within the context of our controversy here in two important respects. There seems to be little doubt that Athens and Syracuse, for example, were independent and "sovereign" entities; there seems little doubt, either, that the scope and intensity of the conflict between Athens and Syracuse, at least, were such that it qualifies as a "war" rather than a skirmish or an incident.

If conflicts that Athens fought with other "democracies" are not to be categorized as wars between democracies, then it is the democratic status of Athens (and/or its opponents, such as Syracuse) that must be brought into question. This, it turns out, is not difficult to do, if the definition of democracy one has in mind stipulates that democratic systems are ones in which the most important national political leaders are selected in competitive elections in which at least half the population is eligible to vote and in which the government's opposition has a chance to win as established by historical precedent. One should consider first the proportion of the population in Athens made up of slaves.[12] Add to that the fact that the female half of the population was not eligible to participate politically, and it is clear that neither Athens nor Syracuse was "democratic" in the sense of the word that suggests that at least half the adult population should be eligible to participate in competitive elections.

Of course, the stipulation that at least half the adult population must be eligible to vote will exclude virtually all the pre-twentieth-century states from the category "democratic" because female suffrage is with only minor exceptions a twentieth-century phenomenon. I have set the suffrage threshold as low as that only to avoid eliminating as without any interest pre-twentieth-century cases that had at least universal adult *male* suffrage. I do not feel that it is capricious to stipulate that at least half the adult population be eligible to vote. Any constitution and/or political system that treats *over* half the population as somehow unfit for participation in politics betrays profoundly antidemocratic attitudes that it is only fair and logical to take into account in attempts to evaluate how "democratic" states relate to one another.

Nevertheless, many pre-female-suffrage states had substantial democratic characteristics, and it would be a mistake to treat all pre-twentieth-century states as totally lacking in interest for students of the behavior of democratic states. In addition, I am not inclined at present anyway to argue theoretically that female suffrage is *the* crucial attribute, the absence of which will make otherwise "democratic" states war prone in their relations with each other.

But the ancient Greek city-states were "undemocratic" in other ways. Many, perhaps most, important governmental leaders in Athens, for example, were not selected in competitive elections, even if we do not insist that at least half the adult population must be eligible to participate if they are to be considered truly fair and competitive. "The administrative side of government [in Athens] was divided among the large number of annual offices and a council of 500, all chosen by lot and restricted to one or two one-year terms, with the exception of the board of ten generals" (Finley 1973, 18). Ironically, this arguably "hyper-democratic" system of selection of governmental leaders by lot meant that those leaders were not really accountable to their constituents. That is, they could not be voted out of office because of unpopular decisions, as there were no elections, much less competitive ones.[13]

Then, too, if the types of regimes are to have an impact on relations between states, there must be a certain minimal amount of information about those regimes available to both sets of political decision makers. It is not clear whether this information was available to the assembly in Athens that voted for war against Syracuse. "When in the winter of 415 B.C., the assembly voted . . . to send a great expeditionary force to Sicily, they were, says the historian Thucydides . . . 'for the most part ignorant of the size of the island or of its inhabitants'" (Finley 1973, 20). This is not the kind of situation where the impact of democracy on bargaining between states, as stipulated by Bueno de Mesquita and Lalman (1992), for example, might be expected to exert its pacifying impact.[14]

Even if there were not these more specific objections, one might justifiably reject examples from ancient Greece as legitimate exceptions to the rule about nonwarring democracies because so many profound changes have occurred in ideas about politics in the last 2,500 years. As Bruce Russett (1990, 123) points out, in classical times, the state was assumed to be legitimately engaged in shaping a society rather than an impartial arbiter, and so such states did not have the modern concept of a citizens' natural rights. In addition, some have argued (Mueller 1989; Ray 1989) that democratic values and opposition to slavery constitute a kind of syndrome of cultural and ethical attitudes that might eventually cause international war initiation to become as obsolete as slavery. The fact that ancient Athens practiced slavery makes it easy to argue that this syndrome of values was yet to be developed 2,500 years ago and, plausibly, might be much more potent in contemporary times. In short, it does not seem necessary to admit that events in ancient Greece involving Athens, Syracuse, and other city-states undermine to any serious extent the validity of the assertion that democratic states have never fought international wars against each other.[15]

Early Wars Involving England

The next wars on our list of exceptions all involve England, and one efficient manner of dealing with them as they relate to the controversy here would involve a focus on the extent to which England might accurately be categorized as a "democracy" in the years from 1780 to 1812. In fact, it turns out to be pretty easy to exclude England's wars against the United Provinces in the early 1780s, the French in the 1790s, and the United States in 1812 from the category of wars between democratic states on the grounds that England during those decades was not democratic. Such a judgment can be based on basic, easily operationalized indicators. Even if we leave aside for the moment the question of women's suffrage, we will find that only a small percentage of adult males were eligible to participate in British elections not only in the late eighteenth and early nineteenth centuries but right up until the end of the nineteenth century. Richard Rose (1974, 482) points out that in Britain the Reform Act of 1832 routed the defenders of the traditional electoral system known as the Old Corruption, in place since the seventeenth century. Even after this rout, "the numbers eligible to vote increased by one-half, but accounted for less than one-fifth of the total adult male population."[16] In addition ballots in England were not made secret until 1872.

This is not to say that there is no logic to the argument that wars between Great Britain, on the one hand, and the United Provinces, France, and the United States, on the other, were wars between democratic states. By 1770, when England got involved in a war with the United Provinces as part of its war against the revolution in the United States, England had developed some democratic characteristics. "Constitutional government in the literal sense, then, dates from the late eighteenth century. Nevertheless fundamental aspects of what we mean by that phrase are a good deal older, and stem from the seventeenth century in Britain. . . . A two-party system came into being . . . admired almost everywhere" (Treadgold 1990, 228).

Of Great Britain's opponent in the first of the wars under consideration here, one historical account of the Dutch role in the American Revolution asserts that while France, Prussia, and Spain were governed by the will of their kings only, "the United Provinces formed a republic in which party spirit rules" (Edler 1911, 11). The French Revolution in 1789 was democratic in its origins, anyway, whereas by 1812 the United States may well have been the most democratic country in the world at that time. There had been by 1812, for example, peaceful transfers of power, one of the keys on which we focus here, from the Federalists to the Republicans (forerunners of today's Democrats). In general, speaking of events in the Netherlands, France, and the United States (as well as Great Britain), R. R. Palmer (1964, 572) writes that "these events of the eighteenth century [were] a single movement, revolutionary in character, for which the word 'democratic' is appropriate and enlightening."

Perhaps so, but as significant as the political developments to which Palmer refers were, they do not compel the conclusion that Great Britain's wars with the United Provinces, France, and the United States were wars between democracies. "Britain in the late eighteenth century was not a democracy. . . . Commons was more powerful than the monarchy, but it was elective only in a restricted sense and would become representative only as the nineteenth century wore on" (Treadgold 1990, 228). The United Provinces in 1770 were headed by a "stadtholder," William V of Orange, who had held this rather kinglike office since 1751 and was at the same time supreme commander of the military and naval forces of the "republic." The United Provinces, further, were dominated by Holland, which was governed in an aristocratic fashion (Edler 1911, 11, 12). (Even as late as 1800, the electorate in the Netherlands was only about 12 percent of the adult population, and elections to the legislature did not become direct until 1849 [Lijphart 1974, 230]).

By the time England became involved in the Wars of the French Revolution in 1793, whether or not the Revolution was leading to "democracy" became an interesting question. The Revolution was adopting a more radical hue. The trial and execution of Louis the XVI led to a break in diplomatic relations between Britain and France (McKay and Scott 1983, 282). "A Constitution of 1793 would have produced democracy but was never put into effect" (Treadgold 1990, 204). The Terror was imminent.

As for the War of 1812, it might be pointed out that Whigs and Tories alternated in the office of Prime Minister of Great Britain with regularity in this era, thus matching the United States in that crucial respect. But whatever democratic characteristics Great Britain possessed (and we have seen that those characteristics were strictly limited) the generation of leaders in power in the United States was not likely to perceive. "The Revolutionary generation remained acutely conscious of the isolation of their [republican, or democratic] enterprise. Not since Rome, so men believed, had there been in the world a successful and permanent republic of major size. . . . The downfall of the French republic . . . left the United States as the only remaining republic by the turn of the century" (Brown 1964, 2).[17] To American decision makers at the time, the War of 1812 was thought to be literally a second "War for American Independence" against a predatory monarchy (whose clutches they had only recently escaped). The idea that it was a war between democratic states would have seemed quite inconceivable to them.

Wars between Belgium and Holland and in Switzerland

The next two "wars between democracies" on the alleged exceptions list are mentioned in a fairly fleeting manner in a paper by John Mueller (1991) and neither necessitate extended comment. The war between Belgium and Holland could not qualify as a war between democratic states because they were in 1830 united in one political entity, albeit reluctantly, as a result of actions by the Great Powers as the Napoleonic Wars wound down in 1814 and 1815. "The two peoples most involved were not consulted; had they been they very probably would not have approved the union" (Vandenbosch 1959, 52–53).[18] Not a very democratic arrangement. Nor was William I, the head of this reluctant union a very democratically oriented man. "He regarded his ministers as servants. . . . Only in 1823 was a Cabinet . . . established, but it was not allowed to take decisions nor to consider questions except those which the King himself put on the agenda" (Kassman 1978, 16). In short, the conflict between Belgium and Holland does not qualify as an international war between democratic states because Belgium and Holland were not independent states, the federal-like state they comprised was not democratic, and in any case it is uncertain at best that the conflict was sufficiently lethal to qualify as "war."[19]

Much the same kind of judgment seems warranted regarding the "Swiss Civil War" in 1847. In the first place, this was a civil, not an international (or interstate), war, taking place within the state of Switzerland. Admittedly, the semi-independence of the cantons making up the country, and the democratic way at least some of them were governed, makes this case worthy of at least a moment's consideration. In addition to the basically domestic character, though, its lack of substantial violence seems to rob this case definitively of any serious chance of being categorized as an international war between democratic states. "In the whole struggle there were only seventy-eight dead. . . . It was, therefore . . . a singularly bloodless affair" (McCracken 1892, 333; other estimates that corroborate this one can be found in Lloyd 1958, 66; Luck 1985, 362; Craig 1988, 5).

The War of the Roman Republic

This war is listed in the article by Melvin Small and J. David Singer (1976) as a war between democratic states, which has brought it to the attention of several others. It was a war with the Papal States on one side and Two Sicilies, France, and Austria-Hungary on the other. France is categorized as democratic, as are the Papal States, by Small and Singer (1976), thus making this, in their terms at least, a war between democratic states.

That it was an international war (involving about 2,000 battle deaths) between independent political entities seems not in doubt. The ambiguities of this case stem from the categorization of France and/or the Papal States as "democratic." That the ambiguities are substantial is suggested by the fact that Steve Chan (1984) rates France as well as the Papal States as comparatively unfree during this period. (France receives a score of 6 on the democracy index in Polity II for 1849; the Papal States receive the code for "interruption/interregnum/transition.")

A rating of France as "undemocratic" in 1849 is defensible but not beyond dispute according to the criteria used here. There was a revolution in France, which ended a monarchy in February 1848. The new republic adopted universal manhood suffrage for the election of a National Assembly in April 1848, and that National Assembly selected Louis Eugene Cavaignac as the leader of the government. "Political democracy was . . . fundamental to the republicans as a form of government, and under Cavaignac this second great conquest of February was not only preserved but egalitarian principles were extended to various national institutions" (de Luna 1969, 231).

Furthermore, in the first election for president held under the new constitution, Louis Napoleon defeated the currently ruling (although only provisionally and indirectly elected) Cavaignac, thus arguably meeting the stipulation that the regime establish by historical precedent that the governing leaders can be replaced by means of an election.

A counterargument would insist that the regime in question was not really established until its first president was elected under the new constitution in December of 1848 and that its democratic character, in terms defined here, hinged upon the question of whether Louis Napoleon (or successors in the same party) could be replaced by election. About that possibility there was doubt right from the beginning. "Politically, the election of Louis Napoleon was a defeat not only for Cavaignac, but for the [republicans] who had been in power since February, and in a sense for the February revolution itself" (de Luna 1969, 389–90). Hearnshaw (1919, 252) says of the new republic that came into being in 1848 in France that "while democracy was burning itself out in Central Europe and Italy, in France also it was hastening towards self-extermination."[20] Another historian points out that the first parliament under the new "Republican" constitution contained an "immense monarchical majority," and that "Louis Napoleon . . . desired, above all, to weaken the republic [and] encouraged a combination of all the monarchists to reduce the rights secured by the revolution" (Schevill 1940, 507).

Admittedly, these are judgments made in part with the benefit of hindsight, but even at the time the election of Louis Napoleon created lots of doubts in the minds of contemporary observers about the democratic character of the new regime.[21] And I would conclude that the new regime set up in France in 1848 ultimately failed on the key test of establishing by historical precedent that the governing party can lose an election and be replaced. Louis Napoleon "was keenly aware that he could not carry [his principles] out in the four years granted him under the constitution of 1848. He therefore made it his first task to get the Constitution changed, and to convert his transitory office into a permanent and hereditary possession" (Hearnshaw 1919, 102). Napoleon's activities along these lines led to a coup in 1851, and he eventually declared himself emperor in

1852. If we add to this the fact that the Roman Republic against whom France fought was ruled by a revolutionary regime under Mazzini that did not come close to surviving a sufficiently long time to establish its democratic credentials via a peaceful transfer of power, it seems safe to exclude this conflict from the category of international wars between democratic states.

The American Civil War

This is one of those conflicts that comes closest, perhaps, to being a war between democratic states. It was one of the bloodier wars, international or civil, in the last two centuries. Small and Singer (1982, 317) acknowledge that "it could almost qualify as an extra-systemic war," thus acknowledging also that its categorization as a civil war is not an easy call. As the quote by Blainey (1988) in the alleged exceptions list suggests, it is certainly conceivable that if the Confederacy had won the war, it might now generally be perceived as an international war *and* a war between democratic states.

In any event, it is categorized as a civil as opposed to an international war, according to Small and Singer's (1982) criteria, because the Confederate States never achieved the status of an independent state; in Correlates of War project terms, this means Great Britain and France did not establish diplomatic missions in the Confederacy. If that were the only reason that the Civil War did not qualify as a war between democratic states, that would constitute a rather technical victory for the nonwarring democracy principle at best. The Confederacy came very close to getting official recognition of sovereign status. "On May 13 [1860] Queen Victoria issued a proclamation of neutrality recognizing the belligerency of the Confederacy, meaning that England recognized the South as having a responsible government capable of conducting war" (De Conde 1963, 243).

Such a step might be interpreted as tantamount to "foreign recognition of the Confederacy as an independent nation, [but] it was not. It was merely a customary proclamation of impartial neutrality" (De Conde 1963, 243).[22] And this distinction between the South as an independent nation, or a rebelling section of an independent state, should not be construed as trivial within the context of the controversy regarding relationships between democratic nations. Surely lurking somewhere in the background of the ideas about the pacifying character of democracy is the notion that democratic political leaders are more likely to respect legal principles in political conflicts (especially in conflicts with other "legitimate" democratic regimes), a tendency that would make them more reluctant to violate international legal norms regarding the avoidance of force to resolve disputes and to invade the sovereign territory of independent states. These war-inhibiting factors did not play a role in the conflict between the United States and the Confederate States of America.

Doubts about the assertion that the Civil War in the United States was really an international war between democratic states focus most pertinently on whether or not the Confederacy was a democracy. A prima facie case can be made that it was. "The Confederate Constitution can legitimately be viewed as an amended Constitution of the United States . . . The two documents are for the most part identical" (Holcombe 1992, 63).[23] By the time the conflict between the North and the South began, in South Carolina in April 1860, the Confederacy had approved a provisional constitution and had selected Jefferson Davis as president in February 1861. He was selected by representatives selected in turn by secession conventions in the separate states. Each state, technically, in its own eyes, "sovereign," was given one vote.

Thus Davis was selected in a process that was at least vaguely democratic but not based on "competitive, fair elections" precisely in the way that we are using those terms here. This was, admittedly, only a temporary arrangement. "President Davis and Vice-President Stephens were merely provisional officers elected only for a year at most" (Coulter 1950, 27). If this means that the war cannot be considered a war between independent, democratic states at its beginning (since the Confederacy had not had time to hold democratic elections before April 1860), it might still be argued that it evolved into a war between independent democratic states, as the Confederacy itself evolved in a democratic direction.[24] The Confederacy held an election in the Fall of 1861, but "obsessed with the feeling that there should be harmony, the Confederacy provided only one ticket, and of course, Davis and Stephens were re-elected" (Coulter 1950, 104). There were two candidates for Congress in *some* districts. But especially when one considers that not only the proportion of the population that was female but also the 35 to 40 percent of the population of the Confederacy that were slaves (*Historical Statistics of the United States: Colonial Times to 1970* 1975, 22, 24–36),[25] were excluded from the (one party) elections, it does not seem necessary, even in an attempt to bend over backwards to be fair to those who argue that this was a war between democratic states, to categorize this election as "democratic." And, of course, the Confederacy never came close to demonstrating that it was "democratic" in the sense of establishing by historical precedent that the governing party could be defeated in an election. It ran out of time before Jefferson Davis's term was completed.

The Spanish-American War

This was clearly a military conflict involving independent states with over 1,000 battle deaths. Any doubts about its candidacy for inclusion in the category of wars between democratic states must involve the types of regimes in power in the United States and Spain at the time. Women did not vote in the United States, but it is still true that "at least half " the population, i.e., the men, were eligible to vote in elections where two independent parties presented candidates and where peaceful transfers of power between those parties took place with regularity.

Was Spain democratic? There is a case to be made in the affirmative. A new constitution was adopted in Spain in 1876 with definite democratic characteristics and potential. Under that constitution, for example, "a sweeping law on the freedom of the press was passed in 1883 and lasted until 1936" (Treadgold 1990, 256). By 1890 universal male suffrage was established in national level elections. By the time the war with the United States occurred in 1898, trade unions had been legalized and trial by jury was in effect (Treadgold 1990, 256). Most impressively, it was clearly established in the Spanish regime as the twentieth century approached, by repeated historical precedents, that peaceful transfers of power between different, independent political parties could and did take place. The Liberals and the Conservatives alternated in power peacefully with each other, and in fact, "a new and liberal Spanish government had come into power in October [1897]" (De Conde 1963, 342), a transfer of power that one might plausibly argue should have reassured American decision makers about Spain's democratic status, that should have in turn had (in theoretical terms articulated, for example, by Bueno de Mesquita and Lalman 1992) an important pacifying effect on negotiations between the United States and Spain as the crisis unfolded in 1898. In short, it seems that when David Lake (1992, 33), to cite perhaps the most influential recent example, categorizes the Spanish-American War as one in which democratic states fought against each other, his decision was justified.

But appearances that Spain was a democracy in 1898 when it became involved in a war with the democratic United States are, to some important extent, deceptive. It is true that *most* national political leaders (executive and legislative) were selected in competitive elections with at least two formally independent political parties competing. Further, at least half the adult population was eligible to vote, since there was universal male suffrage. And, to repeat, the "Liberal-Conservatives" and the "Liberals" did alternate in power.

But those peaceful transfers of power between the independent political parties were *arranged* by an explicit agreement between the leaders of the two major parties and the monarch. This "innovative feature" of the regime established by the constitution of 1876 was referred to as the "turno pacifico" (the "peaceful alternation"), and it was an "arrangement between the major political parties . . . guaranteeing alternating control of the government" (Share 1986, 10). "As in eighteenth century England," one historical account notes, "governmental changes preceded elections. Their outcome largely depended upon negotiations between national party leaders and local *caciques* who offered support to the Government in exchange for local political office" (Medhurst 1973, 4).

In other words, what is within the framework being developed here *the* crucial concrete indicator of a "democratic" system, that is, the peaceful, constitutional transfer of power between independent political parties based on results in fair, competitive elections, was manipulated in gross and obvious ways in the Spain of 1898 so as to make the system *look* "democratic." "Periodically," Richard Herr (1971, 115) explains, "as the political situation became difficult, the party in power resigned, and the monarch appointed a minister of the opposition and then dismissed the Cortes [the Spanish parliament] and called for new elections . . . [T]he new minister could ensure the electoral victory of his party . . . but . . . he was careful to allow the leaders of the opposition to be reelected."

Herr (1971, 115) goes on to explain how these electoral results could be manipulated in such detail. "The *turno pacifico* depended on a refinement of the system of controlled elections which originated under Isabell II. . . . The system is known as *cacequismo,* from the word *cacique,* meaning originally an Aztec chief. . . . When the Cortes was dissolved, the minister of *gobernacion* gave instructions to the local *jefe politico* . . . who was his appointee, and the *jefe politico* worked with the *caciques* to produce the desired majority."[26] As Donald Share (1986, 10) concludes, "the *turno pacifico* required an elaborate system of electoral manipulation and vote fraud."[27]

Spain in 1898, then, did not "really" have a system whose "democracy" was established by peaceful transfers of power in response to fair, competitive elections. But the elections were "fair" and "competitive" in terms of most of the operational criteria I have established here, i.e., independent political parties participated, at least half the adult population was eligible to vote, and elections did produce peaceful transfers of power between the independent political parties. And looking beneath the surface of those indicators, as I have done here with respect to the Spanish case, is to some extent, a violation of the rules of the game that I have established at the beginning of this effort. Yes, it is clear to me that the peaceful transfers of power between independent political parties in the Spanish regime of 1898 were a sham and a fraud and that Spain was therefore not "really" democratic. But I am equally aware that analogous arguments could be made about transfers of power within *any* political system, even the most pristinely democratic. I am committed here to an attempt to categorize regimes in simple, concrete, and operational terms that do not require such relatively subtle, detailed, interpretative analyses. I want to rely instead entirely on the most straightforward, simple criteria involving the selection of political leaders through elections in which at least two independent political parties participate, in which at least half the adult population is eligible to vote, and in which it is clear, because of historical precedent, that the government can be defeated in an election. Does not Spain qualify as a "democracy" if one adheres to the austere, simple categorization process to which I have committed myself?

The answer is no, and not entirely because (as I could argue without grossly violating my own guidelines) the peaceful transfers of power in Spain were manipulated in such obvious ways. Spain was not democratic in 1898 because many of the most important political leaders in the legislative and executive branch were not subjected to the possibility of defeat even in corrupt, grossly manipulated elections. First, in the Senate, a coequal portion of the Cortes, half of the members were "Senators in their own right" or "Senators for life appointed by the crown." "Senators in their own right" were the "sons of the king" or "the Grandees of Spain . . . [with] a proven annual income of 60,000 pesetas" (Verduin 1941, 9). ("Senators for life appointed by the crown" seems self-explanatory.)

Even more important, at least in terms of the criteria that the nature of the controversy in question requires us to adhere to, Spain does not qualify as a "democracy" because not only was half the Senate not selected by voters in competitive, fair elections but neither, of course, was the King. And the King of Spain, according to the Constitution of 1876, was not a mere figurehead. As Carr (1982, 349) notes, "The Constitution of 1876 was drawn up by a committee composed of all shades of monarchical opinion . . . Its centre was Article 18: 'The legislative power lies in the Cortes with the king.'"[28] Charles Chapman, (1948, 506) having analyzed the evolution of the constitutional regime launched in 1876, even after universal manhood suffrage was introduced in 1890, concludes that "the net result was a centralized monarchy in the control of the conservative elements." Donald Share (1986, 10) asserts: "The Constitution of 1876 marked the start of a regime that was remarkably stable. The stability . . . however, was based on a set of authoritarian political structures. *Foremost among them was a powerful monarch, subject neither to the legislative control of France's Third Republic nor to the 'conventions' of England's political system*" (emphasis added).

The impact of this point is diluted by the fact that at the time of its confrontation with the United States in 1898, Spain did not have a king in power. Rather, Spain was ruled by a regent, the mother of the king-to-be (Alfonso in 1902), Maria Cristina of Austria. But the fact that the role of the monarch happened to be filled by a temporary person who may not have had much influence herself does not negate the fact that the role and the powers delegated to it were available for others to use in an undemocratic fashion. This, one can surmise, is one reason, for example, that whereas Gurr et al. (1989) give Spain a relatively high score of 7 on their democracy scale (which is why Lake, 1992, and Cole, 1990, refer to the Spanish-American War as a war between democratic states), Chan (1984), for example, rates Spain in 1898 as "relatively unfree." In short, considering the relatively obvious ways that the electoral system in Spain was manipulated, and more important, the fact that half of the Senate and a relatively powerful monarch were selected in clearly undemocratic ways, outside of the (rather transparently fraudulent) electoral system, the argument that the Spanish-American War in 1898 was a war between democratic states does not seem compelling.

The Second Philippines War

A conflict growing out of the Spanish-American War that might be construed as a war between democratic states was the Second Philippines War between the United States and the Philippines from 1899 to 1902. Having wrested control of the Philippines from Spain in 1898, the United States government decided to maintain control of it rather than liberate it. This was clearly a rather undemocratic thing to do and I think despicable in many ways. That it was a war between democratic states is doubtful. The Philippines did not become an independent state until 1946. But, on a more substantive level, was it not a nascent democratic state in being that the democratic United States decided to annex in 1899?

The Philippines in 1899 was, probably, a nascent democratic state, but it was not yet "in being." Emilio Aguinaldo was the leader of an insurrection against the Spanish that, when the islands were taken over the United States, transformed itself into an insurrection against the United States. "On May 24, 1898 . . . Aguinaldo set up a government to direct the course of the revolution against Spain. . . . The government was dictatorial. The conduct of affairs was to be by decrees set forth under Aguinaldo's sole responsibility" (Pacis et al. 1971, 157).

By January 1899, the revolutionary movement did adopt a more democratic constitution (at Malolos),[29] but there was no time or opportunity to select the new leaders of this aspiring country by way of elections or otherwise establish the existence of this "republic" (Pacis et al. 1971, 168; Miller 1982, 38; Karnow 1989, 116–20). And, of course, this means that it was a long way from establishing its democratic character in the sense of demonstrating by historical precedent that the governing party could lose an election. To say this is neither to blame the Filipinos nor to exculpate the Americans. It is merely to categorize the political regime in power in the Philippines at the time; clearly in the sense of the term relevant to the discussion here, the Philippines was not a democratic state.

The Boer War

In this war, democratic Great Britain invaded two arguably "democratic" republics in southern Africa—the Transvaal or the South African Republic and the Orange Free State—defeated them, and ended their existence as indepen-

dent republics by 1902. This war does not count as an interstate war, in Correlates of War project terms, because the republics in South Africa did not have a
(white, at least) population of 500,000 and/or perhaps because they did not
receive diplomatic recognition and missions from Great Britain and France.
But it was an international war, resulting in 22,000 deaths on the British side
alone (Small and Singer 1982, 86). Thus, it was clearly bloody enough to count
as a "war."

Whether or not it was a war between democratic states is a question that
needs addressing in two parts, because of the differences between the Transvaal,
the main British opponent in the war, and the Orange Free State, which became
involved as a formal ally of the Transvaal. One difference has to do with whether
the two republics were independent. There is no question that the Orange Free
State's independence, at least, was fully recognized by Great Britain and had
been since 1854. Whether or not the Transvaal was independent is a more interesting question, but it can be answered in a fairly definitive manner, according
to the *Oxford History of South Africa:* "The quasi-legal basis for the British
intervention was the claim that Britain had suzerainty over the South African
Republic. Suzerainty had indeed been included in the preamble to the Pretoria
Convention of 1881; but it was not mentioned in the London Convention and
Chamberlain's claim that it still existed . . . was contrary to the facts" (Wilson
and Thompson 1971, 322).

Thus, the confrontation between the democratic Great Britain and the possibly democratic South African Republic was arguably a conflict between two
independent states. Furthermore, since 1881, the Transvaal had selected all of
its leading government officials, including its president, by means of competitive elections. All white males, with exceptions to be noted, were allowed to
vote in these elections.

But the South African Republic was not "democratic" in our terms for
several important reasons. The first was, ostensibly at least, a major issue leading to the war. A discovery of gold had attracted a large influx of English speaking
immigrants into the South African Republic. "By 1896, the 44,000 white alien
men, who became known as Uitlanders, may have outnumbered the Afrikan
males in the Transvaal" (Thompson 1990, 136). The South African Republic
refused to let these people vote,[30] which, ostensibly, was one of the grievances
that Great Britain had when it went to war with it in 1899.[31]

The South African Republic was undemocratic in other ways. To repeat,
Uitlanders could not vote. Neither could women. Add to this the fact that blacks,
a substantial if difficult-to-determine proportion of the population, were also
not allowed to participate politically, and it becomes clear that the South African Republic in 1899 was a long way from being democratic in the sense that
"at least half of the population is allowed to participate in elections." In addi-

tion, since 1881, when the republic had gained independence from Great Britain, it had not demonstrated by historical precedent that the president, or his governing party, might lose control of the presidency by way of election. "By 1899, [Paul] Kruger . . . had been President and virtually undisputed ruler of Transvaal for 16 years" (Belfield 1975, 5). Kruger, as head of a triumvirate, negotiated independence from Great Britain in 1881 and then won the first election for president in 1883. Winner of all subsequent elections, he was still in office in 1899 when the war with Great Britain occurred.[32]

But the Orange Free Republic, Great Britain's other opponent in the Boer War, was arguably quite a bit more democratic. In fact, it was arguably *ideally* democratic: "The Free State was the sister republic of the Transvaal. . . . And how enviable was its history in comparison with the Transvaal's. The British had long regarded it as a model republic: a show-piece of tolerance and good sense" (Pakenham 1979, 34).[33] The Orange Free State, like the Transvaal, had immigrants, or Uitlanders. It dealt with them quite differently. "The Uitlanders in the Free State had all the political rights denied their counterparts in the Transvaal" (Pakenham 1979, 34).

Also, unlike the Transvaal, different people, and opposing political views, contended for and won the presidency. For example, "At the . . . presidential election in 1896, President Steyn, the candidate of the Africander Bond, defeated M. J. G. Fraser, the able representative of the policy identified with President Brand" (Cecil 1900, 21). (Brand was a predecessor of Steyn's in the president's office.) Add to all this the declaration that "the constitution [in the Orange Free State] stipulated that justice would be administered according to Roman-Dutch law and that private property, personal freedom, and the freedom of the press would be guaranteed" (Van Schoor 1986, 236), and it would appear that here, in the conflict between Great Britain and the Orange Free State in the Boer War of 1899, we have a promising candidate for the so-far null category of international wars between democratic states.

The fly in the ointment, so to speak, however, is the fate of black Africans in the Orange Free State. They constituted a considerable if difficult-to-pin-down proportion of the population of the state: it was probably about one-third.[34] Even a noticeably sympathetic account of the political history of the Orange Free State provides enlightening comments on the role of blacks during this period. Van Schoor (1986, 244) acknowledges that the "White Free Staters did keep the Basuto subordinate chiefs under White control in their tribal areas."[35] "All arrangements and relations with the indigenous non-Whites were determined by the principles of differentiation and guardianship," according to Van Schoor. (He does not elaborate on these principles, but one can infer with some confidence that they were not democratic principles.) Blacks could not own or purchase land. In short, "the Blacks were therefore subject to the authority of

Whites throughout the Republican period. They were given no say in the political or economic sphere" (Van Schoor 1986, 250).[36] Since women also were not allowed to vote or otherwise participate in political life in the Orange Free State, it was not "democratic" in the sense that at least half the population was allowed to participate in the selection of the important leaders of the government.

This may seem rather like a technical knockout of this case, as the Orange Free State was apparently quite democratic, except for its exclusion of blacks and women, at a time when women voted virtually nowhere, and not too long after the United States abolished slavery. Further, it is not clear why or whether the exclusion of blacks and women by the Orange Free State had an impact on the process leading to war between that state and the United Kingdom in 1899. But the Orange Free State was neither sufficiently large nor important enough to be recognized as an independent state by the criteria adopted here. In addition, the importance of this case as a near-exception is diluted to some extent, perhaps, by the indirect way it became involved in this war, as an ally of the Transvaal, the initial belligerent, along with the United Kingdom. And it is surely not unreasonable to insist that, at a minimum, a state ought to allow at least half of its adult population to vote in its elections if it is to be categorized as "democratic" or sufficiently democratic so as to avoid wars against other democratic states. By those criteria, the Orange Free State in 1899 was not (or, at least, not sufficiently) "democratic."

World War I

"Imperial Germany," Michael Doyle (1983, 216) suggests, "is a difficult case." But Doyle disposes of it, especially in terms of our criteria here, quite easily, in fact. As Doyle also acknowledges, the argument that Germany, going into World War I, was democratic, is not ridiculous. The legislature was elected by universal male suffrage. German citizens were accorded civil rights. But, to an extent even more clear than was the case with the Spanish king in 1898, the German emperor was no mere figurehead. As Doyle (1983, 216) points out, the chancellor in the German system was appointed by and could be dismissed by the emperor. Furthermore, "the emperor's direct authority over the army, the army's effective independence from the minimal authority of the War Ministry, and the emperor's active role in foreign affairs . . . together with the tenuous constitutional relationship between the chancellor and the Reichstag made imperial Germany a state divorced from the control of its citizens in foreign affairs" (Doyle 1983, 217).

Germany is even more easily declared undemocratic in terms of the criteria stressed here because such an important political leader as the emperor was not selected in fair, competitive elections. There was obviously no chance that *he* could be defeated in the next election, and he exerted a significant amount of power within the system, especially with respect to foreign affairs. In Bueno de Mesquita and Lalman's (1992) terms, states involved in conflicts with Germany could not be expected to perceive Germany as "democratic" and therefore "dovish," because of the amount of power concentrated in the hands of the emperor, and the army's obvious influence on the emperor. World War I was not a war between democratic states.

World War II

Bueno de Mesquita and Lalman (1992) make the useful point that there are no guarantees that democratically elected leaders will keep their states at peace with democratic states. Adolf Hitler was democratically elected and, of course, became extremely belligerent toward democratic states. This example, too, serves as a useful reminder that even a world full of democratic states might not be forever peaceful, even if democratic states never do fight wars against each other, because democratic states might come under the control of despots, even democratically elected ones. But it is obvious that by the time Hitler became involved in war against democratic states in World War II he had expressly, overtly, and officially terminated Germany's democratic political system.[37] Thus the conflicts between Germany and several democratic opponents were not wars between democratic states.

Finland versus Great Britain (and Other Allies), Second World War

As a result of hostilities between Germany and the Soviet Union in 1941, "Britain was compelled to declare war on Finland . . . in order to satisfy her Russian ally" (Eskelinen 1973, 57). Some have cast doubt on the assertion that this war between Great Britain and Finland was between democratic states on the grounds that Finland was transforming itself at the time in the direction of fascism, as a result of its cooperation and alliance with Germany. But Hugh Shearman (1950, 97), at least, insists that "in spite of German domination of Finnish foreign and military policy, the internal regime of Finland continued to follow the western democratic pattern." Shearman also asserts, however, that in the view of the Finns (as reflected in the Finnish press), "Finland was fighting for its own free and democratic social order against Russian autocracy," and that "Finland's war with Russia was a separate incident and involved no hostility to Britain." Similarly, W. R. Mead (1968, 173–74) explains that "throughout the war Finland had accepted that it was a co-belligerent with Germany but asserted that it was engaged in an entirely separate war."[38] Even more important is Mead's (1968, 174) statement that "there was never any direct action between Britain and Finland." Since the proposition of interest here is that democratic states never *fight* wars against each other, this episode in which at least two democratic states (Great Britain and Finland) did find themselves officially on opposite sides of a complex multilateral war, but whose military forces never actually engaged each other in conflict, need not count as disconfirming evidence.

Israel versus Lebanon, 1948

Small and Singer (1976) categorize Lebanon (and Syria) as "bourgeois democracies," and the assumption that Israel is a democracy on the other side of this war fought in the wake of Israel's creation has led several to offer this is an example of a war between democratic states. However, in Polity II Lebanon only receives a score of 4 on the 10-point democracy scale in 1948 (Syria receives a 5), and in Chan's (1984) data, both Lebanon and Syria are categorized as "relatively unfree." Since Small and Singer do not categorize Israel as a democracy going into the war in 1948, because the country had not as yet had elections, this turns out not to be one of the more interesting cases. (Israel would not, of course, in terms of our criteria, have yet had time to demonstrate that it was democratic in the sense that precedents would have established that the governing party can lose an election.)

India versus Pakistan, 1948

This is categorized as a war between democratic states in Wilkenfeld, Brecher, and Moses (1988, 122). Whereas India was arguably democratic, Pakistan was in a very nascent status and never did establish a democratic system. (In Polity II Pakistan receives a score of 3 on the 10-point democracy scale in 1948, and Chan [1984] rates it as relatively unfree.) In any case, according to Small and Singer (1982), this initial clash between Pakistan and India did not involve a sufficiently large number of battle deaths to qualify as an international war.

Lebanon versus Israel, 1967

This case is raised and disposed of quite definitively by Doyle (1983, 213). Lebanon did send jets into combat against Israel at the beginning of the 1967 war, but they were repulsed and Lebanon engaged in no additional hostilities against Israel. Lebanon is not listed as a participant in the 1967 war in the Middle East by Small and Singer (1982, 93). (In addition, in 1967, Lebanon receives only a score of 4 in Polity II's democracy scale and is categorized as relatively unfree in the Chan [1984] data set.)

Turkey versus Cyprus, 1974

This is listed as a war between democratic states in Chan (1984). It might have been listed as a war between democratic states by Lake (1992), also, depending as he does on Polity II data to categorize regimes. But in the Polity II data set, Cyprus is recorded as achieving a 7 on the 10-point democracy scale for six years leading up to 1974 (which would have qualified it as a "democracy" for Lake [1992]); for that particular year the "missing data" code appears. In any case, this is clearly an interstate war, as defined by Small and Singer (1982), between two states that were arguably democratic.

Whether or not Cyprus was "democratic" at the beginning of 1974 is an interesting question.[39] But whether or not the Turkish invasion of Cyprus on July 20, 1974, precipitated a war between democratic states is not, it turns out, sufficiently subtle to be a very interesting question, for reasons nicely summarized by Markides (1977, xiii): "On July 15, 1974, the Republic of Cyprus collapsed after fourteen turbulent years of independent life. In a bloody coup instigated by the military regime then ruling in Greece, hundreds of loyalists were killed and thousands were wounded or arrested. Archbishop Makarious, the president of the republic, barely escaped assassination as he fled. . . . A week later, on July 20, Turkey landed troops on the north coast of the island."[40]

It is still possible to argue that this war *became* a conflict between democratic states, because in July 1974 the leader of the coup in Cyprus stepped down to be replaced by a representative of the previously elected government there, and the war heated up again (for two days, according to Small and Singer 1982, 94) in August of 1974. However, this turns out also to be a relatively weak argument. In the first place, the person who took over in Cyprus from the coup leader "did not take the oath of office in accordance with the 1960 Constitution. . . . Moreover, in his cabinet he retained most of the [coup leader's] men, none of whom had been appointed in accordance with Article 46 of the 1960 Constitution" (Necatigil 1989, 87). If, even in the face of that evidence, one is inclined to argue that the legitimately elected government of Archbishop Makarios was in power (indirectly) when the war between Cyprus and Turkey resumed for two days in August of 1974, then one must deal (in terms of the criteria stressed here) with the fact that the democratic character of the regime under Archbiship Makarious had never been established by historical precedent involving a peaceful transfer of power. Makarios had up to that time always been in power, rather autocratically according to some; in the most recent election before this war (in 1968) Makarios had received 95.45 percent of the vote (Mayes 1981, 195). In addition, there had been a military coup in Turkey in 1971, with full civilian government restored only after elections in October 1973. So, by 1974, whether or not it was democratic according to the definitional criteria advocated here (or in the eyes of their counterparts and opponents in Cyprus) was also not established (Hale 1990, 53–77). This war, then, neither began as nor became (for two days in August 1974) a war between democratic states.

Peru versus Ecuador, 1981

Michael Doyle (1983, 213) points out this case and dismisses it on the grounds that, for both Peru and Ecuador, "the war came from within one to three years after the establishment of a liberal regime, that is, before the pacifying effects of liberalism could become deeply ingrained." I could dismiss it in a similar but simpler and more operational fashion by pointing out that in both Peru and Ecuador, relatively recent liberal regimes had been established, in neither of which had it been demonstrated by way of historical precedent that the government could be defeated in an election. In Ecuador, a new constitution was approved (after a military dictatorship had been overthrown) in January of 1978. Jaime Roldos Aguilero became president of this new regime in 1979 and was in office when a military clash with Peru occurred in early 1981 (Dostert 1990, 93). Similarly, in Peru, Fernando Belaunde was elected president in 1980, after twelve years of military rule from 1968 to 1980 (Lincoln 1984, 137).

But the main reason that this conflict does not constitute a "war" between democratic states involves its quite limited nature. It did not produce enough battle deaths to be categorized as a "war" by the Correlates of War project (Singer 1991, 63). Reports in the *New York Times* in January and February of 1981 of two, one, one, and eight soldiers killed suggest that there were far fewer than 1,000 battle deaths in this conflict, another reason not to categorize it as a war between democratic states.[41]

Conflict in the Post-Communist World in the Former Soviet Union and Eastern Europe

The end of communism in the former Soviet Union and in Eastern Europe, Yugoslavia in particular, has created conditions rife with conflict in those regions, perhaps even wars between democratic states. Many of the post-Communist governments are elected, at any rate, and there have been bloody conflicts between Serbia and Croatia, Serbia and Bosnia-Herzegovina, and Armenia and Azerbaijan, to mention only the most prominent to this date. These conflicts are fraught with ambiguities for the issues in focus here. Are they international or civil wars? Have they resulted in 1,000 battle deaths? Finally, and most difficult to deal with, are the governments involved democratic? The conflicts in question are so recent and complex that only tentative answers can be attempted here.

Tentatively, first, I would assert that Serbia, at least, is not democratic, and so none of the conflicts involving it are wars between democratic states. Slobodan "Milosevic . . . rose to power through the Communist Party's apparatus and has deflected criticism and held power by appealing to Serbian nationalism and controlling the republic's large enterprises and most influential media" (*New York Times* June 1, 1992, section A, p. 8.) Even if we assume that this *Times* story exaggerates the extent to which the Milosevic regime represents a continuation of the Communist regime that preceded it,[42] it is quite clear that the Serbian regime (as well as regimes of Croatia, Slovenia, and Bosnia-Herzegovina, for that matter) has yet to establish that it is democratic in the sense that current rulers can be ousted in an election.

The former Soviet republics of Armenia and Azerbaijan both have governments elected in multiparty elections, so their war over Nagorno-Karabakh might be seen as a war between democratic states. *Freedom in the World 1991–92,* however, rated political rights and civil liberties in both places as "5" on a 7-point scale (with "1" being most democratic).[43] Details of electoral processes in both places are hard to come by at this stage. although Azerbaijan did elect a new president in June of 1992, which could be construed as a step in the direction of establishing by historical precedent that governing parties can be defeated in fair, competitive elections. However, the previous government was driven from office by civil unrest, so the currently elected government exists within a system or regime whose ability to produce a peaceful, constitutional transfer of power between independent political parties is still unclear. Armenia currently has an elected, non-Communist president, Levon Ter-Petrossyan, but here too it is unclear whether the regime can produce or sustain a peaceful transfer of power between independent political parties.

It might be stressed here that conflicts such as the one between Armenia and Azerbaijan and others in the post-Communist world (assuming it stays post-Communist) promise to pose crucial tests for the idea that democratic states will not war against each other. The hypothesis was originally formed—and my efforts here at conceptual clarification have been based in part and inescapably—on a knowledge of the history of conflicts between democratic and near-democratic states. Therefore, it is impossible to deny the possibility that the hypothesis itself, and my clarifications, have been tainted, so to speak, by that knowledge. More stringent tests of the hypothesis, its theoretical basis, and refinements such as occur in this chapter will occur in the future, as a possibly greater number of "democratic" states interact and conflict with one another.

The conflict between Azerbaijan and Armenia foreshadows probably some of the controversies and issues that will arise in attempts to evaluate the validity of "predictions" based on the democratic peace hypothesis in the light of the conflicts and possibly the wars that will arise among the newly independent states in the post-Communist world. Let us imagine, for the sake of discussing this point, that Azerbaijan and Armenia have recently become "democracies" according to the criteria here and the war continues. This would make it, according to this thought experiment, a war between two democratic states. But would that conflict have become an exception to the "rule" about the lack of wars between democratic states? That is debatable, because the war arguably began as a civil war as long ago as 1988. Does the democratic peace hypothesis suggest that international wars that emerge out of civil wars should cease once the participants become independent and democratic? The theoretical argument by Bueno de Mesquita and Lalman (1992) suggests that the democratic character of conflict participants should have a pacifying effect on negotiations and bargaining between states *before* the war begins. It is not clear, in fact, that any of the relevant theoretical discussions suggest that democracy should terminate ongoing wars between states that entered into those wars as undemocratic states. Perhaps the proposition, then, of greater relevance and interest is not that democratic states never fight wars against each other but that democratic states never *initiate* wars against each other.

In any case, at this point, with respect to the conflict between Armenia and Azerbaijan, and others in this area of the world (such as, at this writing, in Moldova and Georgia), it is reasonably safe to conclude that there have not been and are not yet wars between democratic states taking place, if one of the criteria for "democracy" involves peaceful constitutional transfers of power between opposing political parties.

Conclusion

Skeptical, or perhaps even simply disinterested readers may conclude, by this point, that the sheer number of ostensible exceptions to the proposition that democratic states *never* fight international wars against each other undermines its credibility. "Where there is so much smoke, there must be at least a little fire" would be an understandable reaction. But I have been perhaps excessively zealous in my attempt to deal with every possible exception that I have read (or heard) about, and I think that the number of proposed exceptions does not serve as a sound basis for rejecting the democratic peace proposition in its strongest form. *Most* of the alleged exceptions are "international wars between democratic states" only if very minor military conflicts are counted as wars and/or if states displaying superficial, even ephemeral democratic characteristics are categorized as democratic states. In fact, of all the cases discussed here, only the American Civil War, the Spanish-American War, and the Boer War (with the War of 1812 deserving honorable mention) come sufficiently close to being international wars between democratic states to provide a basis for extended debate. And, if democracy is defined as a type of political system in which the identities of the leaders of the executive branch and the members of the national legislature are selected in elections involving at least two independent political parties, in which at least half the adult population is eligible to vote, and in which the possibility that the governing party will lose has been established by historical precedent, then none of those cases should be categorized as international wars between democratic states. Interestingly, all of those relatively close calls occurred in the nineteenth century. (The closest calls in the twentieth century are, arguably, all in the process of developing in the post-Communist world in the former Soviet Union and in Eastern Europe.)

This does not mean, of course, that I have definitively established that there have been no international wars between democratic states according to the criteria for "wars" and "democracy" that I have proposed here. A more convincing way of establishing that point would involve relatively independent generation of data sets regarding wars and regime types that would cover all countries and all years of interest based on those criteria and then the analysis of those data sets to see if any overlaps occur. (Small and Singer 1976; Chan 1984; and Maoz and Abdolali 1989 all approach this ideal to varying degrees.) Furthermore, until and unless that is done, it will be impossible to establish whether or not the category of democratic states I have developed here is sufficiently inclusive that the absence of war among them is statistically significant. What I have accomplished here is a kind of spot check of many (but probably not all) of the possibilities brought up in the writing and discussion of the democratic peace phenomenon over the last ten to fifteen years. There might be, for example, extrasystemic wars (to use the Correlates of War project terminology) that I have not examined closely that would appropriately be categorized as international wars between democratic states. But I have reviewed here, in some detail, a list of cases sufficiently interesting that they have prompted consistent or prominent mention in the literature or discussions among participants in the debate about the democratic peace proposition. My conclusion is that none of those cases is appropriately categorized as an international war between democratic states.

Notes

1. Maoz and Russett (1992, 264) assert that democracies "rarely" go to war with each other, but they also note that "it is noteworthy to point out that some studies . . . have found *no* incidence of war between democracies"; they also acknowledge that theirs is one of those studies.

2. In an era when it was passionately argued that the only "true" democracy involved a dictatorship of the proletariat, enforced with the most stringent autocratic means, it was probably quixotic to pursue a definition of democracy with anything close to universal acceptance. But that era may be over.

3. Interestingly, Gastil (1990, 49) notes in a recent article about the annual Freedom House reports that "the claim for lack of institutional bias may not be valid for surveys produced after July 1989," when apparently, Gastil's association with the organization was terminated.

4. A "competitive" system in this coding scheme is one in which "*relatively* stable

and enduring political groups regularly compete for political influence and position with little use of violence or disruption. No *significant* groups are regularly excluded" (Gurr, Jaggers, and Moore 1990, 80; emphasis added).

5. Maoz and Russett's (1992, 250) index of democracy is based on the formula "Democracy = (Demlevel - Autolevel) x Concentration," where "demlevel is a 1–10 scale of the level of democracy in a political system, autolevel is the level of autocracy in a system, and concentration represents the extent to which the set of attributes specific to a regime are well-defined."

6. It should be said in defense of Maoz and Russett (1992) that they do analyze carefully the categorizations of states according to their threshold to determine whether those categorizations are sensible and intuitively appealing, and the results of those analyses are encouraging.

7. I use the admittedly awkward phrase involving the "determination of the identities" of the leaders of the executive branch in particular, rather than a more straightforward phrase such as "selected in elections" or simply "elected," in order to deal precisely with parliamentary systems where prime ministers, for example, are typically not directly "elected" or selected in elections but selected by heads of state and/or approved by the parliament. Any definition that stipulates that the heads of the executive branch be directly elected would eliminate such countries from the category "democratic"; the United States, with its Electoral College, would also be eliminated.

8. The stipulation that the political parties be only "formally" independent makes it unnecessary to deal with the impossible task of evaluating the validity of arguments to the effect that the Democrats and Republicans in the United States, for example, are virtually indistinguishable, not "really" different, etc. Such arguments may well have merit on a philosophical level, but if "formal" independence of the type exemplified by Democrats and Republicans in the United States is not sufficient to establish some requisite level of "real" independence, then "formal" democratic procedures are only superficial in their impact in any case. And I would acknowledge that formal "parties" are not necessary for democracy. "Factions" or "coalitions" or other groupings are sufficient, as long as they are at least formally independent (i.e., *not* within the same political party, especially if it is the *only* political party).

9. The case of Japan, in the context of this definitional issue, is sufficiently important to warrant a comment. It is not entirely clear that the peaceful transfer of power criterion would have excluded Japan from the democratic category as defined here, even before the most recent developments there. In 1955, there was a transfer of power from the "Liberals" to the "Democrats." The elections of February 27 of that year "made the Democrats for the first time the plurality party. The Liberals lost about half of their Diet seats" (Reischauer 1964, 274). Admittedly, subsequently the Liberals and the Democrats did coalesce into the Liberal-Democratic party (in November of 1955), which ruled Japan until very recently, but those parties were at least formally independent going into the 1955 election.

10. Rummel (1979, 53) also asserts that "we should sew on our underwear the understanding that power corrupts, and absolute power corrupts absolutely." The corrupting influence of power clearly plays a major role in Rummel's thinking and, I believe, in the theorizing of almost everybody who deals with the connection between regime type

and international conflict. Constitutional transfers of power based on election results should serve as a good indicator of the ability of a political system to deal effectively with the corrupting influence of the concentration of power that governing requires.

11. There are some minor exceptions to these rules. See Small and Singer (1982, 43–45).

12. Admittedly, just how large this proportion was is an issue debated even in current times. See Meigs, 1972.

13. It might also be argued that "representative" or "republican" democracy constitutes a more pacific form of government than "direct" democracy, or one in which governmental leaders are chosen by lot. Chris Brown (1992, 32) points out that Kant regarded "direct democracy" as a "form of despotism. The lawful state must be 'republican,' which to Kant means that it must be based on the separation of executive and legislative powers—it is because democracy, as he understands the term, fuses these powers that it is despotic."

14. Spencer Weart (1991, 5) asserts that "they [the Athenians] knew little about affairs in Sicily, for the distance was tremendous and communications rudimentary. They did know that the island was bitterly divided. Rightly or wrongly, when the democrats of Athens launched their invasion they did not believe that they were going against people of their own political stripe."

15. There are a couple of historical settings in which "wars" between "democracies" might have taken place that I will mention here only in passing. One involves the "Forest Cantons" of medieval and early modern Switzerland, where, according to Spencer Weart (1994, 303), "democratic" cantons "conducted an autonomous foreign policy in response to the votes of an assembly of peasants and cowherds." After an analysis of the histories of these cantons, Weart concludes that the democratic cantons "never once warred against one another." Another setting where democratic wars might have occurred would involve the Italian city-states from 1200 to 1600. According to Weart (1994, 306–7), at least, it is not clear whether any of those "republican" city-states were democratic, as opposed to oligarchic, and in any case, warfare between the "republics" disappeared between 1350 and 1380 when republican governments became "well-established" in their competition with other corporate bodies such as groupings based on kinship ties and personalistic leaders.

16. Though the percentage of adults eligible to vote in British elections was clearly small, just how small is a matter of controversy. If, as Rose suggests, one-fifth of males could vote as of 1832, that would constitute some 10 percent of the total (male and female) adult population. But Small and Singer (1976, 54) assert that "between 1832 and 1867, only three percent of the electorate was eligible to participate in British elections."

17. Historian Donald R. Hickey (1989, 27) makes the same argument: "The United States was the only democratic republic in the world, and even though most Americans were confident that they were riding the wave of the future, they were acutely conscious of how fragile republican institutions were." Furthermore, England's desperate struggles with Napoleon at the time led it to take desperate measures that made it even more unlikely that Americans would perceive it as a "democracy." "In resisting Napoleon, whom many regarded as the devil incarnate, Englishmen honestly thought they were

fighting for the liberation of the entire world. Ironically, as the struggle became longer and harder, liberties were increasingly suppressed in Britain while the sense of the world mission became even more potent" (Coles 1965, 3).

18. Vandenbosch (1959, 52) goes on to explain that "the Belgians, Catholic almost to a man, did not accept the Protestant King with enthusiasm. . . . The Netherlands were scarcely more pleased with the union. They feared that Belgian industry might be favored at the expense of Dutch commerce."

19. "On 23 September Prince Frederich marched into Brussels at the head of his troops. . . . The attack on Brussels began too late and was half-heartedly carried out. . . . The losses of the armed forces and the resistance fighters ran into the hundreds" (Kossman 1978, 154). On the other hand, a Belgian source says that "for three days there was terrible street fighting, and on the night of September 26–27 Prince Frederich, with at least 1,500 killed and many wounded, admitted his defeat and left Brussels" (VanderEssen 1916, 154). According to this source, at any rate, this would seem to qualify as a "civil war," as defined by Small and Singer (1982, 210–13). Presumably their decision to exclude this conflict from their list of civil wars was based on such sources as Kossman, 1978, whose estimates of casualties are lower.

20. Hearnshaw (1920, 99) also points out that "although on the one hand a legislature based on universal suffrage was set up, on the other hand it was given no control over the executive." If this judgment is accepted, and as I have argued above, judgments on this criterion are inherently debatable, the categorization of France in this period as a "democracy" according to the criteria used by Small and Singer (1976) is also debatable.

21. For example, de Luna (1969, 397) points out that "the formation of a ministry under the man who had been the last premier of the founding July Monarchy on February 24 dramatized the antirepublican significance of the election of Louis Napoleon."

22. Nevertheless, it is true that if the Confederate States had been more successful militarily, it is probable that at some point Great Britain and France would have recognized their independent status and the war might have evolved into an international war.

23. This was not an accident or a coincidence. "From the beginning those attending the [Confederate Constitutional] Convention intended to base the Confederate Constitution on the Constitution of the United States" (Holcombe 1992, 763).

24. "As the Provisional Government should function for one year or less, Congress provided that elections should be held on the first Wednesday in November 1861, for President, Vice-President, and Congressmen. Now for the first time people would have the right to choose their officials" (Coulter 1950, 103).

25. Some states had a majority of black residents. Mississippi, for example, was 55 percent black, and South Carolina, where the rebellion began, was almost 60 percent black (*Historical Statistics of the United States: Colonial Times to 1970* 1975, 24–36).

26. Herr (1971, 115) elaborates: "After 1890 under universal suffrage peasants and landless workers, many of them illiterate, voted when and for whom they were told to. There were many districts firmly in the hands of *caciques* where candidates ran unopposed."

27. Share bases his conclusion in part on a rather detailed discussion of *caciquismo* in Carr (1982, 355–79).

28. Carr rather emphasizes the traditional limits on the role of the monarch, but he does so in a way that also makes clear his official powers, and by emphasizing the restrictions placed on the monarch by the oligarchical Conservative leader of the time, Antonio Canovas de Castillo.

29. "In the opinion of contemporary American and foreign observers, a stable democratic republic could not have been maintained under the Malolos constitution, because the fundamental elements from which democratic government springs were not possessed by the people of the Philippines in 1899. Nevertheless, this organic law was a free expression of the type of state to which the articulate Filipinos aspired at the end of the Spanish regime. This state was democratic and liberal and was pledged to a careful regard for the protection and development of the masses of its citizens" (Hayden 1942, 32). When he wrote this, Hayden was professor of political science at the University of Michigan. He served as vice-governor of the Philippines from 1933 to 1935.

30. "Kruger [the president of the Transvaal] and the Volksraad [the legislature of the South African Republic] never hesitated; they progressively raised the franchise qualifications until by 1894 no uitlanders could vote in presidential elections" (*Encyclopedia Britannica* 1990, 651).

31. In May 1899, Milner [the British high commissioner in South Africa] sent Chamberlain a telegram declaring that "the case for intervention is overwhelming, since 'thousands of British subjects [were being] kept permanently in the position of helots'" (Thompson 1990, 140).

32. "In the Volksraad, or Parliament, Kruger abused his immense prestige, crushing and terrifying anyone who opposed him" (Belfield 1975, 7). For more on Kruger's "despotism," albeit from an obviously biased source, see Amery (1900, 129).

33. Similarly, Fisher (1900, 129) declares: "The Orange Free State, in law and administration, has always been a model of what a Boer republic might be. The purity of its government has never been questioned."

34. "[President] Brand declared during the London Conference in 1876: The Free State has no native problem: we have already settled it. The Whites are against the natives as two against one" (Van Schoor 1986, 244).

35. Typically, Van Schoor (1986, 244) adds that "the republic never considered the Blacks in the Free State to be a 'problem.'"

36. Upbeat to the end in his discussion of this topic, Van Schoor concludes: "The personal approach and attitude of the majority of Whites towards the Blacks reflected a sound relationship between master and servant" (1986, 251).

37. "[In 1933] Hitler asked for and got new elections that, under systematic terrorization, gave him (with some minor allies) a bare majority; he used it to suspend the constitution, and for the remainder of the Nazi era, the country was ruled by decree. All parties but the Nazi party . . . were eliminated" (Garraty and Gay 1972, 1055).

38. Both Eskelinen (1973, 57) and Mead (1968, 174) declare that Finland was never officially at war with either France or the United States.

39. Reddaway (1986, 162) succinctly describes the fate of Turkish Cypriots in the Cypriot Republic in the decade before the Turkish invasion.

40. This account of events is supported in numerous sources, among the more authoritative and convincing of which is Necatigil (1989, 75). Necatigil (1989, 101–24)

also discusses whether or not Turkey's invasion was justified in terms of international law by a Treaty of Guarantee signed by the United Kingdom, Greece, Turkey, and Cyprus in 1960.

41. These reports appeared in the *New York Times* on January 30, 1981, section A, p. 6; February 2, 1981, section A, p. 1; and February 10, 1981, section A, p. 2, respectively.

42. The 1991–92 annual report from Freedom House explains the origins of the war in what used to be Yugoslavia this way: "On the surface the war seemed to be precipitated by declarations of independence by Slovenia and Croatia on 25 June, but in reality the conflict was an outgrowth of age-old Serbian-Croatian animosities exacerbated by Serbia's anti-reformist Communist President Slobodan Milosevic's repeated calls for a resurgence of a Greater Serbia" (*Freedom in the World, 1991–92* 1992, 508).

43. *Freedom Review,* published by Freedom House in February 1993, gives Armenia ratings of 4 and 3 on political rights and civil liberties respectively, still giving Azerbaijan ratings of 5 in both categories. As I have reviewed the facts surrounding this case, it has often occurred to me that more than ten years ago, while discussing the validity of the claim that no two democratic states have ever fought a war against each other, I asserted that the fact that "no two [democratic] states have . . . fought wars against each other . . . may be no more remarkable than the fact that since 1816 no two states whose names both begin with the letter 'A' have fought each other" (Ray 1982, 178). This was, of course, a thinly veiled but remarkably prescient forecast of the current conflict between Armenia and Azerbaijan.

Chapter 4

Case Studies, Covering Laws, and Causality

Case studies, in some eyes, constitute "telling stories," as opposed to serious research. Case studies can be defended, perhaps, as a source of ideas (or even hypotheses), but it is less clear that they are accepted, by most quantitatively oriented scholars at least, as legitimate sources of *evidence* regarding the validity of hypotheses. And, of course, there are those who believe that *only* the close analysis of a case, or two or three, provides a legitimate base for knowledge about causal relationships. As Bruce Bueno de Mesquita (1985, 123) has observed: "An important methodological division within the field of international conflict that bears directly on criteria for judging advances in knowledge exists between those who subscribe to the belief that knowledge is advanced by the in-depth study of a very small number of cases and those who believe that many cases must be examined before knowledge can be acquired."[1]

Nevertheless, if pushed sufficiently hard, many political scientists will adopt the conciliatory position that both large-N and small-n studies are important. Someone as closely identified with quantitative analysis as Bruce Russett (1970, 426–27, 431) has asserted, for example, that "the so-called nomothetic-idiographic dilemma is an artificial one; neither the case study nor the general kind of systematic analysis I shall call correlational study can alone provide the basis for reliable and valid generalizations about international politics. . . . The crucial point is that both kinds of studies are critical to the development of scientific knowledge."

Differences between Small-n and Large-N Advocates

Despite the fact that such broad-minded conciliatory statements are rather common, there *is* a gulf between those who favor intensive study of a few cases and those who more typically analyze relatively large numbers of cases. Certainly one of the more prominent defenders of the utility of close analysis of a few cases is Alexander George. He, too, makes conciliatory statements about the complementarity of small-n and large-N studies.[2] But in the course of his defense of case studies and how they complement quantitative analyses of large numbers of cases, George asserts that "political scientists employing statistical methods for analyzing a large number of cases have *come to recognize* [emphasis added] the necessity for assessing whether the correlations among variables discovered in such studies are genuinely causal." Such a statement gives the impression that this is an insight that quantitatively oriented political scientists came to only after years of overzealous pursuit of statistical analyses. In fact, even beginning students in a course on research methods will almost certainly learn within the first few weeks that "correlation does not mean causation" because the correlation might be spurious.

George goes on to assert that case studies are useful in attempts to find out whether a correlation is spurious or not. Specifically, he suggests that "to assess whether a statistical correlation between independent variables and the dependent variable is of causal significance, the investigator [should subject] a single case in which that correlation appears to more intensive scrutiny, as historians would do, in order to establish whether there exists an intervening process, that is, a *causal nexus,* between the independent variable and the dependent variable" (George 1979, 46). Such a suggestion is likely to seem strange to most quantitatively oriented scholars, who will wonder what George could possibly mean when he refers to a "correlation" between variables occurring within the confines of a single case, since correlation by definition refers to covariation or co-occurrence of variables across a number of cases (or at least across a number of observations, or points in time, larger than the one that is utilized in most intensive case studies).

James Fearon (1991, 194) makes this point succinctly and clearly. "Quite commonly, researchers . . . assert that their dependent variable is X, where X is some *particular* event or phenomenon. X might be the failure of the U.S. to play the role of international hegemon between the world wars, a change in the nuclear proliferation regime, the dominance of the Liberal Democratic Party in Japan, or the collapse of communism in Eastern Europe. Analysts explaining such events need to understand that *none* of these are variables. They [are] *values* of variables." Quantitatively oriented analysts will also wonder how one can possibly identify a *causal nexus* (much less a spurious correlation) if one restricts one's view to a single case, within which one cannot possibly perceive one of the most essential elements of such a nexus, i.e., a relationship between variables over a number of cases or observations.[3]

Ultimately, George provides a rather clear answer to such questions. "The utility of explanations developed in case studies," he explains, "rests upon their plausibility" (George 1979, 58). However, this is likely to strike at least some advocates of large-N studies as an admission of fatal weaknesses in case studies, since from their point of view the hallmark of almost all interesting questions in the social sciences is opposing hypotheses that are quite consistently of equal plausibility.

Causal Variables and Explaining Single Cases

The gulf between advocates of small-n and large-N studies revealed in these comments by George (and in my comments about his comments) has its roots in conflicts and/or not very clearly formulated ideas about the notion of "cause" and what constitutes an "explanation." And I do not mean to suggest that it is only the naivete or lack of knowledge on the part of small-n advocates that is the source of the problem. It seems, on the contrary, that advocates of large-N studies often do confusing things or make confusing arguments.

For example, a standard textbook description of "cause" asserts the following: "In order to infer that one or more independent variables causes one or more dependent variables, it is necessary to show three things: (1) the independent variable(s) occurred before the dependent variable(s); (2) the independent variable(s) and the dependent variable(s) vary together in some consistent nonrandom manner; (3) no other independent variable(s) could cause the same observed variation in the dependent variable(s)" (Jones 1971, 20).

In short, this means that the identification of a causal relationship between factors A and B involves establishing that there is a nonspurious correlation between those two factors in which temporal order has been established. Congruent with this notion of "causality" is the standard social scientific practice of referring to the extent to which variation in Factor A "explains" variation in Factor B.

Problems arise in this notion of causality when it is applied to "explanations" of single events. Surely, part of what it means to *explain* the outcome of a given event is to specify what *caused* it. But if causation, by definition, can only be inferred from *covariation* across a number of cases (or observations), how does one identify a causal nexus within the confines of a single case (observed only once)? An answer espoused by some is that one cannot, and this means that no self-respecting "scientist" is really interested, at least while wearing his or her "scientist's" hat, in *a* case. Single events cannot be "explained." Who really cares, this point of view suggests, why Joe Smith voted as he did in the election of 1992? Who really cares even about, say, the Franco-Prussian War in particular, from a "scientific" point of view?

Simplifying Assumptions and Tracing Causal Processes

Another source of confusion in arguments offered by defender's of large-N studies invokes the assertion by some (formal modelers, usually) that "*descriptive inaccuracy*' . . . is a mark of all powerful theory" (Friedman 1953;

cited in Allison 1971, 75). In discussing and defending his expected utility approach, for example, Bueno de Mesquita insists that "I do not suggest that decision-makers *consciously* make the calculations of the expected utility model. Rather, I argue that the leaders act *as if* they do" (Bueno de Mesquita 1988, 63). Having disavowed any interest in whether or not "real world" decision makers actually make the calculations stipulated by this theory, though, Bueno de Mesquita rather consistently attempts to demonstrate (in a confusing, if not contradictory, way) that in fact decision makers *do* make calculations of the type incorporated into his expected utility theory. For example, in the same article in which he disavows any claim that decision makers consciously make the calculations in his expected utility model, he *also* argues that "the concepts of equation [5] can be seen at work in the decision of Istvan Tisza, the Magyar premier, in July 1914, to endorse military action against Serbia" (Bueno de Mesquita 1988, 643).[4] Similarly, in *War and Reason,* Bueno de Mesquita and his coauthor (Bueno de Mesquita and Lalman 1992, 225–43) seem obviously quite intent on demonstrating that the calculations of Bismarck and other decision makers involved in the Seven Weeks' War in 1866 between Prussia and Austria paralleled quite closely those stipulated by the international interaction model developed in that book. Readers might well wonder, with all the emphasis that these modelers put (in typical formal modelling fashion) on the "as if " assumption, why they should emphasize precisely how decision makers think and calculate in the crises being analyzed.

Causes of Single Events

With regard to the possible confusion regarding the relationship between correlation, causation, and the explanation of single events, let me begin by asserting that I accept the idea that single events cannot be "explained" in isolation. My position on this issue can be illustrated most helpfully in an initial stage, perhaps, by engaging in an imaginary debate with a historian about the causes of a specific event.

Let us imagine, for the purposes of this debate, that Anatolia initiated a war against Catalonia in 1859.[5] Imagine further that the historian has concluded that the leader of Anatolia initiated the war against Catalonia primarily to deal with domestic political problems for himself. In short, he (the leader of Anatolia) had felt that his tenure was insecure and that he might evoke a substantial "rally round the flag" effect if he involved his nation in a military conflict against Catalonia.

From my vantage point as a social scientist, I would find this "explanation" of Anatolia's attack on Catalonia in 1859 more credible if the historian could provide corroborating details about the situation in Anatolia at the time, such as evidence suggesting that dissident groups were active, concern by the leadership about those activities, and so forth. But the historian would not be able to induce in me any important level of acceptance of the legitimacy of his or her "explanation," no matter how many details he provided me about the event *in isolation*. To that extent, to repeat, I accept a declaration to the effect that "single events can't be explained."

From my point of view, if Anatolia's attack on Catalonia is to be "explained," it must be compared to a representative sample or the relevant population of cases. In other words, that event must be shown to fit into a pattern. If I were, for example, to generate data on all states in 1859 on the extent of internal unrest and the initiation of wars, and if I were to find in fact that states, like Anatolia in 1859, with greater amounts of internal unrest were more likely to initiate wars against other states, that kind of evidence would lead me to have more confidence that the historian's explanation of Anatolia's attack on Catalonia was valid.

But let us imagine, for the sake of probing further into this pattern-based notion of causality and explanation, that I do generate data regarding the relationship between internal unrest and war initiation in 1859, and I discover in fact that there is a *negative* relationship between those two variables in that year.[6] Under those circumstances I would not accept the historian's explanation of Anatolia's attack on Catalonia in 1859.

Most historians, I suspect, if they were to be informed about this skepticism regarding their explanation and the basis of that skepticism, would regard the criticism as misguided and misinformed. They would feel that their extensive familiarity with the particulars of the situation in Anatolia in 1859 provides a sounder basis for analyzing the factors involved in bringing about the attack by Anatolia on Catalonia than any aggregate data analysis and that in fact such analyses are largely irrelevant to an understanding of that particular attack.

But let us imagine further, in order to extend this discussion for whatever illumination it might generate, that the historian in this example is willing to search for common ground with my social scientific approach to the analysis of Anatolia's attack. The historian might, if he or she were in a conciliatory mood, explain that though it might be the case (as my data indicate) that, for states in general in 1859, internal unrest made states less, not more, likely to launch an attack on other states, the unrest in Anatolia *did* evoke its attack on Catalonia. If I were also in a compromising mood, I would point out to the historian that to me his position suggests that he feels that Anatolia is different from states *in general* (at least in 1859) in ways that have an effect on the relationship between internal unrest and external conflict. How, specifically, I might ask the historian, do you feel Anatolia was different from other states in general in a way that would cause its leaders to react differently to internal political unrest?

A cooperative historian might reply that perhaps Anatolia responded to internal unrest in a manner unlike other states in general in 1859 because the regime there that year was a military dictatorship. Military dictators, perhaps, are especially prone to solve internal political problems by fostering external conflict. I might then control for regime type and find that, indeed, for those states that were military dictatorships in 1859, internal unrest did apparently make war initiation more likely, and the historian and I could agree, then, that internal unrest in Anatolia was a cause of its attack on Catalonia in 1859.

But if I found that even among military dictatorships, internal unrest was associated with a *lower* probability to initiate wars, the historian and I would still disagree. He or she would feel—because of his or her familiarity with that single case and his or her epistemological notion that plausibility is the most stringent, perhaps the most persuasive characteristic (a la Alexander George, perhaps) that we can expect of explanations of human behavior—that internal unrest in Anatolia was an important cause of its attack on Catalonia. I would feel that in the absence of any evidence that internal unrest is systematically related to the increased probability of war initiation within any set of states to which Anatolia belongs, the historian's conclusion is unjustified. We might resolve this dispute if the historian claimed that Anatolia was different from most military dictatorships in that it was, say, a predominantly Catholic country, and if I found that among military dictatorships in predominantly Catholic countries, those with internal unrest were indeed more likely to initiate wars.

But if I found instead a negative relationship between internal unrest and the probability of war initiation even among military dictatorships in predominantly Catholic countries, and the historian insisted that Anatolia was different from most military dictatorships in Catholic countries in general because it was an *Iberian* Catholic military dictatorship, the historian and I will have closed in on the nub of our epistemological disagreement. He or she will feel that, by closely examining *a* case, it is possible to identify causal linkages or to explain the outcome of an event such as Anatolia's attack on Catalonia in 1859. I will feel that no "explanation" is worthy of the name unless it alludes to a pattern into which the event in question fits. If the historian accuses me of possessing peculiar attitudes in such matters, I might refer him or her to the *Handbook of Political Science,* which states the following: "The unique explanation of a particular case . . . can rest on general hypotheses. Indeed, it *must* rest on them, since theoretical arguments about a single case, in the last analysis, always proceed from at least implicit general laws about a class or set to which it belongs, or about universal attributes of all classes to which the case can be subsumed" (Eckstein 1975, 99).[7]

If I further inform the historian that there were so few Iberian Catholic military dictatorships in 1859 that it is impossible to establish whether or not there was a pattern involving internal unrest and external conflict within that category of states, the historian is likely to be unperturbed. He or she will feel that my search for patterns is misguided in any case. The situation regarding Anatolia's attack on Catalonia in 1859 was so different from those surrounding other war initiations, he or she might patiently (or impatiently) point out to me, that attempts to fit it into a pattern are most likely to be futile. The best we can hope for, he or she might conclude, is to make a case for *plausible* assertions about causal connections, as Alexander George does in his defense of analyses focusing on a very small number of cases.

In a final (desperate?) attempt to persuade me he or she is right about Anatolia's attack on Catalonia in 1859, the historian might reveal to me that he or she has come across a secret diary kept by the military dictator of Anatolia of that period in the years up to and including the year of its attack on Catalonia. This diary has an entry, it turns out, written in the week before the attack, in which the military dictator asserts that "the internal unrest in the country endangers my future as the leader of Anatolia. In light of that danger, next week I will order a military attack on Catalonia, in the hope that the resulting war will solidify support for my regime, and provide me a rationale for crushing the domestic opposition to my regime." To the historian, this might seem the ultimate proof of the validity of an "explanation." This would especially be the case if the historian believed in the hermeneutic approach to the analysis of social behavior. "The central hermeneutic theme [is] that *action must always be understood from within* . . . [T]he investigator needs to know what the agent intended by and in performing the action: why this agent played this move in the 'game'" (Hollis and Smith 1990, 72).

Perhaps it is more likely that the historian will share the attitudes of well-known philosophers of history, such as R. G. Collingwood or William Dray. Collingwood (1974, 25–26) explains that "when a historian asks 'why did Brutus stab Caesar?' he means 'what did Brutus think? what made him decide to stab Caesar?' The cause of the event, for him, means the thought in the mind of the person by whose agency the event came about: and this is not something other than the event, it is the inside of the event itself. . . . All history is the history of thought." William Dray (1974, 68–69), in defense of what he labels "rational explanation" (the kind of explanation, he asserts, that is predominant in and most appropriate to history), argues that "to achieve understanding, what he [the historian] seeks is information about what the agent believed to be the fact of his situation, including the likely results of taking various courses of action considered open to him, and what he wanted to accomplish: his purposes, goals, or motives. Understanding is achieved when the historian can see the reasonableness of a man's doing what this agent did, given the beliefs and purposes referred to; his action, can then be explained as having been an 'appropriate' one." These philosophers of history, then, argue that "explanations" are to be judged primarily by their plausibility, and that their plausibility in turn depends primarily upon how well they can reconstruct thought processes engaged in by the agents bringing about the event to be "explained."

But I, on the other hand, would wonder first if the military dictator of Anatolia might have been lying, for the sake of history, perhaps, when he wrote that diary entry. And if the historian is able to establish that the dictator of Anatolia had, before he wrote the crucial diary entry in question, ingested a truth serum of some sort, I would then wonder if the military dictator really understood his own motives. Or it might be that his motives in this case were irrelevant, that the decision to attack Catalonia was *really* made elsewhere in the government and that the dictator was merely developing a rationalization for going along with the controlling faction within his regime.[8] In any case, I would not be convinced by *any* evidence restricted in its scope to one case. I would insist, instead, that no explanation is deserving of serious credence (or in fact can appropriately be classified as an "explanation") unless it demonstrates that Anatolia's attack on Catalonia in 1859 was merely an example that fits into an established general pattern.

Carl Hempel and "Nomological" Explanation

Obviously, in pushing the imaginary historian to such extremes of exasperation, I would be adhering to a notion about causality and explanation advocated most prominently by Carl Hempel. Hempel (1965, 231) argues that "general laws have quite analogous functions in history and in the natural sciences." He also states that "the assertion that a set of events, say of the kinds C_1, C_2, . . . , C_N have caused the event to be explained, amounts to the statement that, according to certain general laws, *a set of events of the kinds mentioned* is regularly accompanied by an event of the kind E" (232). To put Hempel's point in my own words, I would stipulate that an "explanation" is a statement (or set of statements) that demonstrates that the outcome of a particular event is merely an example of an established general pattern. If the historian is going to convince me that internal unrest led to a war initiation by Anatolia against Catalonia in 1859, he or she must demonstrate to me that internal unrest *generally* does increase the probability of war initiation among a class of states to which Anatolia belongs. "Historical explanations" Hempel (1965, 235) asserts, "aim at showing that the event in question was not a matter of chance, but was to be expected in view of certain antecedent or simultaneous conditions." The only way, in my view, to show that the event in question was "to be expected" (i.e., "explained') is to demonstrate that the antecedent or simultaneous conditions are associated with the outcome to be explained with regularity.

This kind of explanation, which "amounts to a deductive subsumption of the explanandum under principles that have the character of general laws"

(Hempel 1962, 10), is referred to by Hempel as a nomological explanation. "What Carl Hempel has called . . . nomological [explanation]," according to Jeffrey Isaac (1987, 189), "remains the dominant view of causality and scientific explanation in political science."

Why, then, in light of the fact that Hempel's views on the matter are so important, does one encounter within the social scientific community that idea that single events cannot be "explained." (After all, Hempel's *definition* of explanation pertains specifically to the concept as it applies to *an* event.) My impression is that resistance, when it occurs, to the idea that single events can be "explained," has its origins to an important extent in the impact of David Hume's well-known argument: "I shall venture to affirm, as a general proposition which admits of no exception, that the knowledge of this relation [that is, between a cause and an effect] is not, in any instance, attained by reasonings *a priori,* but arises entirely from experience, when we find that any particular objects are constantly enjoined with each other" (Hume 1748, in Hendel 1955, 42). All we can see is that one phenomenon (say, a war initiation) follows another (internal unrest). We cannot see, within the confines of a single event, no matter how intensely we investigate that event, (or no matter how much we delve into the minds and recollections of those involved in that event, even in their secret, totally honest diaries) the *causal nexus* that explains the outcome of that event. As Mohr (1990, 6) observes, Hume challenged his contemporaries to identify any substance, power, or mechanism they actually see that can be labeled a "cause." Hume's challenge, according to Mohr, "has never been answered."

The appropriate inference, however, from the well-known Humean argument is that *causation* can never be perceived directly, or inferred, within the confines of a single case or observation. It is clearly an error, at least from the viewpoint of Carl Hempel, to go from this premise to the conclusion that the outcomes of single events cannot be *explained.* The outcomes of single events can be explained, in Hempel's view, but only within the context of general laws and empirical regularities whose validity can only be established by observation of a larger number of cases.

Challenges to Hempel

Hempel's views on causality and explanation have never been universally accepted, even though it is true, as Mohr (1990, 7) observes, that "if there can be said to be a prevailing view of causality in philosophy at present, the regularity theory undoubtedly fills the role." It is striking, and rather reassuring for someone like myself who has definite ideas on the subject, but does not follow the most specialized literature on a continuing basis, the extent to which Hempel's ideas still serve as a major focus of debate on these issues, even though they were presented at least as long ago as 1942.[9] But Caldwell (1982, 63), for example, declares that though "covering-law models of scientific explanation were once thought to be sufficient for the description of all the legitimate types of explanation existent in science," recently, "some . . . question the adequacy of covering-law models." And in sources more closely related to the field of international relations, there is a challenge to covering law models from those who advocate hermeneutics and/or "scientific realism."

One of the more prominent advocates of scientific realism (which is unrelated to and within the field of international politics typically opposed to realism or neorealism as theories of international politics) and critics of nomological view of explanation in standard international relations outlets is Alexander Wendt. According to Wendt (1987, 353), "traditionally, there have been two competing ideals of scientific explanation: the empiricist or 'nomothetic' view that explanation involves the *subsumption* of a phenomenon under a lawlike regularity; and the realist or 'retrodictive' view that involves the identification of the underlying causal *mechanism* which physically generated the phenomenon."[10] Wendt criticizes those who adhere to the nomothetic view of what constitutes an explanation for a lack of interest in "underlying causal mechanisms which make an event naturally necessary," and concludes that "whereas the empiricist explains by generalizing about observable behavior, the realist explains by showing how (often unobservable) causal mechanisms which make observable regularities possible *work*" (Wendt 1987, 354). Similarly, David Dessler (1991) contrasts "causal" with "correlational" science and calls for more penetrating insights into causal processes than can be provided, in his view, within the nomological causal framework. "[C]ausal knowledge cannot be captured," Dessler (1991, 345) asserts, "within the confines of the deductive-nomological framework. Causal explanation [which Dessler contrasts with nomological explanation] shows the *generative* connection between cause and effect by appealing to a knowledge of the real structures that produced observed phenomena, and it is this generative connection that gives the notion of cause meaning beyond that of simple regularity." Dessler may be alluding here, at least in part, to what some refer to as "genetic" explanations. "Explanations that give the history of an event by presenting the phenomenon as the final stage of a developmental sequence are called *genetic explanations*. They begin at the 'genesis' with the most remote cause and proceed through the history of the event to the most proximate cause" (McGaw and Watson 1976, 71). What Dessler has to say also resonates with defenders of case studies and "narratives" such as Howard Becker: "Developing imagery is a process in which we try to understand what we want to understand better. We do not search for causes so much as look for stories that explain what it is and how it got that way. When an analyst of causes has done his job well, the result is a large proportion of variance explained. When an analyst of narrative has done the job well, the result is a story that explains why it is inevitable that this process led to this result" (Becker 1992, 212).

I have three main reactions to these arguments by Wendt, Dessler, and scientific realists, as well as philosophers of history such as Collingwood and Dray, or defenders of "narratives." The first is that, in my opinion, the idea that causal mechanisms can be identified and understood without relying on comparison and the identification of regularities and correlations is illusory. The second is that if Wendt, Dessler, Collingwood et al., and those who agree with them feel that nomologically inclined analysts have no interest in the finer details or intricacies of thought process, causal mechanisms, or even "stories," that impression is understandable and based on justifiable interpretations of some arguments by those who advocate a covering law approach to explanation. Finally, my third reaction is that although it is understandable that Wendt, Dessler, and others believe that those who utilize nomological explanations have no interest in the intricate details of thought processes or other kinds of causal mechanisms, that belief is mistaken.

The Epistemological Foundations of a Theory of Home Runs

Let me deal with the first point within the context of the simple anecdotes of the type that seem to characterize much debate on these matters. Imagine that I return to my seat at a major league baseball game just in time to see the ball fly out of the park, with the batter in the early stages of his home run trot around the bases. If I ask my companion, who has seen the event transpire, what happened, he might tell me that the pitcher threw a high hanging curveball. My companion might well feel that he has directly observed the *causality* in a causal mechanism at work, but my feeling is that the sequence of the high hanging curveball followed by a home run takes on the appearance of a causal connection because this fan has often seen high hanging curveballs hit for long distances and/or because he is aware that high hanging curveballs often result in disaster for the pitcher. In any case, *I* will feel that the result has been "explained" because I will have been provided with a statement demonstrating that the outcome in question (the home run) is merely an example of an established general pattern, that is, high hanging curveballs are regularly hit high and far. And the more confidence I have in the existence of the regularity and the strength of that general correlation, the more confidence I will have in the validity of the explanation of the particular outcome at hand.

Let us imagine alternatively (or counterfactually) that I return to my seat another day at another game just in time to see another home run leave the park and on this day I am accompanied by a friend who is much less familiar with baseball. When I ask this friend for information about what has occurred, he might respond, "Well, the pitcher threw a fastball about one hundred miles per hour that was a little bit outside and just below the knees." This person will have seen *that* kind of pitch hit out of the park and will have assumed that he has perceived a causal mechanism at work that connects one-hundred-mile-per-hour fastballs that are outside and below the knees to home runs. His perception of a causal mechanism at work will *seem* as vivid as the perception by my friend at the previous game who asserted that the delivery by the pitcher of the high hanging curveball resulted in the home run. My second friend will by imputing causality to a sequence of events based on the *structure* of the single event he has perceived in a way that is *logical* but almost certainly erroneous. The smack of the bat on that fastball that was a little bit outside and a little below the knees was undoubtedly real, and having witnessed a real event, it is logical to attribute causal power to the speed and the location of the pitch, on the one hand, and the home run that followed, on the other.

But no knowledgeable baseball fan (i.e., one with a good theory of baseball or at least a knowledge about its empirical regularities) will be persuaded that, within this event, the extremely hard fastball off the outside corner of the plate and a little below the knees *caused* the home run, no matter how compelling the structural argument based on analysis of the outcome in question might be. The sounder conclusion, and one that can only be based on an attempt to subsume the occurrence of this home run into a larger pattern, is that the batter that day hit a home run *in spite of* the fact, rather than because of the fact, that the pitch was extremely fast, a little outside, and somewhat below the knees.

I hope that these examples will increase the intelligibility of my assertion, then, that I cannot understand and therefore do not believe that it is possible to achieve knowledge about or develop valid explanations based on causal mechanisms in the absence of familiarity with the regularities (or correlations) that are the only visible manifestations that allow one to differentiate between causal connections and random or highly unlikely co-incidences. I know that this assertion seems quite counterintuitive to some. Mohr (1990, 8), for example, insists that "the regularity theory is not right because we all know that it is wrong. When one billiard ball smacks into another one on the table, the smack is real, and the resulting movement of the billiard balls does not occur because of a followed-by rule or a trick of the mind." However, at the risk of seeming perverse, I would acknowledge that though the movement of the billiard balls (or the flight of the baseball out of the park after the equally compelling smack of the bat) does not occur because of a trick of the mind, a strong intuitive feeling that the movement of the balls has occurred *because* of the smack of another ball is the result, most importantly, of a perception that movements of that kind regularly result from smacks like that, and *not* the result of any direct perception of causal mechanisms at work based on some deeper knowledge of the structure of billiard balls (or baseball games) developed independently of a knowledge about regularities.[11]

Now a scientific realist will undoubtedly object that I have structured my example regarding scientific observations of home runs in a biased way so that the "scientific realist" (i.e., the baseball fan who does not base his or her explanation on knowledge about regularities and covering laws) is not only disinclined to "explain" the outcome of events by subsumption but is also ignorant about the causal mechanisms at work with respect to the phenomenon in question. The fan of the nomological, or nomothetic, bent, in contrast, is much more familiar with the game, and so his or her "explanation" is not only based on a covering law but is also much more credible.

That would be a fair criticism of the examples I have used to support my point, except to the extent that it suggests that the greater familiarity with the game of the nomologically inclined fan is an accident, or nothing more than a coincidence imposed arbitrarily in order to make the example come out right. From my point of view, it is not necessarily an accident or a coincidence that the nomologically inclined baseball fan *also* is intensely familiar with the nuances in the game beyond a superficial knowledge of its empirical regularities.

The hermeneutically inclined analyst, or a historian adhering to approaches like those of Collingwood and Dray discussed above, might object to the "home run" example on the grounds that the explanation of the event in question is inadequate or not even an explanation because it provides no information about what the principles (the pitcher and the batter) were *thinking* or perceiving at the time. Perhaps, for example, the pitcher and the batter were colluding in order to determine the outcome of the game for the sake of a lucrative arrangement they had made with gamblers, and the pitcher threw the high hanging curveball by prearrangement and on purpose. Only if we are provided that kind of information, from this point of view, do we really have an explanation and a valid understanding of the event in question.

I would agree that information about the thought processes and intentions of the principles in the event would complement the explanation based on (or at least alluding to implicitly) a pattern involving hanging curveballs and home runs, but I would still insist that the event is explained only if knowledge of the pattern exists and the event fits into that pattern. In *this* case, the pitcher intended to throw a hanging curveball and for the batter to hit a home run. In most cases, the pitcher throws such curveballs by accident. In *all* the cases, regardless of the varying thought processes of the principles involved, there is a correlation between hanging curveballs and well-hit balls, which is almost certainly indicative of a causal connection (rather than a spurious correlation). Similarly, if democracies in disputes avoid wars with each other (to hark back to the theme of the book before it is forgotten entirely), the thought processes of the principles involved in the disputes may vary widely in content. But an explanation of any particular peaceful outcome of a dispute between democratic states based entirely on those widely varying thought processes is inadequate, and not really an explanation at all, unless the democratic structures that provide the context for those thought processes—and apparently help produce the peace—are included, thus bringing into the picture the pattern into which that particular peaceful outcome can be embedded.

The "As If" Assumption and Causal Mechanisms

If Wendt, Dessler, and other critics of covering laws as the basis for explanations believe that "positivists," "neopositivists," and/or "neorealists" are really only interested in regularities in observable behavior, and not about the subtleties of causal mechanisms, that may well be the fault, at least partially, of those who believe in the utility of the nomological approach to explanation. When Milton Friedman (1953) and Bueno de Mesquita (1988), for example, insist with fervor that they do not believe that decision makers actually make the calculations stipulated by their models but *only* that decision makers behave *as if* they do, they might justly be accused of creating the impression that all they are interested in is regularities in observable behavior.[12] The defense of the *as if* assumption, at least, certainly appears to be a disavowal of interest in the specific causal processes that bring those regularities about. Similarly, when Milton Friedman (1953), for example, makes his famous claim that a model should be judged *only* by the accuracy of its predictions and not by the plausibility of its typically simple, unrealistic assumptions about the processes leading to the predicted outcomes, one should not be surprised if this creates the impression that modelers of his "positivist" stripe are interested only in regularities in observable behavior, and not in the intricacies of the processes which undergird those regularities.

Causal Mechanisms and Covering Laws

Such impressions, to repeat, are perfectly understandable, but I want to argue that they are quite clearly *mis*impressions. On the most fundamental, perhaps even superficial, level, advocates of explanations based on covering laws are not interested in just *any* observable regularities in behavior. They are particularly interested in nonspurious correlations in which temporal order has been established,[13] an interest that automatically leads them to be interested in causal mechanisms involving several factors in addition to those associated with each other within the covering laws in question. And even nonformal modelers are more impressed with explanations that rely on covering laws if the regularities to which those laws refer are buttressed by a detailed theory that provides plausible accounts of additional, related regularities, i.e., a theory which provides details about the causal mechanisms connecting the original factors of interest, as well as related phenomena. Julian Simon (1969, 449) notes, for example—in a discussion that seems, without actually citing Hempel, to adhere to a covering law notions regarding causality and explanation—that "the more tightly a relationship is bound into (that is, deduced from, compatible with, and logically connected to) a general framework of theory, the stronger is its claim to be called 'causal.'"

And Bueno de Mesquita indicates his intense interest in the intricacies of causal mechanisms in at least two ways. One is in the detailed descriptions he provides, as we have noted above, of specific examples in which he stresses that decision makers (despite his stress on the "as if" assumption) make calculations that parallel quite closely those stipulated by his expected utility model. The other involves his emphasis on the importance of the theoretical basis of the regularities he points out. He is quite clearly not interested in regularities for regularities' sake, or just for the sake of providing covering laws and their subsumptive potential. He, on the contrary, is only really interested in regularities that are produced by causal mechanisms he describes in meticulous, logical detail in the course of presenting his model. In his own words:

> *Formal, explicit theorizing takes intellectual, if not temporal, precedence over empiricism.* Rigorous "tests" of casual hunches seem to me to carry little more weight than do casual "tests" of those same hunches. In the absence of the careful specification of the exact logical linkages among the terms in one's hypotheses, even the most rigorous empirical analysis is doomed to be inchoate . . . The difficult task of making precise the meaning of each term in a stipulated relationship, so that the propositions are clear and so that the *explanatory component* can be evaluated, is essential. (Bueno de Mesquita 1985, 128–29)

The Realist or Neorealist Concept of "Explanation"

According to Wendt (1987. 351), Bueno de Mesquita (1985) provides the "most explicit recent discussion of the philosophy of science underlying neorealism." But Bueno de Mesquita himself, in *The War Trap* (1981, 140–45, is one example) as well as in *War and Reason* (Bueno de Mesquita and Lalman 1992, e.g., 274–76) specifically rejects both realism and neorealism. (As we discussed in chapter 1, there are substantial areas of overlap between realism and Bueno de Mesquita's approach, so Wendt's impression is understandable.)

Perhaps the argument by Wendt that realists or neorealists are interested only in regularities and not in causal mechanisms would be supported if we looked at "real" realists or neorealists?

Interestingly, Morgenthau (1967, 7) declares very early on in *Politics among Nations* the following: "The difference between international politics as it actually is and a rational theory derived from it is like the difference between a photograph and a painted portrait. The photograph shows everything that can be seen by the naked eye; the painted portrait does not show everything that can be seen by the naked eye but it shows, or at least seeks to show, one thing that the naked eye cannot see; the human *essence* of the person portrayed." This passage contains, first, what seems to be a sophisticated defense of simplifying assumptions, the legitimacy and utility of which we shall turn to more specifically below. But it also seems to display an interest in causal mechanisms, in their *essence,* which is quite realist—that is, scientific realist—in flavor.

If we go to the heart of neorealism and look for an epistemological rationale (instead of someone like Bueno de Mesquita who denies that he is a neorealist), we find that Kenneth Waltz declares the following: "What do I mean by *explain*? I mean explain in these senses: to say why the range of expected outcomes falls within certain limits; to say why patterns of behavior recur; to say why events repeat themselves, including events that none or few of the actors may like. The structure of the system acts as a constraining and disposing force" (Waltz 1986, 57).

Alexander Wendt (1987, 354) as we have seen above, declares that "whereas the empiricist explains by generalizing about observable behavior, the realist explains by showing how the (often unobservable) causal mechanisms . . . *work.*" He also asserts that "scientists work backward from the observed phenomenon to a postulated entity or causal mechanism" (1987, 358). Similarly, David Dessler (1991, 349–50) says that "causal theory [i.e., causal theory as conceptualized by 'scientific realists'] does not purport to identify the conditions associated with the occurrence of a specified type of outcome. . . . In general a causal theory is vindicated 'by showing that the best explanations of relevant phenomena appeal to instances of mechanisms in the repertoire of the theory.'"[14] Dessler points to Darwin's theory of evolution as an example of the kind of causal theory he is talking about. He asserts that Darwin's "claims are causal, not correlational," that "correlational science plays no role" in Darwin's work, and that for that reason, philosophers such as Popper (1974) have denied Darwin's ideas the status of a "scientific" theory (350). Both Wendt and Dessler, I will argue, offer accurate descriptions in such arguments of the modus operandi and the epistemological basis of the work of Kenneth Waltz.

For example, one of the most fundamental causal claims made by Waltz in *Man, the State, and War* (1959, 159) is that "with many sovereign states, with no system of law enforceable among them, with each state judging its griev-ances and ambitions according to the dictates of its own reason or desire—conflict, sometimes leading to war, is bound to occur." This claim may have correlational implications, but they are quite indirect. Mostly it is an "explana-tion" in the sense that it emphasizes how the system "*works*," a la Wendt. An-other quintessentially Waltzian causal claim, or "explanation," from *Theory of International Politics* (1979, 166), points out that "it is important to notice that states will ally with the devil to avoid the hell of military defeat." Correlational implications might be teased out of this assertion, but it is quite clear in Waltz's discussion that he does not consider this a covering law of that type. Rather, what he argues is that he has put his finger on a *causal mechanism* that explains alliances between states of opposing ideologies and regime types throughout the history of international politics, which has its roots in the anarchic nature of international political systems, in a manner similar to Darwin's arguments on behalf of this theory of evolution. Waltz's theory even has, like Darwin's, a "survival of the fittest" theme, as when he argues that "competitive systems are regulated . . . by the 'rationality' of the more successful competitors . . . [S]ome do better than others—whether through intelligence, skill, hard work, or dumb luck. . . . Either their competitors emulate them or they fall by the wayside" (1986, 66). In short, it is quite clear that Waltz is (almost certainly unwittingly) a "scientific realist," as opposed to an "empiricist."

Alexander Wendt is aware of this possibility, at least to some extent, ac-knowledging at one point that "it could be argued that neorealists . . . are . . . at least in some respects, 'closet' scientific realists" (1987, 351). He dismisses the possibility, however, with the declaration that "the explicit metatheoretical state-ments" of neorealists "remain within the empiricist discourse" (351). But the example he adduces in support of this claim is an essay by Bueno de Mesquita (1985) who, as we have seen, explicitly rejects neorealism.

Inescapable Covering Laws

An attentive reader might well feel by now that the "story" I am telling (my "explanation," as it were) is getting confusing. To the claim by scientific real-ists like Wendt and Dessler that empiricists and neorealists are only interested in regularities and not the intricacies of causal mechanisms and the structures that produce them, I have retorted that nomologically inclined empiricists are in fact as interested in causal mechanisms as scientific realists and that neorealists behave, or at least Kenneth Waltz actually behaves in print, as if he were a scientific realist.

I certainly cannot claim to be able to resolve all the confusing issues at hand.[15] However, I will claim that the notion of a covering law does at least create some coherence among conflicting ideas about knowledge and causality, even though that notion is explicitly rejected by scientific realists as well as at least some philosophers of history. I say this despite an uncomfortable awareness that it smacks of arrogance to claim that one's understanding of how other people think is better than those people themselves are capable of. But it does seem to me that *comparison* of an event to be understood and explained with other events is logically impossible to avoid. As Hempel (1965, 235–37) argued in his classic article, "While most historians do suggest explanations of historical events, many of them deny the possibility of resorting to general laws in history. It is possible, however, to account for this situation." He accounts for it by arguing that, in some cases, the universal hypotheses or covering laws in question are *assumed* to be so familiar to everybody that they literally go without saying. In other cases, it is difficult to state the hypothesis resorted to without obviously weakening the "explanation" being offered because not all the relevant evidence supports the "covering law" in question. Thus, the historian feels more comfortable leaving the general hypothesis unstated. "All [historical explanation] rests on the assumption of universal hypotheses," Hempel (1965, 237) concludes, "but in many cases, the content of the hypotheses . . . are tacitly assumed."

James Fearon (1991, 171) points out, in what I see as a similar argument, that even analysts who give close scrutiny to a single case have no logical option but to compare (perhaps only subconsciously) that case to *something* if they are to provide assertions that strike people as being "explanatory." In arguing that C was a cause of an event E, Fearon suggests, "analysts have available a choice between two *and only two* [emphasis added] strategies for 'empirically' assessing the hypothesis. Either they can imagine that C had been absent and ask whether E would have (or might have) occurred *in the counterfactual case;* or they can search for other *actual* cases that resemble the case in question in significant respects, except that in some of these cases C is absent." In other words, even those analysts who focus on a *single* case must compare it to *something* in order to "explain" it, even if it is an imaginary counterfactual case, in order to make the explanation plausible, or to give the intended audience the feeling that the event has been explained.

David Dessler (1991, 350), at least tacitly, makes the same point when he declares that "in causal comparison [of the type carried out by "scientific realists"], theory justification is typically punctuated with 'what else could it be?' argumentation." "What else could it be" argumentation consists of comparisons of the world as it is (according to, for example, Darwin's theory of evolution) with, in Fearon's terms, a counterfactual world. "If the world were not as I say it is," such arguments contend, "then it (the 'real' world) would not operate in the way my theory predicts." In other words, a world structured differently (i.e., a counterfactual world) would operate differently. This is the structure of Darwin's principle arguments on behalf of his theory of evolution and of most of Waltz's arguments on behalf of neorealism (Ray 1992, 532).

As Fearon also notes, this mode of reasoning undergirds explanations even though the analysts in question may adopt that kind of comparative strategy tacitly, or even unconsciously. And in so doing, they are, perhaps again unconsciously, adopting the "covering law" notion regarding "explanation." That is, the comparison of a single case to a counterfactual case only provides a persuasive basis for an "explanation" if the results of that comparison provide evidence in favor of the tacit hypothesis or covering law that is being appealed to in order to legitimate or provide a basis for the putative "explanation." In other words, the comparison has to reveal, if the explanation is to be persuasive, a strong "correlation," so to speak, between the presence of the causal mechanism in the "real" world and the outcome (or outcomes) that the causal mechanism allegedly accounts for and the absence of that mechanism along with the corresponding absence of the outcome to be explained in the counterfactual world.

As Wesley Salmon (1985, 651) points out, there are two "venerable intuitions: *explanation as derivation* and *explanation as identification of mechanisms.*" He rightly concludes that "the two viewpoints are equally committed to the covering-law principle." Similarly, Carl Hempel argues, historians who offer explanations based on thought processes or inferences about what reasoning agents think are offering covering law explanations at least implicitly, based on a "descriptive principle stating what rational [or calculating] agents will do in situations of [this] kind" (Hempel 1974, 101).

The Legitimacy of the "As If" and Other Simplifying Assumptions

Despite the interest in causal mechanisms displayed by formal modelers such as Bueno de Mesquita and by neorealists such as Kenneth Waltz, their reliance on the "as if" and other simplifying assumptions does seem contradictory, somehow, to an emphasis on such mechanisms. Perhaps for that reason, but surely also for others, simplifying assumptions such as the "as if" one can evoke considerable hostility, even among those not antagonistic toward correlational analysis or explanations based on covering laws. Philip Schrodt (1990, 754), for example, declares that "the persistent use of empirically unsupported 'as if' assumptions is symptomatic of sloth, not science." If formal modelers (or neorealists) are in fact (as I argue) so interested in the details of causal processes, an attentive reader might wonder at this point why they so consistently (sometimes even rather passionately) insist that decision makers do not actually make calculations stipulated by their models but only behave as if they do?

Wendt (1987, 343) asserts that the "as if" approach to theory building is "untenable" and cites Terry Moe (1979) in defense of that assertion. Moe's attack on the "as if" assumption is a spirited one and takes advantage of the inconsistencies in the arguments utilized by defenders of that assumption.[16] I will argue, though, that the "as if" assumption, as well as other simplifying assumptions (in Waltz, or even Morgenthau) serve a valid purpose for formal modeling or even the more general theoretical enterprise that has been, I will also argue, overemphasized.

As Moe (1979, 233) acknowledges, "there is nothing inherently wrong with 'as if' language." Specifically, he admits that in evaluating a rational choice model, "it makes no difference that actual individuals fail to perform differential calculus or Bayesian estimates." But he concludes that the "as if" assumption is a source of ambiguity and confusion that he apparently would like to see abandoned.

Perhaps, instead, it just needs to be modified or made somewhat less stringent or defended in less zealous or enthusiastic ways. As Moe (1975, 231) points out, "the exclusion of mental processes is all the protection that 'as if' reasoning can provide." But this is important protection, without which rational choice models would clearly not be tenable. That is, rational choice modelers clearly cannot plausibly stipulate that decision makers actually make calculations (based, for example, on differential calculus, Bayesian estimates, or complex computerized calculations) that they might well be incapable of understanding.

But formal modelers go too far if they claim, as they sometimes appear to do, that they have no interest at all in actual "real world" calculations of decision makers. Decision makers will not make calculations that parallel *precisely* those stipulated in a typical rational choice model. However—and this is a point that formal modelers may justly be accused of obscuring, perhaps—if a model is to be credible, decision makers *must* make decisions in a way that contains some essential core that is analogous to, parallel to, or homomorphic with the processes stipulated in that model.

For example, Bueno de Mesquita's (1981) expected utility model of international conflicts stipulates that decision makers estimate the probability of victory in anticipated military conflicts. That probability is further stipulated to be a function (among other things) of the relative military capabilities of the potential initiator and the probable target of the conflict being contemplated. It would be silly for Bueno de Mesquita to insist that decision makers evaluate the probability of victory in precisely the way he does in order to evaluate the implications of this model. In other words, clearly decision makers do not base comparisons of military capability on exactly the same indicators that Bueno de Mesquita utilizes in systematic empirical tests of his model. But his model does imply that decision makers do base their decisions at least in part on the probability of victory in any anticipated military conflict; it may also imply, although this is less clear, that they take military capabilities into account when they estimate those probabilities. Actual decision makers in "real world" situations may use very rough indicators. They may be badly informed. But there must be some essential core of correspondence between the actual calculations made by real decision makers and the calculations stipulated by formal models, or else there is no logical reason to expect that the predictions made by the model (or the "postdictions," for that matter) will turn out to be accurate. In other words, "real world" processes and the processes stipulated by formal models may be grossly different in obvious, even apparently fundamental, ways. That is the point conveyed by, and that serves (adequately, in my opinion) as the rationale for, the "as if " assumption. But a formal model, or any other theory, must in fact capture the fundamentals of real world processes if it is going to produce accurate predictions or valid explanations.[17] Otherwise, the accurate predictions could only be explained as magical, or at least highly mysterious coincidences.

The Legitimacy of Small-n Studies

In short, I confess that I believe that the "as if " assumption and similar simplifying assumptions serve legitimate purposes, even though they provoke hostility in some quarters and create a misleading impression that their advocates have no interest in the details of "real world" causal mechanisms. I also confess to being partial toward the nomothetic notion of "explanation," considered outmoded in some circles. Such a notion requires, if valid explanations are to be developed, analyses of *large numbers* of cases. However, the nomological approach does not imply that one cannot develop explanations of the outcomes in single cases, even though it does clearly imply that causal linkages leave visible traces only over a larger number of cases and/or observations.

Nor does the nomological model of explanation imply a lack of interest in the intense analysis of one or a small number of cases. Intensive analysis of a single case or two or three cases can produce insights about complex causal mechanisms that will not be obvious or even visible in large-N studies. Such analyses can also provide evidence useful for evaluative purposes, in the form of detailed information regarding the intricacies of causal processes, that will not be generated by large-N studies.

Another reason for such intensive analyses of a case, or two, is that for a significant portion of analysts in the field of international politics, such analyses are the preferred method of both identifying causal relationships and evaluating hypotheses regarding putative causal linkages. I might feel (and obviously

I do) that such analyses must necessarily be combined with large-N analyses before even relatively firm conclusions can be drawn, but even in light of the incredibly persuasive nature of the arguments in this chapter, it would be unrealistic to assume that everybody will ultimately agree with me.

In other words, I would prefer that even those who find my epistemological notions naive and/or misinformed would nevertheless entertain seriously the notion that regime type or democracy has a substantial impact on conflict between states. As Mohr (1991, 16) observes about epistemological notions: "We seem to have a strong, well-developed sense of . . . causation, but it can be shown to have flaws. In practice, we patch up the flaws as best we can and proceed with the business of life." Some readers may feel there are flaws in my notions of "causality" and "explanation." My hope is that they will nevertheless be willing to proceed with the "business of life," which in this case is a consideration of the possible impact of regime type on international conflict. My hope also is that analyses in the next chapter, focusing on an intensive analysis of two cases, will be of interest both to those who share my epistemological framework and to those who reject it, at least in part. For the former group (the nomologically inclined), my aim in this chapter has been to help those readers evaluate the analyses in the next chapter by giving them a clearer idea of what I am trying to accomplish there and why. In particular, I have tried to illuminate what I see as the most important aspects of the relationship between large-N studies and small-n studies.

One main reason for doing so is that I believe that the potential contribution of small-n studies is of particular importance for those of us who analyze relatively rare events such as international wars, and arguably even more important by degrees of magnitude for any analysts interested in the impact of democracy on international conflict. Wars are, to repeat, relatively speaking, rare events. In most years, 99.9 percent of the dyads in the international system do not fight international wars against each other. This is a problem for the nomothetic approach to explanation, and it is compounded when an explanatory factor of interest is democracy. Wars are rare; until recently (in recent decades) democratic regimes have been even rarer.

The exact dimensions of the problem (as discussed earlier in chapter 1) are highlighted in the recent analysis by Bremer (1992), in which he focuses on all dyads in the international system in each year from 1816 to 1965. As we observed in chapter 1, after some cases are deleted because of missing data, Bremer has a total of 202,778 dyad-years to analyze, a luxuriously large number for those intent on statistical analyses. But an international war was initiated within only 85, or .04 percent of those dyad-years. There are more than 20,000 uniformly democratic dyad-years to work with from 1816 to 1965. But given the rate of war occurrence among dyads in general, on an annual basis, there would have been only 9 wars between democracies during the 149 years analyzed by Bremer even if democratic states warred against each other at exactly the same rate that states in general become involved in wars against each other.

Fortunately, for the sake of those of us who are interested in the expansion of the number of totally democratic dyad-years available for analysis, there has been a significant increase in the number of democratic states in the international system since 1965. Even so, the number of wars between democratic states that might be expected to have occurred just by chance, if democracy really has no pacifying impact at all, is not very large. Accordingly, the definitions and coding decisions regarding regime types and wars can have a dramatic bearing on how one evaluates the hypothesis that regime type has an important impact on international conflict. In other words, even small changes in the definitions of democracy and war might increase the number of wars observed between "democratic" states by an amount no larger than 2 or 3, but nevertheless quite significant in light of the small number of wars that would be expected just by chance.

This means that the categorization of every case can have a relatively large impact on the outcome of analyses of that relationship. It also means that the number of cases in which the uniformly democratic nature of the regimes might serve as an "explanation" of the peaceful outcome of a dispute is quite small. Every single one of those cases, under these circumstances, merits close scrutiny. Analysts of voting behavior have literally millions of new data points generated every time there is an election. By comparison, analysts of the impact of joint democracy on pairs of nations involved in serious disputes have only a relative handful of cases to work with. It is important to exploit those cases, for insights, for evidence, and possibly for persuasive purposes, to the greatest extent possible, just because there are so few of them available.

Conclusion

Although most political scientists will argue that small-n and large-N studies are complementary, attempts to bridge the gap between them confront difficult questions regarding the nature of causation and the definition of "explanation." I stipulate here that the identification of a causal relationship necessarily involves establishing that there is a nonspurious correlation between two factors in which temporal order has been established and that an explanation is a statement (or set of statements) that demonstrates that the outcome of an event is merely an example of an established general pattern. One of the implications of these definitions is that causal linkages cannot be identified within the context of one case, no matter how much information one might uncover about the genesis of that case, the causal mechanisms that produced it, or the the mental processes of the people involved in its outcome. Another implication is that explanations necessarily invoke "covering laws," in Carl Hempel's terminology.

Hempel's nomological conception of explanations is not universally accepted. Such scholars in the field of international relations as Alexander Wendt and David Dessler, for example, have argued that Hempel's epistemological views are outmoded and that the field should adopt instead "scientific realism." Scientific realists strive to explain by identifying underlying causal mechanisms rather than by subsumption.

However, I argue here that the idea that causal mechanisms can be identified and understood without relying on comparisons, regularities, and correlational analyses (a "scientific realist" idea) is unsound. But I also argue that nomologically inclined scholars have contributed to confusion about their conceptions of causality and explanations, specifically by the arguments they make about the role of simplifying assumptions in the theoretical enterprise.

Critics of nomological notions about explanations can hardly be blamed if they infer from stirring defenses of the *as if* assumption that nomothetically inclined analysts have little or no interest in the intricacies involved in complex causal processes. Defenders of the *as if* assumption might help eliminate this misperception if they would make clear that there is in fact an important core of correspondence between the calculations stipulated by a valid rational choice model and the actual calculations made by decision makers in the "real world." Otherwise, there would be no good reason to expect that predictions based on such models will be valid.

Neorealists such as Kenneth Waltz are singled out by Alexander Wendt as advocates of covering laws, but an analysis of Waltz's causal claims suggests that his approach to explanation is closer to that of scientific realists. Charles Darwin's theory of evolution, according to David Dessler, is an example of a scientific theory with no correlational implications; his theory therefore exemplifies "explanation" in the scientific realist's sense of the term. But the explanations offered by Waltz, Darwin, and analysts of single cases, some of whom explicitly reject nomothetic explanations, nevertheless take a step in the direction of utilizing "covering laws" when they compare (as they must logically do, implicitly or explicitly) the systems or the cases they examine to counterfactual systems or cases.

Small-n and large-N studies, then, are genuinely complementary, and it is particularly important to exploit the possibilities inherent in intensive analysis of small numbers of cases when the phenomena of interest, like international wars and democratic pairs of states, are statistically rare. And, as David Dessler acknowledges, nomological and the scientific realist notions about explanations are also complementary.[18] I would add, however, that because scientific realists necessarily compare (at a minimum, and implicitly or explicitly) actual systems or cases to counterfactual systems or cases, the scientific realist approach to explanation can be subsumed under the covering law approach.

Notes

1. This methodological division is exemplified nicely by two essays immediately following Bueno de Mesquita's in the same issue of *International Studies Quarterly* by Krasner (1985) and Jervis (1985), both of whom express considerable skepticism about Bueno de Mesquita's arguments regarding the superiority of large-N studies over small-n studies.

2. "Controlled Comparison analysis of a small n is neither competitive with nor a substitute for quantitative analysis of a large N. Rather, the two approaches are genuinely complementary" (George 1979, 61).

3. It is logicallly possible that what George is referring to here is the observation of a single case over many points in time, and thus the correlation of variables over time, but it is rather clear from a reading of his argument that that is not the kind of "correlation" he has in mind.

4. Bueno de Mesquita goes to some length here to demonstrate that the calculations made by Premier Tisza paralleled quite closely those in the equation derived from his model.

5. I base this discussion on an entirely imaginary event in order to prevent issues of substance from intruding in inconvenient, counterproductive ways into this primarily epistemological discussion.

6. I realize that, alternatively, I might generate and analyze data on internal unrest and war initiations by Anatolia over time, or data on those two variables for all states over time, or engage in cross-sectional analyses of each of the last two hundred years, or of all serious disputes in the last two hundred years, etc. But the discussion is already sufficiently complex without introducing questions regarding the relationships between cross-sectional and longitudinal studies or analyses on different levels of analysis. For the purposes of this discussion I would suggest that we assume that all possibly relevant types of systematic empirical analyses of relatively large numbers of cases produce similar results, i.e., there is no important relationship between internal unrest and war initiation among any population or sample of cases in which Anatolia can be included.

7. Eckstein here quotes Verba (1967) in support of this position.

8. Discovering that this was actually the case, i.e., that the formal leader of the country had not actually made the decision to go to war, would not be of particular concern to me even if I were a formal modeler who had assumed that such decisions are made by a unitary actor. That assumption does not necessarily imply that the unitary actor in question is the *formal* political leader of the country.

9. See, for example, Tuchanski (1992).

10. Wendt cites several sources in support of his interpretation of scientific realism, among the more prominent of which are Wylie (1986), McMullin (1984), Harre and Madden (1975), and Hausman (1983).

11. In order to deprive antagonistic readers of the pleasure of imagining that I naively believe that my argument here is original, let me cite David Hume once more: "We fancy that, were we brought on a sudden into this world, we could at first have inferred that one billiard ball would communicate motion to another upon impulse, and that we needed not to have waited for the event in order to pronounce with certainty upon it. Such is the influence of custom that where it is strongest it not only covers our natural ignorance but even conceals itself, and seems not to take place, merely because it is founded in the highest degree" (Hume 1748).

12. Such an accusation might be leveled with even more justification at J. David Singer, so well identified with correlational analyses in the field of international politics, when he says (as Dessler 1991, 346, notes with, perhaps, a certain glee): "We would do well to drop the mystical concept of causality from our epistemological repertoire" (Singer 1979, 15). My definite impression is, however, that Singer's views on causality are rare, if not unique, among those who engage in correlational analyses in the field of international politics. In Singer's defense, it might be argued that he adheres more closely to Hempel's views on these matters than most nomologically inclined analysts; Dessler (1991, 344) points out, apparently with some justification, that "for Hempel there is nothing to causation beyond correlation; in the deductive-nomological approach causation is a redundant concept that is ultimately dispensable." In defense of those, like me, who admire Hempel's nomological approach to explanation but are reluctant to give up the notion of causality (and who, in fact, find it very hard to understand how those two concepts can be divorced from each other), I would point out that Hempel's (1965, 231) *definition* of explanation, cited above, does refer to an explanation as an assertion that "a set of events . . . *caused* the event to be explained."

13. A word about the rather awkward phrase "in which temporal order has been established" might be in order here. According to a standard textbook argument, one may conclude that A is a cause of B if A occurs before B, A correlates with B, and the correlation is not spurious. (One can never, of course, be entirely confident about the last point.) But Mohr (1990, 5) argues quite persuasively, in my view, that a viable definition of "cause" must allow for simultaneous causation. "If ball X hits stationary ball Y," Mohr explains, "and then there is a pause, and then Y begins to roll, we are at a loss to know why it began to roll just when it did, or even why it began at all. There can be no pause, which means that the cause and the effect were simultaneous." Mohr also suggests that when "a bowling ball is placed on a piece of foam . . . [it] takes on a cup-like indentation around the ball. . . . [W]hich occurs first? The ball cannot make the indentation until the indentation is made, but neither can the indentation be made until the ball makes it. They are simultaneous." Mohr's arguments persuade me, at least, that one should stipulate that A can be said, logically, to be a cause of B if it occurred before, or simultaneous with B, but not if it occurred after B.

14. Dessler here is citing a passage from Miller (1987, 140).

15. For example, Wendt (1987, 351) accuses Bueno de Mesquita and other "empiricists" of harboring unsophisticated, antagonistic attitudes about the role of "unobservables" in scientific explanations, and then points out a few pages later that one of the more important unobservable causal entities that plays a key role in much contem-

porary scientific research is utilities (354). Bueno de Mesquita certainly cannot be accurately categorized as one who is unaccepting of the utility of utilities.

16. However, as Achen and Snidal (1989, 158) point out, correctly in my opinion, Moe's criticism of the "as if" assumption is based on a comparison of a rational choice theory to an empirical generalization (Galileo's law), rather than a natural science theory, like Newton's. ("Had [Moe]—more logically—" Achen and Snidal conclude, "compared the causal structure built into rational choice with the causal structure built into Newton's theory (which explains Galileo's Law), his conclusion would have been reversed."

17. As Anatol Rapoport (1961, 46) asserts regarding a physicist who utilizes "false" assumptions, "In return for sacrificing precision . . . he gains simplicity, and what is more important, he gets at the fundamentals (almost in the Platonic sense of the word) of the situation." Jack Levy (1989, 306) asserts (speaking specifically of Bueno de Mesquita's expected utility approach) that "the *as if* assumption is not too damaging to a theory if and only if there does not exist an alternative theory that provides equally accurate empirical predictions and that is also based on assumptions that are more congruent with empirical reality." But how does one assess the congruence with empirical reality of assumptions (not hypotheses)?

18. Specifically, Dessler (1991, 346) asserts that "the two explanatory formats [i.e., the nomological and the scientific realist] examined here . . . do not present us with an either/or choice, as some philosophers have argued."

Chapter 5

Comparing the Fashoda Crisis and the Spanish-American War
A Pseudo-Experiment Regarding the Impact of Joint Democracy

This chapter will be devoted to a comparison of the Fashoda Crisis involving Great Britain and France in 1898, with the Spanish-American War, also occurring in 1898. The initial question that might be asked about such a comparison is "Why analyze only two cases?" I hope that question has been answered, or at least usefully addressed, in the previous chapter. To reiterate briefly, I would point out here that large-N studies are indispensable for establishing the existence of a causal linkage within individual cases. And I would not be inclined to embark upon this analysis of only two cases were it not for the fact that several excellent large-N analyses (e.g., Rummel 1979; Maoz and Abdolali 1989; Maoz and Russett 1992, 1993; Russett with Maoz 1993; Bremer 1992, 1993) have presented substantial evidence that there is a correlation between the regime type of the disputants and the probability of conflict escalation on the dyadic level of analysis. I am also encouraged to allocate resources to the close analysis of a couple of cases because several of those large-N studies have dealt energetically with the possibility that the correlation might be spurious, and by the fact that Rummel (1979), Bueno de Mesquita and Lalman (1992), Russett (1993), and Weart (1994) have provided a detailed theoretical basis for the argument that the correlation is causal.

Provided that research as a basis, an analysis of a couple of cases can reasonably be expected to provide at least a couple of benefits. It might provide insights into the causal process connecting the types of regimes involved in international disputes and the probability that a dispute will escalate to war. This defense of the comparative analysis of two cases is analogous to the arguments made by Lijphart (1971, 691) in defense of "hypothesis generating case studies" and/or by Eckstein's argument regarding the "heuristic" value of case studies discussed in the previous chapter. However, I would also argue (with Eckstein 1975, 106) that "too much is made of heuristic case studies." If the potential of the comparative study in this chapter were limited to "teasing out" (Bueno de Mesquita 1985, 134) patterns or relationships between variables related to the question of the impact of regime type on conflict escalation I would not consider the project deserving of the time and energy I will allocate to it. What makes the endeavor worthwhile, in my view, is that "case studies . . . are valuable . . . at the stage of theory building where least value is generally attached to them: the stage at which candidate theories are 'tested'" (Eckstein 1975, 80). Mohr (1992, 11) argues even more strongly that "the case study is a design that is not only pertinent but is well suited to establishing causality in social science."

Why the Fashoda Crisis
and the Spanish-American War?

An implication of any large-N study is that the difference in the outcomes of any two cases where the causal factor in question is present in one but not in another (or present to a greater degree in one than the other) can be "explained" in part by that causal factor. As we discussed on several occasions, Bremer (1992) shows that if there had been no democratic states in the international system between 1816 and 1965 (or alternatively, if democracy had had no impact on international conflict), there would have been nine more wars than actually occurred. Because only nine or some other relatively small number of "nonwars" (or peaceful resolutions of conflicts) can be explained by the "democratic peace proposition," it is important to examine all of the relatively rare cases with care in order to achieve the best possible understanding of the causal processes of interest here.

But this is a counsel of perfection and, strictly speaking, an illogical one. It is not possible to identify those nine disputes (or whatever the number is) occurring between 1816 and 1965 (or more recently) that would have escalated to war had it not been for the democratic character of the regimes involved. Joint democracy, assuming it systematically exerts that impact (on conflict escalation), exerts that impact on every dispute in which it exists. Whether it prevented any given dispute from escalating to international war is a function of the extent to which it is present (which we can estimate with some ostensible validity) *and* the extent to which all the other factors impacting on conflict escalation or resolution exerted their impact, which we cannot be expected to estimate with much accuracy. In other words, even a dispute between two states that are marginally democratic might have been prevented from escalating to war by the joint democracy effect if all the other factors pushing it in that direction were not pushing too hard. On the other hand, even the presence of full-fledged democracies on both sides of a dispute might have no impact at all on the peaceful resolution of that dispute if it were highly unlikely to escalate to war regardless of the type of regimes involved in it. And, of course, joint democracy might arguably exert its most profound pacifying impact by preventing serious or militarized disputes from arising between democratic states in the first place, thus conjuring up the interesting task of identifying those nondisputes that "resulted" in the nonwars of interest to us. Perhaps, when Joseph Nye (1993, 40) asserts that "the idea that democracies do not fight *other democracies* . . . need[s] exploration via detailed case studies to look at what actually happened in particular instances," he implies that he knows how such cases of nondisputes leading to nonwars might be identified. (But I doubt it.)

However, despite all those logical difficulties confronting the task of isolating cases in which joint democracy might have made a crucial contribution to the peaceful resolution of serious disputes (or the avoidance of serious disputes), one could argue that it is likely to have made its most visible and important contribution in disputes that almost escalated to war. It is among such cases that the type of most interest to us (i.e., disputes that might have escalated to war *but for* the democratic nature of the regimes involved) would be found. Furthermore, the causal processes of greatest interest here might arguably be most clearly brought into view by comparing a dispute between democracies that almost escalated to war with a dispute between a pair of states that were almost uniformly democratic that did escalate to war.

The logic on which that assertion is based was formulated first, perhaps, and influentially by John Stuart Mill; it is commonly referred to as the "method of difference." Mill's statement of this principle from his *System of Logic* is as follows: "If an instance in which the phenomenon under investigation occurs and in which it does not occur have every circumstance in common save one, that one occurring only in the former, the circumstance in which alone the two instances differ is . . . the cause, or an indispensable part of the cause of the phenomenon" (cited in Meckstroth 1975, 133).

In words relevant to the issue at hand, this suggests that if we can find two disputes involving pairs of states that are exactly alike in every respect except that the regimes involved in one dispute are both democratic, and in the other dispute they are not, then the differences in the outcomes of the disputes (e.g., the dispute between the democracies was resolved peacefully, but the dispute between the autocratic regimes was not) could, according to the "method of difference," be attributed to the differences in the regimes involved in the disputes.

Of course, we are never going to find two disputes in which the pairs of states involved are *exactly* alike, except for the differences in their political regimes. For that reason, Przeworski and Teune (1970, 32–46) suggest avoiding such "most similar systems" designs (based, confusingly enough, on the "method of difference" logic), in favor of a most different systems approach. This approach would lead to the comparison of disputes between pairs of states that were extremely different in virtually every respect, except that they were all democratic. Then, if despite the fact that the pair of states were vastly different in virtually every respect except regime type but they still resolved their disputes peacefully, the peaceful resolutions of disputes could be traced, logically, to the types of regimes involved in the disputes.

But the argument by Przeworski and Teune in favor of a "most different systems" as opposed to a "most similar systems" design depends ultimately on a levels of analysis transition that I am reluctant to deal with at this stage of the game. Przeworski and Teune (1970, 32) argue that "the most different system designs eliminate factors differentiating social systems by formulating statements that are valid regardless of the systems within which observations are made." They support eliminating the proper names of social systems in the course of research as a basic step toward general theory. In other words, they are interested in showing that on the *individual* level of analysis, variable A is (causally) related to variable B regardless of whether the sample of individuals analyzed is drawn from France, the United States, or China.

If scholars of international politics had more than one international system to analyze, the Przeworski-Teune approach might be applicable to our problem here. If, for example, there were an international system on Mars as well as the one on Earth, and the two systems differed substantially with respect to their war proneness, one might explain the difference in war proneness by pointing to differences in the political cultures of Earth and Mars. This would be using the proper name of social systems as explanatory factors in the way to which Przeworski and Teune object. In that situation, one might compare the regime types of pairs of states in both the Martian and the Earthian Systems and find that democratic pairs of states relate to each other peacefully within both systems and that it is the existence of more democracies on Earth that makes its international system more peaceful than that on Mars, and not some system level difference between Earth and Mars. The proper names of the system, Earth and Mars, might then be eliminated as explanatory factors in the manner advocated by Przeworski and Teune.[1]

But of course we do not have two international systems to compare. We could compare regional subsystems, and strive to eliminate "Latin America" or "Asia" or other proper names of regional subsystems in explanations of international war and conflict, but as hardly anybody that we are aware of seriously proposes regional subsystemic characteristics as major factors accounting for conflict escalation or war, that does not seem a very promising strategy.

So we will focus here on a "most similar systems" design. That is, we will focus on a pair of disputes, one between two states that were democratic and that came close to war (the Fashoda Crisis) and another involving a pair of states that were almost uniformly democratic that did escalate to war (the Spanish-American War). The argument for this strategy suggests that if we compare a dispute between a pair of states that were close to being uniformly democratic and that ended up in war with a dispute between a fully democratic pair of states that almost ended up in war, the relatively small number of differences between the political systems of the dyads, on the one hand, and the gravity of the disputes, on the other, ought to make it possible, first, to specify more precisely or to formulate hypotheses about which characteristics of the regimes we focus on were more crucial to the avoidance of war and the occurrence of war. It might also be easier to evaluate the argument and the evidence regarding the proposition that it was the uniformly democratic nature of the disputants that accounted for, in part, the peaceful resolution of the conflict between the democratic states.

Even if the general logic of that argument is accepted, it still leaves open the question of why it is useful to compare the Fashoda Crisis and the Spanish-American War in particular. The Spanish-American War commands attention in part because of its role as a possible exception to the rule that democratic states never fight wars against each other. Its designation in the article by Lake (1992) as an exception to that rule enhances its interest. And a perusal of the list of interstate wars that have occurred from 1816 to the present suggests that the Spanish-American War is the most extensive international war that has occurred between two states that were almost uniformly democratic, as well as indubitably independent, during that time. In other words, there has been no other war causing as many battle deaths between two states as close to being uniformly democratic as the Spanish-American War. It is arguably an "outlier"; it might even qualify as a "crucial case" in the sense of that term in Eckstein's (1975) defense of case studies. Finally, there is the happily serendipitous fact that there is (at least) one case study of the Spanish-American War already, by John Owen (1993), conducted with the explicit purpose of evaluating the democratic peace proposition.

In looking for a case to which compare the Spanish-American War, the "most similar systems" design suggests that one should look for a case involving states as similar to the United States and Spain as possible except that they were *both* democratic, rather than only almost uniformly democratic, and involving a dispute that is as nearly like the one involving the United States and Spain as possible, except that it did not end up in war. One possibility is the dispute between the United States and Great Britain regarding a boundary dispute between Great Britain and Venezuela over territory claimed by both Venezuela and British Guiana, in 1895. This dispute, like the Spanish-American War, involved the United States and another European power, at about the same time, and over territory in roughly the same part of the world. The United States intervened in the dispute with a message to the British government that "with its time limit and belligerent tone had the characteristic of an ultimatum." Further, when President Grover Cleveland delivered an address to Congress on the matter, it was sufficiently bellicose that it might accurately be described as "the language of war" (De Conde 1963, 332).

Although this dispute between the United States and Great Britain in 1895 was serious enough to merit closer scrutiny, ultimately I decided that the Fashoda Crisis of 1898 between Great Britain and France would be a better case for comparison with the Spanish-American War. Like the United States and Spain, Great Britain and France in 1898 were both relatively large, politically important states. As was the case with the Spanish-American War, the Fashoda Crisis involved a kind of sphere-of-influence conflict over which state would predominate in territory outside the boundaries of both parties to the dispute. In other words, in neither case did the dispute involve territory that was an integral part of one of the disputants but coveted by the other. Finally, two practical considerations favored the Fashoda Crisis. That crisis was a more prominent event than that between Great Britain and the United States in 1895, and materials about it are more readily available. And, finally, again fortuitously, there already is a case study of the Fashoda Crisis, focusing on it with a view toward evaluating the democratic peace proposition, by Hongying Wang (1992).

The Structure of the "Pseudo-Experiment"

In general terms, what I will engage in here is a "thinking experiment" of the kind that Bruce Russett and Harvey Starr, for example, carried out with respect to the question of why it is that the relationships among democratic states, especially since 1945, have been so peaceful. As they imply, "it is a purely analytical exercise, unlike the clinical or laboratory experiments where one may vary conditions to see what effect the changes have" (Russett and Starr 1985, 416).[2]

It may be useful and an attempt will be made here to demonstrate that it is useful to structure such analytical exercises in one's mind as if they were true experiments. They might be called "quasi-experiments," except that in our case the control, or the elimination of confounding variables, is so modest that even that less ambitious title is probably unwarranted. According to Donald Campbell (1988, 191), "we can distinguish quasi-experiments from true experiments by the absence of random assignment of units to treatments." Obviously, in our case, we cannot randomly assign pairs of countries to experimental and control groups, assign democratic "treatments" to one group and autocratic treatments to the other, and observe which groups produce international wars at which rates. It is not even clear that we will be able to structure our comparisons in a way that fits one of Campbell's "quasi-experimental" designs. What we will engage in here will best fit what Campbell and Stanley (1963, 12) refer to as a "static group comparison." It might be called a "pseudo-experiment."[3]

There are two advantages to structuring thinking experiments as "pseudo-experiments" and comparing the structure of pseudo-experiments to that of true experiments. One is that it helps to highlight the reasons that the results of the thinking experiment may be misleading. Or, to put it in language more similar to that of Campbell, it makes it easier to focus on confounding variables that make it appear that the hypothesized causal connection exists when actually it does not. Also, conceiving of thinking experiments as pseudo-experiments may lead one to ideas about how one might alter the structure of one's thinking and observation in such a way as to move the pseudo-experiment closer to the structure of a true experiment, or at least a quasi-experiment, and thus provide a stronger basis for the evaluation of the proposition being analyzed.

Static Group Comparisons: Pros and Cons

The structure of a "static group comparison" in Donald Campbell's (1988) terms is depicted in figure 9 (Thomas Cook and Donald Campbell [1979, 98] refer to this as "nonequivalent control group" design).

Figure 9
A "Static Group Comparison"
(from Donald Campbell, 1988)

$$X \qquad\qquad O_1$$

$$O_2$$

"In this design," according to Campbell (1988, 155), "there is a comparison of a group which has experienced X with a group which has not, for the purpose of establishing the effect of X." "X" in our case is joint democracy in a pair of states. The "group" above the line of dashes (which in Campbell's approach symbolizes the lack of equalization of the two groups being observed through random assignment) consists of the pair of nations England and France as they are involved in the Fashoda Crisis in 1898. "O_1," indicates the observation of England and France as they are involved in that crisis; what we observe is that the crisis is resolved peacefully. The control group, the United States and Spain in 1898, is "untreated," in a sense. That pair of nations at that time is not jointly democratic. "O_2," indicates the observation of this pair of nations in the serious dispute between them that occurred also in 1898. And what we observe, as our hypothesis about the impact of joint democracy on relationships between pairs of states would suggest, is that the crisis ends up in international war, i.e., the Spanish-American War in 1898.

On the surface this "experiment" indicates that "X," joint democracy, had the hypothesized effect. But this is obviously a weak conclusion. As Donald Campbell and John Stanley (1963, 64) point out, "design 3 [i.e., the static group comparison] is a correlational design of a very weak form, implying as it does the comparison of but two natural units, differing not only in the presence or absence of X, but also in innumerable other attributes. Each of those other attributes could create the differences in the Os, and each therefore provides a plausible rival hypothesis to the hypothesis that X had an effect." England and France, unlike the United States and Spain in 1898, were jointly democratic. But those two pairs of states, and the disputes in which they were involved, were different in many other ways, any one of which might be the factor (or factors) that caused one dispute to end peacefully while the other ended up in international war. How can we make even modest progress toward strengthening the argument that it was joint democracy, in the case of England and France, that caused the dispute to end peacefully while it was the absence of joint democracy in the case of the United States and Spain that played a role in leading that dispute to end in international war?

Campbell and Stanley (1963, 64) assert that "we are left with a general rule that the differences between two natural objects are uninterpretable." One practical solution to this problem proposed by Campbell and Stanley (1963) is to expand the number of observations so that there are numerous independent natural instances of X as well as numerous examples of not-X. And I agree wholeheartedly with the implication that in the *absence* of large-N studies, a detailed comparison of the crises involving England and France in 1898, on the one hand, and the United States and Spain in 1898, on the other, with a view toward making a case for the proposition that joint democracy had an impact, would be entirely quixotic.

However, in the light of the numerous analyses indicating that there has been a consistent, nonspurious correlation between joint democracy and peaceful outcome of disputes, close analysis of one of the pairs of observations that contributes to that correlation may increase our confidence in and intuitive appreciation of its hypothesized causal character. In the course of conducting that analysis we will attempt to increase confidence in our intuitive appreciation of the alleged causal connection between joint democracy peace in three basic steps. First, we will consider the list of potentially confounding variables developed by Campbell and Stanley (1963) and Campbell (1988) with a view toward determining which contain threats to the proposition that joint democracy played a role in producing the peaceful outcome of the dispute between England and France, whereas the absence of joint democracy contributed to the unpeaceful outcome of the dispute between the United States and Spain. Then we will consult both theoretical and empirical work on the democratic peace proposition in order to create a list of more specific alternative factors that might also have accounted for the different outcomes of the disputes. Finally, we will conclude by sorting and sifting through historical materials on the *process* involved in the unfolding crises in search of evidence that it was, or was not, joint democracy, in our first case, and the lack of joint democracy, in the second case, that explains the different outcomes of the two disputes we analyze in this chapter.

Categories of Confounding Variables

The list of major classes of confounding variables presented in Campbell and Stanley (1963, 8) are (1) history, (2) maturation, (3) testing, (4) instrumentation, (5) regression, (6) selection, and (7) mortality. Several of these are relevant to an evaluation of whether "X" had an effect only if the "X" is a treatment under the control of the investigator. Others are relevant only if the two groups in question are observed before and after "X" has been applied to the experimental group.

For example, "testing" is not a confounding variable of much concern in the kind of thinking pseudo-experiment with history we are discussing here. It is "the effect of a pre-test" (Campbell and Stanley 1963, 9). If one gives a pre-test in order to evaluate the impact of some kind of training program, the subjects might do better the second time the test is given, after the training program has been implemented, simply because of the practice of taking the pre-test.

"Instrumentation," in Campbell and Stanley's (1963) terms, involves differences that occur primarily because of measurement error or "autonomous changes in the measurement instrument" during the time the "experiment" takes place. We have seen in chapter 2 that there seems to be an implicit change in the standards that Gurr, Jaggers, and Moore (1989) use when they classify countries as "democratic" over the nearly two-hundred-year period they analyze. (The United States receives the same score in 1845 and 1985.) If the pairs of countries in our pseudo-experiment were observed at very different times, then those pairs of countries might have been given very different democracy scores even though they were essentially very similar regimes, or vice versa. In other words, a difference between the pair of countries that we assumed reflected a difference in regime types would actually be a function instead of "changes in the measurement instrument" over time.

However, this is one of several problems and one type of confounding factor that we avoid in our particular pseudo-experiment. Any measures of democracy or war or other potential confounding variables might produce inconsistent, invalid results when applied to quite different points in time. Such problems do not arise here because both of our pairs of countries are observed during the year 1898.

Campbell and Stanley (1963, 5) note that "regression" can be a confounding variable "when groups have been selected on the basis of extreme scores." If, for example, a group of students are selected for an experiment because they did poorly on an achievement test, they will be likely to do better on the test after any remedial treatment, not because of the effectiveness of the treatment but because of regression toward the mean. Analogously, regression toward the mean might complicate the interpretation of a pseudo-experiment focusing, say, on France and Germany, in an attempt to evaluate the impact of joint democracy on that dyadic relationship. We might select the France-Germany dyad just because it has historically been so conflict prone. We might "observe" France and Germany before 1945 and then again after 1950, that is, after joint democracy had been established. As the democratic peace proposition would imply, we would find that France and Germany were very war prone before joint democracy was established and not at all war prone after both became democratic. (An analogous argument might in fact be made for the whole of Western Europe. See Smith and Ray 1993, 36.) The peaceful relationship between France and Germany (and among all Western European states) since 1945 might be a result of the democratic nature of the regimes, but it might also have occurred because of regression toward the mean. Having fought so many significant wars against each other, in such a relatively short time, they were bound, just by the luck of the draw as it were, to experience a relatively prolonged period of peace. The tendency toward peace might be reinforced also by war fatigue or the lessons learned from such painful war experiences rather than by the nature of their regimes. But regression toward the mean is not a problem in our particular pseudo-experiment involving the United States and Spain, and Great Britain and France.

"History," as a confounding variable in Campbell and Stanley's (1963, 5) terminology, refers to "specific events occurring between the first and the second measurement in addition to the experimental variable." It creates problems when the experimental group, as well as the control group, are observed before and after a "treatment." In Ray (1981), for example, an attempt was made to evaluate the impact of the fact that the Soviets brought socialism to Eastern Europe in and around 1945. Data on economic growth rates in the Eastern European states before and after 1945 were analyzed. But the worldwide Depression, and World War II might well be historical events that could confound the results of these observations. World War II brought devastation to Germany and Japan, for example, but they both experienced prolonged periods of rapid economic growth after the war that Mancur Olson (1982) argues were not coincidental but a result in important part of the breaking up of various rent-seeking interest groups during the war (and the postwar occupation). Thus, any improvement in economic performance in Eastern Europe after the imposition of socialism in 1945 might be the result of the war (an example of "history" in the confounding sense), rather than socialism. However, the static group comparison on which our pseudo-experiment here is based utilizes only post-treatment observations and so is not vulnerable to "history" as a source of confusion about the possible effects of "X," in our case, joint democracy.

"Mortality" is a source of potential confusion in static group comparisons, according to Campbell and Stanley. It is the result of "differential loss of respondents from the comparison groups" (1963, 5). If college seniors are compared with college freshmen, for example, to evaluate the impact of a college education, the seniors may be different from the freshmen not because of the impact of a college education but because the senior class no longer contains those who dropped out at some point during the four-year college experience. When Ray (1981) compared the economic performance of Latin American states with that of Eastern European states before and after the Soviet Union established hegemony in Eastern Europe in 1945, it was necessary to take into account the fact that "some of the Eastern European states suffered boundary changes in the course of [the] quasi-experiment, and East Germany was added to the Eastern European group after 1945" (Ray 1981, 129).

"Mortality" could be a factor relevant to the general debate regarding the democratic peace proposition. It is conceivable that comparisons of the war proneness of democratic pairs of states with that of other pairs of states, of the kind we are engaged in here, are misleading because of the process that leads states to drop out of the democratic group. Perhaps, for example, there is a tendency for pairs of states engaged in a hostile relationship potentially productive of warfare to adopt autocratic regimes in preparation for war even though the regime type itself has no causal impact on the probability that the hostilities will escalate to war. Similarly, it is possible that warlike individual leaders impose autocratic regimes on once-democratic states and then lead them into wars, creating the misleading impression that states with autocratic regimes are more warlike when in fact it is the character of the leaders and not the type of regime that is the crucial causal factor.

None of these problems, though, are likely to influence our pseudo-experiment involving England and France, on the one hand, and the United States and Spain, on the other. We have only one pair of states in each "group," so differences between those "groups" are not likely to have been brought about by differential dropout rates in those groups. If Spain, for instance, had been democratic until 1898 and then had become autocratic in 1898 as war tensions with the U.S. increased, our pseudo-experiment would arguably be contaminated by "mortality." In other words, critics of the proposition that it is joint democracy that explains the difference between our experimental group (jointly democratic Britain and France) and our control group (not jointly democratic United States and Spain) could argue that in general, and in our pseudo-experiment, hostilities between countries create conditions that destabilize democracies and eventually lead to war but that the autocratic regimes that are created before the wars begin are only spuriously correlated with the onset of war. The wars, and the autocratic regimes, are brought about by whatever is the prewar source of the hostilities, i.e., the *real* cause of the wars that follow.

But in our case, Spain did not become dramatically more autocratic in the course of its developing hostile relationship with the United States in the months leading up to the war. Thus, it cannot be persuasively argued that the United States and Spain "dropped out" of the population of jointly democratic pairs of states in a way that accounts for the differences between the outcomes of our two crisis, i.e., that "mortality" confounds our results.

The most troublesome category of confounding variables for our pseudo-experiment is "selection," or "biases resulting in differential *selection* of respondents for the comparison groups," in Campbell and Stanley's (1963, 5) terms. The crisis involving England and France in 1898 and the one involving the United States and Spain in 1898 ended differently. But England and France, and the United States and Spain, (as well as the crises in which they were involved) were different in countless other ways that might have had an impact on the difference in the outcomes of their disputes, in addition to the fact that the first pair was jointly democratic and the second was not. What we must attempt to do, somehow, is sort out the impact of regime type from the impacts of all the other possibly relevant factors that might have accounted for the difference in the outcomes of the two disputes.

The Impact of Factors Other than Joint Democracy

Fortunately, we have by now several examples of research, as we have seen in previous chapters, that have focused on the questions of what other factors, in addition to joint democracy, might have an impact on the probability of a dispute escalating to war and how those factors might affect the relationship between joint democracy and dispute escalation. Among the most useful for our purposes here, in my opinion, are those by Paul Anderson and Timothy McKeown (1987), Zeev Maoz and Bruce Russett (1992, 1993), and Stuart Bremer (1992, 1993). My review of that body of work (and other related pieces) leads me to the conclusion that among the more important factors to consider in our comparison of the Fashoda Crisis and the Spanish-American War are *proximity, power ratios, alliances, level of economic development, militarization,* and *political stability.*[4]

Bremer (1992, 1993) and Maoz and Russett (1992) have shown that proximity or contiguity is one of the most important factors that distinguish pairs of states that get involved in wars against each other from those that do not. The finding that neighboring states are more likely to fight wars against each other is not really intriguing, certainly not in a counterintuitive way, but it is also certainly important to control for this basic factor in analyses that focus on additional factors.

The geographic relationship of the two pairs of states involved in our pseudo-experiment should, accordingly, also be taken into account. On the surface, a consideration of the role of proximity or contiguity in the Fashoda Crisis and the Spanish-American War strengthens the case for the putative impact of joint democracy. England and France were and are "contiguous" in Correlates of War project terms because they are separated by twenty-four nautical miles or less of water, but the United States and Spain are not contiguous. In other words, contiguity in simple terms cannot account for the fact that England and France did not get into war and the United States and Spain did because to the extent that contiguity played a role it should have made England and France more likely to war against each other than the United States and Spain. On this level, at least, the geographic relationship between the two pairs of states is not a plausible rival to joint democracy as a factor that accounted for the different outcomes of the two disputes.

But there is an obvious limit to the extent to which we can discount geography as an explanation of the outcome of our pseudo-experiment. Pairs of states can be considered either directly contiguous or indirectly contiguous through their colonial holdings as Siverson and Starr (1991) have argued. In this indirect sense, Spain and the United States, as well as England and France, were contiguous in 1898, as Spain had a colonial holding only ninety miles off the coast of the United States, a geographical fact of life with obvious relevance to the war between these states. Even so, contiguity is not a basis for a plausible rival to our hypothesis regarding the impact of joint democracy in these two disputes because *both* pairs of states were contiguous. This geographic fact, then, cannot account for the *difference* in the outcomes of the two disputes in 1898.

Bremer (1992, 1993) reports that pairs of major powers, or pairs of states with one major power, are more likely to get into wars with each other than pairs of minor powers. England and France were major powers in 1898, by the Correlates of War definition (and by Jack Levy's [1983] definition as well), whereas the United States and Spain were not. An explanation based on the power status of the disputants would predict, or retrodict, the opposite of what actually occurred. i.e., that England and France would get involved in a war with each other but that the United States and Spain would not. As a basis for explaining the difference in the outcomes of these two disputes, the power status of the participants is clearly not a competitor with joint democracy with respect to the disputes we are analyzing.

Both Bremer (1992) and Maoz and Russett (1992) report, as Bueno de Mesquita (1981) hypothesized, that allied pairs of states are more likely to fight wars against each other than are unallied pairs. However, Bremer (1992) finds that allies are less likely to fight when other factors (such as joint democracy) are controlled for. The possible lack of clarity about this relationship is not a concern here. Neither England and France nor the United States and Spain were allied in 1898, so the impact of alliance bonds on disputes is not relevant to our effort to explain the difference in the outcomes of the two disputes we are comparing.

Maoz and Russett (1992) find that wealth does not affect conflict among specific types of regimes and assert that "the notion that democracies do not fight one another because they are rich is flatly rejected" (257). Their analyses focus on the time period from 1946 to 1986, and they use a GDP-based measure of wealth. Bremer (1992, 1993), however, focuses on the time period from 1816 to 1965 and finds that "dyads composed of two more developed states are . . . five times *less* likely to originate wars than dyads that contain one or fewer less developed states" (1993, 245). Bremer's analyses, focusing on a space-time frame that includes the two pairs of states in our analysis here, are probably more relevant. He categorizes states as "developed" (or wealthy) if their share of system-wide "economic capability" in the Correlates of War material capabilities set is greater than their systemwide shares of "demographic capability." In other words (for the sake of those not familiar with the Correlates of War capabilities data set), Bremer calculates for each state its share in the world of total population and urban population and considers the average of those percentages as an indicator of "demographic capability." He calculates also for each state its share of the world's iron/steel production and its share of energy consumption and utilizes the average of those two percentages as an indicator of a state's economic capability. Any state whose share of economic resources is found to be greater than its share of the population in the world he counts as "developed."

By Bremer's measures, in 1898, England, France, and the United States were developed, but Spain was not. Thus, the war between Spain and the United States can logically be attributed in part to the fact that Spain and the United

States were a mixed dyad, that is, one developed and one not developed state (or wealthy and not wealthy). Conversely, as Britain and France were both wealthy states on this dimension, they were less likely to become involved in war with each other.

Bremer (1993) finds that a pair of "militarized" states are at least somewhat more likely to become involved in wars against each other. He categorizes states as militarized if their share of system-wide capabilities, measured in terms of military expenditures and military personnel, is greater than their share of total population and urban population. By that indicator, France and Spain were militarized in 1898, but the United States and England were not. However, Spain's share of military capability is only .3 percent larger than its share of demographic capability. And both England and the United States miss being categorized as militarized by quite small amounts. In any case, there is no clear distinction between England and France and the United States and Spain with respect to the extent to which they were militarized. So it seems safe to conclude that military preparedness is not a factor that competes with regime type or joint democracy as an explanation of the different outcomes of the Fashoda Crisis and the dispute between the United States and Spain in 1898.

Maoz and Russett (1992) report that politically "stable states are far less likely to fight one another . . . regardless of their regime type." They measure stability in terms of the number of years that a regime persists, as reported by Gurr et al. (1989). In 1898, according to Polity II, the regimes in England, France, the United States, and Spain had been in place for 209, 21, 109, and 22 years, respectively. In other words, with respect to political stability, the two pairs of states on which we focus here are substantially similar. The Fashoda Crisis and the crisis leading to the Spanish-American War were both confrontations between states that had regimes that had persisted for over 100 years (England and the United States) and for almost exactly 20 years (France and Spain). Political stability, at least as captured by that indicator, seems unlikely to be a factor that might account for the *differences* in the outcomes of the disputes we analyze.

However, Spain and France had regimes that were unstable in certain respects. France was besieged by the Dreyfus Case. The Spanish regime feared a military coup. Instability seemed to have opposite effects, however, in these two cases, a point to which we shall return in the conclusion of this chapter.

Bremer (1992, 1993) and Maoz and Russett (1993) report that large power disparities measured in terms of Correlates of War project indicators of military-industrial capabilities (total population, urban population, military expenditures, military personnel, iron/steel production, and energy consumption) decrease the probability of wars between pairs of states. If we look at England

and France in 1898, we find that England enjoyed a substantial margin of military superiority over France, with England holding about 16 percent of the world's capabilities, and France about 8 percent. The United States, though, enjoyed an even greater margin of superiority over Spain, with the ratio of capabilities being about 12 to 1 in that case. In other words, the United States held almost 20 percent of the world's capabilities, whereas Spain held only 1.7 percent. In the most straightforward terms, then, we can discount the ratio of capabilities between the disputants as a competitor with joint democracy as an explanation of the different outcomes of the two disputes. According to the findings of Bremer (1992, 1993) and Maoz and Russett (1993), England and France, being much more equal in power than the United States and Spain, should have been much more likely to go to war against each other than the United States and Spain. A prediction about the outcomes of these two disputes based on simple power ratios is exactly wrong. I shall elaborate on the significance of this result produced by our pseudo-experiment to an evaluation of the democratic peace proposition in the conclusion of the chapter.

But there are at least two additional basic factors that ought to be taken into account in any attempt to evaluate the impact of the ratios of capabilities of disputants on the probability of conflict escalation. They are the geographic location of the dispute, and the possible impact of allies. The Fashoda dispute focused on a location in Africa that was a long distance from England and France. In short, distance does not affect the conclusion that they were relatively equal in power (relative, that is, to the United States and Spain). However, this dispute between the United States and Spain, focusing on Cuba right off the coast of the United States (ninety miles, as we all know, from numberless political speeches on the topic), accentuated the power disparity in favor of the United States that should, everything else being equal, have made the dispute *less* likely to escalate to war. But it did not. Or, more precisely, if it did make the dispute less likely to escalate to war, the war occurred anyway. What role potential allies might have played in the unfolding dispute between England and France and between the United States and Spain is a question best addressed in the context of a more detailed description of the processes leading to the resolution of each of these disputes.

In sum, our static group comparison has enabled us to rule out several categories of confounding variables, such as history, maturation, testing, instrumentation, regression, and mortality. "Selection," however, is a category full of factors other than joint democracy that might have accounted for the results of our pseudo-experiment. Our first, static look at the two crises in question, relying on previous, large-N analyses as a source of ideas regarding which of these factors deserve closest attention, suggests first that proximity, or the geographical relationships of the two pairs of states on which we focus here is not a plausible rival to joint democracy as a factor that accounted for the different outcomes of the two disputes. A hypothesis based on the power status of the disputants (major powers or not) would predict the opposite of that which actually occurred, i.e., that England and France should have been more likely to become involved in a war against each other. The same is true of a hypothesis based on power disparity; since the power disparity between the United States and Spain was greater, it was *not* the pair of states that, according to this hypothesis, should have been the one to go to war.

Neither the United States and Spain nor England and France were allied to each other or much different in the extent to which they were militarized, so those two factors do not compete with joint democracy as an explanation of the outcome of our pseudo-experiment. Measured in terms of longevity of regime, the two pairs of states in our pseudo-experiment were not much different, either, in terms of "stability," so that factor, too, is not a plausible rival to joint democracy. However, we will look below the level of our operational indicator of stability in our review of the two crises below. Finally, level of economic development is a factor that would account for the outcome of our pseudo-experiment. England and France were more developed, and they did not go to war. We would have to acknowledge, at least, that the level of economic development is a factor that *also* might have had an impact on the different outcomes of the two crises we are analyzing. This might, though, have been an impact in addition to, rather than instead of, one exerted by joint democracy.

Comparing the Processes Leading to War, and a Peaceful Resolution

Let us turn now to a more dynamic and detailed analysis of our two crises. As we review the processes and the interactions involving each pair of states as the Fashoda Crisis and the dispute leading to the Spanish-American War unfolded, we will be particularly attentive, of course, to the possible impact of joint democracy (or the lack of it) in those two crises. The role of public opinion, for example, will be analyzed in both crises. We will also analyze the impact of important, apparently influential interest groups within each state. We might also expect the impact of joint democracy to make itself visible through bureaucratic policymaking processes. We might find that impact of joint democracy, also, on bargaining and negotiations that took place as the crises unfolded. Finally, we could expect that joint democracy might have an impact on the attitudes of leaders of the countries involved in these conflicts. (We will try to be sensitive also to the possibility that joint democracy can be seen to have an impact on the outcomes of these two crises in ways we do not expect.)

The Background of the Crises: The Spanish-American War

Cuba was a Spanish colony for about four hundred years. "By 1515 Havana was the headquarters of Spanish power in America" (Kantor 1969, 279). Spain lost all her colonies in a series of rebellions from 1812 to 1824, except Cuba and Puerto Rico. But in 1823, there were foreshadowings of problems to come for Spain's hold on Cuba when John Adams asserted: "There are laws of political as well as physical gravitation, and if an apple, severed by the tempest from its native tree, cannot but fall to the ground, Cuba, forcibly disjoined from its irrational connection with Spain and incapable of self-support, can gravitate only toward the North American Union, which, by the same law of nature, cannot cast her off from its bosom" (Herring 1972, 396).

There was a rebellion in Cuba starting in 1868, which dragged on for ten years, in which Spain lost 100,000 soldiers (Small and Singer 1982, 96). Another Cuban insurrection began in 1895. The previous rebellion, from 1868 to 1878, had been more costly to Spain than the war in Vietnam was for the United States (a *lot* more, proportionately). And yet faced with further unrest in the same, faraway place some seventeen years later, Spain again launched a massive repressive effort.

The effort was personified by General Valeriano Weyler, who arrived in Cuba in February 1896. "Weyler ordered the peasants to leave their homes and villages and to relocate in towns and cities where the Spanish military could control them" (Offner 1992, 13). The result was a disaster of considerable proportions. The camps for the "reconcentrados" were not prepared for them, lacking food, sanitation facilities, and medical care. By March of 1898 (the war was to begin in April), a common estimate, accepted even by the Spanish, was that 400,000 Cubans, about one-fourth of the population, had died in those camps (Offner 1992, 241). The actual number was probably smaller,[5] but arguably the most important factor to keep in mind in estimating the impact of this carnage on the process leading to the war is that "regardless of the exact number of deaths . . . Cubans, Spaniards, and Americans believed the death toll was extremely large and growing" (Offner 1992, 241).

The crisis escalated in February 1898 when a letter from the Spanish minister to the United States to a friend in Cuba was published in William Randolph Hearst's *New York Journal.* The letter described President McKinley in extremely undiplomatic terms. This created a poisoned atmosphere in U.S-Spanish relations, which were strained almost to the breaking point when the USS *Maine* was blown up in the harbor at Havana, killing 260. These two events might seem in retrospect to have made war "inevitable," but actually, John Offner (1992, 126) argues that: "Both Washington and Madrid handled these difficult dramas well. They settled the de Lome affair [de Lome was the ambassador who wrote the disparaging letter about McKinley], and within two days the government directed the *Maine* disaster into routine investigative channels. If, at the end of Washington's inquiry, the American naval court had concluded that the *Maine* had exploded as a result of spontaneous combustion, which was what McKinley expected, both episodes might have faded into the background."

But on March 21, 1898, the American inquiry concluded (almost certainly wrongly) that a submarine mine outside the *Maine* had been the source of the explosion that caused it to sink. This initiated about a month of negotiations between Spain and the United States, and between President McKinley and the U.S. Congress, with many complicated twists and turns, some of which we will turn to in more detail below. The denouement of this affair, in simple but not misleading terms, was that toward the end of March 1898, the United States issued a virtual ultimatum to Spain insisting that Cuba be given its independence. Spain responded in a conciliatory but not entirely unambiguous fashion. (Specifically, it was not clear when, if ever, Cuba would be granted independence.) On April 22, President McKinley ordered a naval blockade of Cuba. Spain declared war on April 24, 1898. The next day, the U.S. Congress passed a resolution declaring that a state of war had existed between the United States and Spain since April 21, 1898.

The Background of the Crises: The Fashoda Affair

The Fashoda Crisis arose as a result, in most general terms, of the extensive binge of imperialism in which virtually every major country of the world engaged in the three or four decades after 1870. (The Spanish-American War could also be seen as an example of that binge.) More specifically, this particular crisis arose because of imperialistic competition between Great Britain and France in Africa, over the fate of Egypt. In 1870, Egypt was nominally part of the Ottoman Empire, but was in fact ruled as part of an Anglo-French condominium. By 1881, there was a revolt in the Sudan, south of Egypt, which the British managed to suppress, without help from France.

Egypt then became a virtual British protectorate, even though formally the British kept promising that they would leave Egypt. Egypt and the British lost control of at least part of the Sudan in 1895 as a result of an uprising by Muhammad Ahmed (the Mahdi), who captured Khartoum. In 1898, the British sent a mission to the Sudan under the leadership of General Horatio Kitchener; he defeated the Mahdi's successor, the Khalifa, at the Battle of Omdurman.

In the meantime, the French were planning to reestablish at least a semblance of French influence in Egypt. In 1893, they conceived the idea of building a dam on the White Nile that could be used to control the flow of water to the Lower Nile. The point at which they decided to build the dam was at Fashoda, located some four hundred miles south of Khartoum. Two initial French ventures to reach Fashoda were aborted. But in July 1896, Captain Jean-Baptiste

Marchand set out for Fashoda from the French Congo on the west coast of Africa. After a rather incredibly arduous and adventuresome journey of two years and some three thousand miles, "on July 10, 1898, Marchand, accompanied by a half a dozen European officers and some hundred and twenty Senegalese troops, arrived at Fashoda on the Nile and raised the French flag on the ruins of the old Egyptian fort" (Langer 1965, 539).

Unfortunately for Marchand, he was confronted in late September 1898 by a rather obviously superior force under the leadership of General Kitchener. There ensued several weeks of tense negotiations, culminating in French capitulation in early November 1898. The French agreed to evacuate Fashoda, unconditionally.

If the Fashoda Crisis could not have ended in war, then it is obviously impossible to argue (as, ideally, I would like to argue) that *but for* the fact that both England and France were democratic, the Fashoda Crisis would have led to war. It is particularly important to address this issue in light of the fact that Darrell Bates (1984, 186), in one of the most recent and apparently more authoritative historical accounts of the crisis, asserts that "there is really no evidence in the archives in London or Paris that either government seriously considered going to war over Fashoda."[6]

But even Bates (1984, 124) points out that French foreign minister Gabriel Hanatoux, on the eve of Marchand's departure for Africa (and ultimately for Fashoda), assured him that "you are going to fire a pistol shot on the banks of the Nile; we all accept the consequences." And Roger Glenn Brown (1969, 72), in another authoritative historical account of the Fashoda Crisis, reveals that on the British side in January of 1898, Lord Salisbury ("a cautious Prime Minister who also headed the Foreign Office"), having authorized Kitchener to advance to Khartoum, gravely remarked that "within six months we will be at war with France."

Patricia Wright (1972, ix), in another historical account of the crisis, observes that "in October 1898, rumors were rife in Paris . . . reservists were being secretly mobilized, emergency hospitals set up and stores ordered . . . one thing was clear: war was very near." Wright (1972, ix) also says that "in Britain public opinion was even more bellicose and newspaper comment, if possible, even more uninhibited and virulent . . . [E]ven the *Times* declared sedately that the 'elements of compromise do not exist.'"

Finally, T. W. Riker (1929, 54), in an article published in the *Political Science Quarterly* a sufficiently long time after the crisis to provide him a substantial amount of historical perspective, expresses the opinion that "the long-accumulated exasperation engendered by the colonial rivalry of France and Great Britain during the last decade of the century should, if we weigh the strength of historical forces, have produced a terrific explosion over the question of the possession of the Nile." The absence of war between Great Britain and France in 1898, then, does seem worthy of inclusion in that category of events, like the dog that did not bark to which Sherlock Holmes allegedly turned his attention. They both create a need for an "explanation."

The Role of Public Opinion in Two Crises

The results of this pseudo-experiment that would be most supportive of the democratic peace proposition are quite clear, when we focus on the role of public opinion. According to that proposition, and at least some important defenses of it, democratic regimes are less war prone because public opinion has a greater impact on policy in democratic states than in autocratic states, the public as a whole pays the greater share of the costs and suffers the most grievous burdens in international war, and therefore exerts a pacifying impact on foreign policies.

If the results of this pseudo-experiment are to support the democratic peace proposition, we should find first that public opinion in France and England exerted a restraining effect on policymakers in both countries, making the peaceful resolution of the conflict more likely. In our second case, one should find, in the ideal-typical case most supportive of the democratic peace proposition, that public opinion in the democratic United States exerted a restraining effect on policymakers who might have otherwise been inclined to greater bellicosity, whereas in Spain a general public less inclined to war than its autocratic leaders was not allowed, because of autocratic characteristics in the regime, to exert its pacifying effect, thus making the war more likely to occur.

The results of our pseudo-experiment, however, diverge quite substantially from the ideal-typical in the view of an advocate of the democratic peace proposition. There is not a *total* lack of evidence that conforms to the ideal-typical. For example, at the height of the crisis leading to the Spanish-American War, "White House mail was running 90 percent in favor of McKinley's efforts to keep the peace," (Offner 1992, 190), thus indicating that there were pressures toward conciliation from the public on the president, as the democratic peace proposition might predict. Then, too, John Owen (1993), in his analysis of the Spanish-American War, reports that "in early 1898, the government shut down Spanish newspapers and forbade public gatherings either for or against war with America," thus exerting autocratic pressures against agitation for peace in the manner that at least some advocates of the democratic peace proposition might anticipate.

But one obstacle to uncovering evidence conforming to the pattern that would be most supportive of the democratic peace proposition is the lack of public opinion polls as far back as 1898. Even with such polls, estimating how the majority of the public feels about a given issue is tricky business. Without them, one must rely on the newspaper press (in 1898) reports about public demonstrations, reports about mail to politicians, and reports about what politicians believed public opinion to be.

Fortunately, for our purposes the last source of information about public opinion (i.e., the perceptions of policymakers about what public opinion is) is arguably quite important for achieving an understanding of the impact of public opinion on policy, almost regardless of how inaccurate those perceptions might be. In any case, the admittedly indirect evidence that exists about the impact of public opinion in the two crises we are examining here does not conform closely to what democratic peace advocates would predict or hope to find. Hongying Wang (1992, 7), in her analysis of the Fashoda incident, concludes that if the democratic peace proposition were valid, "public opinion in democratic Britain and France should have served as a strong force for the peaceful resolution of the Fashoda Crisis. . . . At least in the short run, quite the opposite was true." Such a statement is probably based on accounts such as that by Darrell Bates (1984, 153), who points out that the negotiations between Britain and France at the height of the crisis "were complicated . . . because they had to be conducted against the background of increasingly strident opposition and suspicion in the press and the parliaments of both countries." Bates (1984, 154) also argues that in Britain, "occasional colonial adventures and clashes with foreigners may not have appealed to intellectuals . . . in Bloomsbury and Cambridge but [they] did attract the cheers and votes of large numbers of those who worked with their hands. Little wars in Africa and confrontations with the French and Russians were often more popular with the masses than with the middle classes." And Patricia Wright (1972, ix) asserts that in France "the public . . . was stirred to a deep and resentful bitterness by a vitriolic press." She concludes that in both Britain and France public opinion was "bellicose."

Even if public opinion in Britain and France had been inclined to conciliation, it might have had a difficult time exerting any important impact because the leading policymakers in both countries apparently thought foreign policy was best left entirely to experts and specialists, like themselves. "Lord Salisbury," for example, prime minister and foreign secretary in Great Britain from 1895 to 1900, "believed as a general proposition that foreign affairs were too important and too complex to be left to popularly elected members of parliament or to public opinion" (Bates 1984, 12–13). Similarly, the French foreign minister during the crisis, Theophile Delcasse, "tended to conduct his country's foreign affairs as if they were his private domain, and with as little reference to his officials and his political colleagues as he could contrive" (Bates 1984, 145). Thus, even if there were abundant evidence of public pressure for peace in Britain and France during the Fashoda Crisis, the contempt in which the leading foreign policymakers in both countries held public opinion on foreign policy matters would make it more difficult to argue that public pressure exerted an important force for the peaceful resolution of the crisis in the way that an advocate of the democratic peace proposition would anticipate. As things stand, though, in the absence of evidence of public opinion on both sides that did exert pressure on the policymakers to resolve the crisis peacefully (and in the absence of any good evidence about what public opinion really was), the disdain for public opinion by people like Lord Salisbury and Theophile Delcasse just makes it easier to discount, to some extent at least, assertions such as that by Wang (1993) that the Fashoda Crisis was resolved in spite of public opinion in both countries, rather than because of conciliatory pressures from the allegedly conciliatory masses.

We have seen that the Spanish government did clamp down on the free expression of opinion about the war as the prewar crisis developed. What is difficult to find is any pacifistic public opinion in Spain that was there to be suppressed, or indications, at least, of such opinions and attitudes that were looking for a chance to be expressed. Offner (1992, 191) reports that at the height of the crisis, "Madrid's press reflected the national outrage." Offner also asserts that as war loomed, "the general public [in Spain] joined in excoriating the United States and championing Spanish nationalism. Street demonstrations, some ending in riots, occurred in Barcelona, Valencia, Malaga, Granada, Orense, and Vallolid. Riots continued for six days in Valencia, and in Malaga an angry mob stoned the American consulate and tore the escutcheon off the balcony." In his analysis of this case with a view toward evaluating its relevance to the democratic peace proposition, John Owen (1993, 21) concludes that Spanish "public opinion was overwhelmingly anti-American."

But the newspaper press and street demonstrations are not very reliable indicators of public opinion. John Owen also cites one author, Jose Varela Ortega (1980, 321) who argues that "politicians over-estimated the importance of public demonstrations, rallies, patriotic shows and collections, and fiery press articles. They believed that the country would not put up with any compliance with the American ultimatum and failed to sense a deeper reality concealed by the patriotic agitation." But how Ortega is able to discern what this "deeper reality" was is not clear. And even if he is right about that reality, it may be more important for our purposes to note that even he feels that the leading politicians felt that public opinion was pushing them into, not away from, war. Once again, the perception of public opinion by key decision makers is arguably more crucial to an understanding of processes of this kind than the "deeper reality" of that opinion.

But it is in the United States in the weeks and months leading up to the Spanish-American War that the idea from the democratic peace literature that widespread public opposition to war is an important pacifying force meets apparently strong disconfirming evidence. Virtually all sources suggest that public opinion was overwhelmingly in favor of war with Spain and in fact was a key factor pushing reluctant leading policymakers into the conflict. One of the major themes of Offner's *An Unwanted War* (1992, ix) is that "in the final analysis, Republicans made war in Spain in order to keep control of Washington." Repeatedly, he suggests that President McKinley and other leading Republicans did their best to avoid war but found they could not escape the pressures of public opinion demanding that they liberate Cubans from the oppression of the Spanish. "The Republicans had recently lost various municipal elections, and the prospect of a national election defeat would convert them from peaceful to aggressive ways" (Offner 1992, 139). David Trask (1981, 31) paints a similar picture. "No one in the Administration," Trask insists, "would have entertained the possibility of war, had it not been for the ungovernable uproar throughout the country that followed the destruction of the *Maine*." At another point, Trask (1981, 41) asserts that McKinley chose war in the end "because he decided that a less aggressive option might result in disastrous political consequences at home. Those elements in the nation who stood with him against war had lost control of opinion."

In coming to such a view about the process leading to the Spanish-American War, Trask is obviously highly influenced by Ernest May (1961), whose analysis of the onset of the Spanish-American War in *Imperial Democracy* suggests that public opinion was *the* driving force for war. In a chapter titled "Hysteria," May (142) asserts that in the weeks leading up to the war, "across the country, thousands gave themselves up to emotional excesses like those of tent-meeting revivals." He also notes that congressmen and cabinet officers received increasingly offensive letters, many scrawled in pencil on crude paper" and that "by the seventh week after the *Maine* disaster, these passions were beginning to take the form of anger against the President" (143). May concludes the chapter by declaring that "a frightened elite retreated from resistance to acquiescence" (147). One review of May's book accurately concludes, then, that in May's opinion, "the American intervention in Cuba . . . resulted . . . from the irresistible urge of the American people" and that "Americans went to war because the body of its citizens, overwrought, highly moralistic, and heedless of consequences, insisted upon it" (Stegler 1962, 8).

In a similar vein, Gerald Linderman (1974) portrays the American public in 1898 as rather incredibly war-hungry. To some extent, this hunger may have been created by the image of Spain many Americans picked up in their grammar school books. According to Ruth Elson (1964), at any rate, nineteenth-century American grammar readers usually portrayed Spaniards as barbaric, cruel, and uncultured.

This picture of the broader public pushing a more pacificistically inclined elite into the war runs counter to a common idea that actually the newspaper press and especially William Randolph Hearst's *New York Journal* were more responsible and that if indeed public opinion did seem rabidly in favor of the war, it was only because Hearst's well-publicized tirades had their desired effect on that opinion (Wisan 1934; Tuchman 1966). This common view is not, of course, beyond challenge. In *Public Opinion and the Spanish-American War,* Marcus Wilkerson (1932, 131), who in fact focuses almost entirely on newspaper editorials and coverage of events rather than public opinion more broadly defined, concludes that "the conflict with Spain has often been referred to as 'Hearst's War,' but this accusation is manifestly unjust in view of the activities of such newspapers as Pulitzer's *World,* Dana's *Sun,* Bennett's *Herald,* Medill's *Tribune,* and many publications in all parts of the nation." In fact, Wilkerson feels that Joseph Pulitzer, whose historical reputation, it is probably fair to say, is more politically correct than that of Hearst, actually took the lead on this issue. "Pulitzer originally," Wilkerson (1932, 131) argues, "set the pace in exploiting the Cuban rebellion."[7]

Even more important, several sources seem convinced that the rabble-rousing by the newspaper press was not all that effective and that the extent to which the passions were aroused by newspaper editorials of the time is generally exaggerated. Joseph Offner (1992, 229), for example, declares that "some historians have interpreted William Randolph Hearst's desire to dominate New York City journalism as causing the public hysteria that galvanized the nation to intervene. But sensational journalism had only a marginal impact. Hearst played on American prejudices; he did not create them." David Trask (1981, xiii) also feels that after the sinking of the *Maine,* "popular insistence on immediate action—including, if necessary, war against Spain—became manifest instantly, and it grew by leaps and bounds in succeeding days and weeks. 'Yellow journals' only rode the wave of feeling; they did not create it." The source that Trask cites in support of this assertion is *Imperial Democracy* by Ernest May. Similarly, George Auxier (1940) concludes that the midwestern newspapers of the time were quite consistently prowar but that they were reflecting more than they were shaping public opinion in the midwest.

In sum, certainly on the surface, at least, the results of our pseudo-experiment with respect to the role of public opinion do not support the democratic peace proposition. We find very little public pressure of any kind in the Fashoda Crisis, and what manifestations there were of pressure from public opinion pushed in the bellicose direction. In Spain, we have found some suppression but little evidence of burgeoning public pressure for peace to suppress. In the United States, in the weeks leading to the war, there was, by virtually universal agreement, broad public opinion in *favor* of declaring war on Spain.

Influences by "Special Interest" Groups

But then the democratic peace proposition does not necessarily suggest that democracy exerts a pacifying effect because the *majority* of citizens agitate for conciliatory policies during times of international crisis. Such theorists as Bueno de Mesquita and Lalman (1992) and, even more definitively, Rummel (1979) suggest that democracy might have a pacifying effect because groups within the population that do not necessarily constitute a majority are free to organize, protest, and speak out against bellicose policies in a way that would not be possible in more autocratic regimes.

A contrasting, competing idea (but one that also focuses on the role of subgroups within the broader population) that is obviously relevant to the two crises we are investigating here suggests that within capitalistic regimes, business interests will press for expansionistic and bellicose policies. As we mentioned above, in the last three decades of the nineteenth century, virtually every major power engaged in imperialistic policies, and both the Fashoda Crisis and the Spanish-American War can be seen as part of that broad general pattern. The Spanish-American War, in fact, helped to inspire the capitalism-leads-to-imperialism thesis expounded by John Hobson in his *Imperialism,* published in 1902.[8] Theophile Delcasse, the French foreign minister who was one of the driving forces behind the French policy that helped to create the Fashoda Crisis, was on record as believing that "Europe is stifling within her present boundaries with production everywhere outstripping demand. Its peoples are therefore driven by necessity to seek new markets far away, and what more secure markets can a nation have than countries placed under her own influence?" (Bates 1984, 4). Joseph Chamberlain, the "militant Colonial Secretary in the Conservative government" who during the Fashoda Crisis "pressed the Prime Minister for an immediate showdown with the French" (Wang 1992, 9), had asked in a speech ten years earlier: "Is there any man in his senses who believes that the crowded population of these islands could exist for a single day if we were to cut adrift from us the great dependencies which now look to us for protection and assistance, and which are the natural markets for our trade?" (Langer 1965, 77).

In contrast, then, to the idea that it was joint democracy that preserved the peace between France and Britain in 1898 and the absence of democracy in Spain that led to the war between the United States and Spain in 1898, we have the notion that it was the expansionist interests of capitalism and the business classes that created the crisis between Britain and France, and the business interests in the United States that were the driving force behind the bellicose policies that country adopted in 1898. Admittedly, since the expansionist economic pressures were ostensibly at work in all four countries we are examining in 1898, this theoretical notion may be hard-pressed to account for the *differ-*

ences in the outcomes of the two crises. On the surface at least, a Hobsonian would predict that both crises should end up in war. But the Hobson-Leninist thesis clearly does constitute a plausible rival hypothesis deserving our consideration to the extent that it suggests that it was the presence of capitalism (and the imperialism of capitalist interests) in the United States, rather than autocracy or the absence of democracy in Spain that was the crucial factor leading the crisis between the United States and Spain to end in international war in 1898.

In consideration of this plausible rival hypothesis it is interesting to note first that one recent authoritative account of the Fashoda Crisis argues that the bourgeoisie in France, at least, were a pacifying factor in the Fashoda Crisis. Bates (1984, 155) says that during the crisis in France "there was an underlying, hard-headed bourgeois assessment that no real French interests were at stake in the Nile valley . . . [S]ome of the strongest opposition to the war with England over Fashoda was expressed in the provincial papers of rich, sea-port towns of Marseilles and Bordeaux, and solid centers of trade like Lyons and Toulouse." Bates (1984, 155) further notes that "it was no coincidence that the same point of view was put forward in England in north county journals like the *Manchester Guardian* which did not think that the [Fashoda region] was worth a war and saw no reason why the French should not be allowed to keep it." In contrast to expectations based on a Hobson-Lenin thesis, what we find here is business groups apparently opposed to imperialistic expansion and agitating against a possible war in the manner that a democratic peace proponent such as Rummel (1979) would hypothesize.

The opposition to war by business groups in the United States as the crisis with Spain developed in 1897 and 1898 was even more striking, at least if many of the major sources on the war are to be believed. Alexander De Conde in his *History of American Foreign Policy* (1963, 347) asserts about the crisis leading to war between the United States and Spain that "at one time it was fashionable to place the blame on vested and expansionist business interests, but American investors in Cuba desired peace . . . [B]usiness interests in the United States, with few exceptions, opposed war." De Conde also observes—in one of many examples of evidence that the almost universal perception of leading politicians of the day was that business interests were opposed to war with Spain over Cuba—that Theodore Roosevelt at the time was of the opinion that "we here in Washington . . . have grown to feel that almost every man connected with the big business interests of the country is anxious to court any infamy if only peace can be obtained and the business situation be not disturbed."[9]

Similarly, Ernest May (1961, 118) in his account of the crisis leading to the Spanish-American War argues that the men of his time most admired by President McKinley were businessmen such as John D. Rockefeller, George H. Pullman, and J. P. Morgan, and that "men who fitted this list were generally against any policy that risked war." In the wake of the sinking of the *Maine,* May (1961, 139) reports that "many businessmen had already come out against intervention in Cuba, and business journals promptly called for patience and self-restraint in the *Maine* case." In short, May (1961, 147) feels that the opinion of the business community was one of "resolute disapproval" of war and that business people in general "dreaded an open conflict."

David Trask does not harp on this point as much as other writers, but he too observes that in reaction to the sinking of the *Maine* "Grenville M. Dodge, a leading railroad executive, proclaimed to McKinley that the United States could not afford a war and should not fight unless it had to defend its integrity. Like many businessmen, he believed that warfare would engender economic instability" (Trask 1981, 30). Trask also points out that "hawkish" critics of the time, antagonized by McKinley's attempts to avoid war with Spain, felt that "McKinley's policy reflected self-interested economic considerations—an indication of the public realization that the business community generally opposed intervention in Cuba" (Trask 1981, 43).

Certainly one of the most recent book-length analyses of the Spanish-American War, *An Unwanted War* by John Offner (1992), has as one of its major theses that the most important domestic opponents of war during the crisis between the United States and Spain concerning the future of Cuba in 1898 were among the business community and that virtually all of the important participants in the American political process recognized this to be the case. He discusses a debate on the conflict between Spain and Cuba as early as 1895 during which one congressman "noted that only the business community opposed congressional action in favor of Cuba" and refers to the general "condemnation of the business community for opposing congressional action" (Offner 1992, 21). In 1896, there was another debate in the House on a resolution to recognize Cuba's belligerency, and the leader of the Democrats in the House, Joe Bailey, according to Offner (1992, 45), "accused the Republicans of currying favor with rich business interests . . . [H]e appealed to them to be patriotic and humanitarian." At the height of the crisis, William Jennings Bryant expressed an opinion about the issue remarkably similar to that of Theodore Roosevelt, cited above. "Humanity demands that we shall act," Bryan asserted. "The suffering of [Cuba's] people cannot be ignored unless we, as a Nation, have become so engrossed in moneymaking as to be indifferent to distress" (Offner 1992, 153), Bryan declared, thus voicing a complaint about the generally pacifistic view of the business community and moneyed interests that was apparently perceived by virtually all who came to favor war against Spain over the fate of Cuba. It is apparently at least partly Offner's account that leads John Owen (1993, 5) in his case study of the Spanish-American War to conclude that "when William Jennings Bryan . . . came out for intervention, and most clergy began advocating it on humanitarian grounds, it began to appear that only business interests remained opposed."

Probably the most prominent voice in opposition to this idea that the American business community was an antiwar force in 1898 belongs to Walter LaFeber (1963). He argues that American foreign policy in general during this era was motivated to an important extent by the idea that the American economy would be in more or less permanent trouble unless it could expand its exports to foreign markets. But even LaFeber (1963, 400) acknowledges that "President [McKinley] did not want war; he had been sincere and tireless in his efforts to maintain the peace," and that the business community in the main supported McKinley's efforts, *until* quite late in the game. Speaking of those forces that finally pushed McKinley to conclude with obvious reluctance that a war was necessary, LaFeber (1963, 403) points to "the *transformation* [emphasis added] of the opinion of many spokesmen for the business community who had formerly opposed the war."

Philip Foner also, in his *The Spanish-Cuban-American War and the Birth of American Imperialism* (1972), provides a determined argument against the idea that American business interests generally opposed the Spanish-American War. He asserts that the idea is largely a function of uncritical and unjustified acceptance of a work by historian Julius W. Pratt published in the 1930s (see 289–307). He does establish rather convincingly (as does Lafeber) that at least some important businesspeople were converted to the cause of war late in the process and that some business interests also helped to persuade McKinley that he should not recognize Cuba's independence even though the U.S. would fight for Cuba's liberation from Spain. Finally, it is undeniable that some business interests did take advantage of the results of the war, in the Philippines as well as in Cuba.

But it still seems safe to conclude that a majority of business interests did oppose war with Spain over the Cuban issue until very late in the game and that this was generally perceived to be the case by most of the leading participants in the political process that ultimately led to the war. In sum, there is a rather substantial body of evidence that tends to disconfirm the proposition that it was capitalism and the expansionist, imperialistic interests of the business classes in the United States rather than the absence of democracy in Spain that caused the crisis to escalate to international war.[10]

The Role of Other
Domestic Political Groups and Issues

It is striking—at least to someone sensitized by the current debate between neorealists and democratic peace theorists—how much emphasis many sources on the Fashoda Crisis and the Spanish-American War give to domestic political considerations. That "foreign affairs are the external aspects of domestic questions" (Downum 1971, 162) and that France ultimately backed down rather than confront Britain militarily over Fashoda are the basic themes of *Fashoda Reconsidered* by Roger Glenn Brown (1969), for example. And a major thesis of Offner's *An Unwanted War* (1992) is that both President McKinley and key business leaders closely allied to the Republican party would have preferred to avoid war with Spain but that "in the final analysis, Republicans made war on Spain in order to keep control of Washington. Expansionism, markets, and investments, the sensational press, and national security interests were much less important in carrying the United States into war" (Offner 1992, ix). In other words, it was, in Offner's view, primarily domestic political considerations that led the United States to pursue bellicose policies against Spain in 1898. Offner (1992) and Trask (1981) both argue, even more strikingly in contrast to realist and neorealist principles, that Spain went to war primarily for domestic political reasons. That is, they both argue that Spanish political leaders felt that the enemies of the Restoration would overthrow the government unless they put up a fight over Cuba. They felt that way even though they were under no illusions about the prospect of war with the United States; they knew, in other words, that they were almost certainly going to lose. Let us consider in turn the implications of these arguments about the primacy of domestic political considerations, as it were, for the democratic peace proposition.

The Fashoda Crisis and the Dreyfus Affair

One could logically argue that it was not joint democracy that brought the Fashoda Crisis to a peaceful resolution, but the demoralizing impact of the Dreyfus Affair in France that caused the French government to capitulate and preserve the peace. This argument, though, is vulnerable to criticism on several counts.

First, the argument that France backed down *in spite of* the Dreyfus Affair is about as plausible, in the light of available evidence, as the proposition that it backed down because of it. The affair made the French government fearful that it would fall. In order to forestall its demise, it felt the need to take a strong stand on the Fashoda issue. As Brown (1969, 127) explains it, the French foreign minister Delcasse believed that "domestic attacks against the cabinet could be offset by gaining some concessions over Fashoda." Brown (1969, 130) further argues that "the Fashoda incident became the Fashoda Crisis because of the condition of French politics," referring mainly to the Dreyfus Affair. If the incident had resulted in war, there is little doubt that this case would be pointed to as an example that supports the proposition that internal conflict and instability make a state more likely to pursue bellicose policies, including international war. In any case, the argument that it was the debilitating impact of the Dreyfus Affair that led France to capitulate and preserve the peace rather than the joint democracy of Britain and France that accounts for the peaceful resolution of this crisis is certainly not an overwhelmingly persuasive rival hypothesis.

On the other hand, the Dreyfus Affair did put democracy in France in danger and in so doing provided, perhaps, some evidence in support of the democratic peace proposition. The Right and the military in France might, inspired in part by the Dreyfus Affair, have tried to pull off a military coup against the democratic government. The British Ambassador in France telegraphed London that such a coup might be in the offing. "The British Cabinet . . . had no faith that the French regime would hold. It was when they received [the British Ambassador's] warning that they mobilized their fleet. It was not so much an act of coercion as a defensive preparation in case France should fall under authoritarian control" (Weart 1994, chapter 13). In other words, to the extent that this dispute almost escalated to war, it might be argued that the escalatory tendencies focused on the struggle not between the democratic governments in Britain and France but on the conflict between the democratic government in Britain and the incipient authoritarian government in France.

Domestic Politics and the American Policy toward Spain

The evidence that the United States government pursued its war against Spain primarily to avoid losing the next election certainly does not on the surface provide support for the democratic peace proposition. On the contrary, it seems to suggest that the war occurred to an important extent because the United States was democratic.

But incongruous as it might seem, that evidence can be construed as supportive of at least some versions of the democratic peace proposition and its undergirding theoretical structure. Maoz and Abdolali (1989) and Bueno de Mesquita and Lalman (1992), for example, suggest that mixed dyads can be particularly prone to conflict escalation and war. In contrast, Bremer (1992) reports that mixed dyads (one democratic and one autocratic) are less war prone than purely autocratic pairs of states. The Spanish-American War, though, seems to provide evidence supporting the idea that mixed dyads are particularly combustible. Leaders, pressure groups, and the masses perceived that Spain was not governing Cuba in a democratic way and was in fact engaged in massive repression leading to the deaths of 400,000 people (they thought, and Spain did not deny it), or a quarter of the population. Moreover, Spain was not generally perceived to be democratic. As Bruce Russett (1993, 19) asserts in his discussion of this case, "the Spanish political situation was at best marginal enough that key United States decisionmakers could readily persuade themselves and their audiences that it was not democratic." Similarly, John Owen (1993, 19) concludes from his thorough review intended precisely to determine the extent to which pacifistic arguments and forces in the United States were inspired by "democracy" in Spain that "Some mention was made in Congress and the press of Spanish liberty, actual or potential, as a reason not to fight, but such references were rare. Confrontationists, however, especially in Congress and the newspapers, did justify their stances quite frequently on the fact that Spain was a monarchy; i.e., by traditional American criteria, not a democracy." John Offner (1992, 77–78) discusses an influential article in the November 1897 *North American Review* in which Hannis Taylor argued that "the Spanish government could not give self-government to the Cubans because that was something the Spanish themselves did not have." In short, the fact that there were clearly democratic pressures toward war in the United States as the crisis with Spain unfolded does not necessarily have to be interpreted as evidence against the democratic peace proposition, because it was quite clearly the *combination* of democracy in the United States and perceived (at least) autocracy in Spain that evoked those pressures. This is particularly compatible with some strands of arguments within the democratic peace literature that posit that mixed dyads are particularly prone to conflict escalation.

Spanish Autocracy, Spanish Domestic Politics, and Crisis Escalation

Evidence that Spanish autocracy helped to escalate the crisis would reinforce the argument that it was not democracy in the United States but the combination of democracy in the United States and autocracy in Spain that caused this crisis to escalate to war. Such evidence is not difficult to find. For example, John Offner (1992, 157) quotes approvingly an American envoy's report to Washington during the crisis that "the army [is] still the controlling factor in Spanish politics, and the attitude of the army constituted the real danger." In fact, one of the main themes of Offner's book is that the Spanish government felt it must pursue a hard-line policy in order to preserve the monarchy against a military coup. Ernest May (1961, 163) pursues a similar theme, arguing that "abandonment of the island was simply out of the question. Spain could not desert the loyal Spaniards there. More important, to give up the struggle would be to insult the sensitive and dangerous vanity of the army."

Another piece of evidence that it was the lack of democracy in Spain that made the presence of democracy an apparently combustible element in the crisis between the United States and Spain can be found in an assertion by David Trask (1981, 16) regarding the inability of the Spanish government to understand the policymaking process in the United States. According to Trask (1981, 10), "Spanish leaders . . . found it difficult to understand that public opinion greatly influenced the behavior of the American president" during the crisis that led to the war. This is an interesting commentary on the extent to which Spain was democratic. In other words, it suggests that it was not very democratic, as its leaders found it difficult to understand democratic pressures on the American leader. It also increases the plausibility of the argument that it was autocracy in Spain, combined with democracy in the United States, rather than democracy in the United States, that made this crisis more likely to escalate to war.

Decision-Making Processes and Attitudes among Decision-Making Elites

Even if it is possible to ascertain what public opinion was during these two crises or what impact special interest groups intended to have, it is difficult to be sure what effects public opinion and special interest groups actually had on conflict escalation or resolution. The public and the groups are removed from the key decision makers in distance and time in ways that complicate conclusions about what their impact was, a point to which we shall return in the conclusion of this chapter. On the surface, anyway, it is easier to evaluate the impact of decision-making processes and the attitudes and norms brought to those processes by the leading decision makers.

However, the review of the process leading to the Spanish-American War is more problematic than the review of the Fashoda Crisis because in the former crisis we are evaluating evidence analogous to dogs not barking, i.e., the absence of joint democracy. We might note, though, that Spain in particular made energetic attempts to get the Great Powers, and especially the Vatican, to mediate the dispute with the United States over Cuba. Whether or not the United States ever accepted the offer of the Pope to mediate became a controversy that complicated the crisis. In any case, ultimately, "McKinley emphatically denied that he had asked the Pope to mediate or that he would accept papal mediation" (Offner 1992, 164–65). This means that this case falls into a pattern reported by William Dixon (1993a) as well as by Gregory Raymond (1994) in which jointly democratic states are more likely to accept mediation. If one is inclined to argue that, unofficially (since the Vatican did engage in rather extensive mediation efforts; see Offner 1992, 159–76), then the fact that the mediation efforts failed is congruent with evidence provided by Dixon (1993b) that mediation efforts are more likely to succeed with respect to disputes in which both states are democratic. In either case, the implication is that this case fits into a pattern supportive of the democratic peace proposition.

It is also interesting to note, in a review of the crisis bargaining leading to the Spanish-American War that Russell Leng (1993, 28) reports that "democracies [are] indeed more likely to choose reciprocating [bargaining] strategies than authoritarian regimes" and that reciprocating influence strategies are most likely to be employed by democratic states either defending the status quo or following a change in the status quo in their favor through a fait accompli. Unfortunately, the sample of crises Leng examines does not contain a number of disputes between democracies sufficiently large to enable him to investigate the impact of joint democracy on the selection of bargaining strategies. Nevertheless, it is intriguing, as Leng (1993, 28–29) notes, that his findings are "consistent with the political culture hypothesis that democratic regimes are more likely to choose influence strategies that promote compromise and peaceful settlements." It is also interesting to note that the United States did *not* choose a reciprocating strategy in its crisis involving Spain in 1898 (according to Leng 1993, 14) and that the crisis leading to the Spanish-American War is one of the cases included in the sample leading Leng to the generalization that "reciprocating influence strategies are most likely to be employed by democratic states . . . defending the status quo." We shall argue below that the fact that the United States was *not* defending the status quo in the crisis involving Spain in 1898 may well be one of the key characteristics that differentiates it from the Fashoda Crisis in such a manner as to make it the one that escalated to international war.

Though honesty compels me to admit that I may be overly sensitized to such evidence by my theoretical predilections, I would argue that a review of decision-making processes and cultural or normative attitudes of leading decision makers reveals substantial evidence of the impact of joint democracy on the outcome of the Fashoda Crisis.[11] For example, when Marchand, the leader of the French expedition to Fashoda, met Lord Kitchener at Fashoda for the first time, they both stated the official positions of their governments on the issue at hand and even agreed that the implications of those two contrasting positions might mean war. But having stated those positions, in a respectful manner, "both men were able to move towards a practical and honorable resolution of the situation with which they were faced. They agreed first of all that the rights and wrongs of the British and French positions on the Upper Nile were outside their competence, and should be referred to London and Paris" (Bates 1984, 132). Both men, then, took refuge in the democratic value of subordination of the military to their civilian governments. Having depersonalized the conflict in that way, they then agreed on crucial, time-gaining compromises. "Kitchener would not require Marchand to haul down his flag or retire, while Marchand for his part would raise no objections to Kitchener hoisting the Egyptian flag at Fashoda and leaving a garrison there" (Bates 1984, 132–33). Even Wang (1992, 11), whose general conclusion is that the Fashoda Crisis does not provide much evidence supportive of the democratic peace proposition, concedes that "at the local level, there was . . . specific evidence of democrats' mutual respect and its role in preventing war . . . [H]aving presented their governments' statements, the General [Kitchener] and the Captain [Marchand] relaxed and communicated appreciation for each other. . . . Such restraint shown by the British and the French officers could suggest an unspoken regard they felt for one another as moral equals."

Then, too, the French government under Premier Henri Brisson fell on October 25, leaving that government at the height of the crisis in a confused, weakened state that would not have been duplicated in an authoritarian regime. As Bates (1984, 157) notes, "Such frequent changes of government at moments of crisis in France, caused Salisbury to observe 'in such a confused situation an ultimatum was hardly necessary.'"

Bruce Russett (1993, 8) also notes that though the key decisions during the height of the Fashoda Crisis were based primarily on geopolitical considerations, the crisis did nevertheless evoke norms suggesting that two democratic nations such as Great Britain and France should not fight each other. He cites a quote by Liberal leader H. C. G. Matthew that "most Liberals regarded the Entente with France as the natural result of democratic impulses."

Finally, Bates (1984, 153) describes the attitudes of the French and British foreign ministers at the height of the crisis in terms that might have been evoked by the theoretical analysis of bargaining between democratic states in crisis situations by Bueno de Mesquita and Lalman (1992, 156). Recall that they argue that "when democracies confront one another, it is common knowledge that each has unusually high confidence that the other is likely to be constrained to be averse to the use of force. And that common knowledge about the magnitude of the prior belief encourages states under all but the most unusual circumstances to negotiate with one another or to accept the status quo." According to Bates (1984, 153), at the height of the tension caused by the Fashoda Crisis, the French foreign minister "Delcasse knew that Salisbury . . . *preferred diplomacy to force in the settlement of international disputes* [emphasis added], and that he and his Conservative colleagues wanted to avoid doing anything risky or costly which might . . . put up the rate of income tax." In this brief phrase, Bates highlights a perception of Delcasse that, according to Bueno de Mesquita and Lalman (1992), is a key to the peaceful resolution of conflicts between democratic states and also points to a consideration of democratic political pressures on Salisbury (i.e., a concern about income taxes) that would be likely to make him (Salisbury) amenable to compromise.

Conclusion

There is one important way that the evaluation of evidence produced by our pseudo-experiment with regard to the validity of the democratic peace proposition is more difficult than I have indicated up to this point. The discussion until now has shared an assumption with many other attempts to evaluate evidence from individual cases that is clearly dubious. That assumption is that if the general public or special interest groups in a democracy are "dovish," that is, if they visibly agitate for conciliatory measures and for peace, then this is evidence that supports the democratic peace proposition, or the general idea that democracy is a pacifying force.

"Reality" may be more complicated. Bueno de Mesquita and Lalman (1990, 763) argue that "dovishness can *heighten* the risk that force will be used" and reiterate the point when they argue that "the high domestic constraints faced by democracies makes them vulnerable to the threat of war or exploitation and liable to launch preemptive attacks against presumed aggressors" (Bueno de Mesquita and Lalman 1992, 159). It was at least tacitly assumed during our discussion of the Spanish-American War that any sign of resistance to bellicose policies in the American society, from the general public or special interest groups within the public, was evidence in favor of the idea that democracy has a pacifying impact. However, as Bueno de Mesquita and Lalman argue, whatever evidence of dovishness we found in our review of the American political scene in the years and months leading up to the Spanish-American War (and we did not find much, except among business groups) might actually have made the democratic United States more, not less, likely to become involved in a war with Spain over the Cuban issue.

In general, though, our review of public opinion and special interest groups in the United States, Spain, Great Britain, and France during the crises we have analyzed did not turn up much evidence of Kantian-like resistance to war. On the contrary, the more visible signs of political expression from those quarters in each case seemed to be rather more bellicose than conciliatory.

A possibly important exception to that rule involved business groups in the United States in the months leading up to the Spanish-American War. The democratic peace proposition would suggest that that is crucial in important part because the political regime in Spain was autocratic, or, at least, because of the combination of regimes (democratic and autocratic) involved in that crisis. A plausible rival hypothesis is that it was not the lack of democracy in Spain but the presence of expansionist capitalism in the United States that led to the war. But the evidence of opposition to the war by business groups in the United States and the possibly even more important evidence that business interests were almost universally perceived to be opposed to the war (by leaders in both the Republican and Democratic parties in particular) inflicts some important damage on the credibility of that plausible rival hypothesis. That doubt is reinforced at least marginally by the evidence of an autocratic crackdown in Spain against public expressions of opposition to the looming war during the peak of the crisis.

Another plausible rival hypothesis suggests that it was weakness caused by the Dreyfus Affair in France, rather than joint democracy, that led to a peaceful resolution of the Fashoda Crisis. But a review of the dynamics of the decision-making process in France as they related to the Dreyfus Affair reveals that the argument that the Fashoda Crisis was resolved peacefully in spite of the Dreyfus Affair is at least as plausible. Then, too, the Dreyfus Affair made it seem possible that the French democratic government might be victimized by a military coup, a possibility clearly perceived by the British. To some extent, the potential for this crisis to escalate to war stemmed from the conflict between the democratic government in England and an incipient authoritarian government in France, thus relieving to some extent the burden of this "near war" from the democratic peace proposition.

My review of evidence relating to decision-making processes and cultural or normative attitudes among the political leaders involved in these crises is, perhaps, generally more supportive of the democratic peace proposition than my review of evidence focusing on the role of public opinion and interest groups. This is partly because public opinion was apparently rather bellicose—and because of the difficulty we have described regarding the evaluation of the impact of "dovish" pressures in the general public or special interest groups. Resistance to mediation efforts and the lack of success of what mediation efforts there were in the crisis leading to the Spanish-American War are congruent with and supportive of the proposition in the democratic peace literature that democratic states are more likely to accept mediation and to have disputes successfully resolved by mediation (Dixon 1993a, 1993b; Raymond, 1994). The attitudes of British and French leaders on the spot in Fashoda (Marchand and Kitchener) and their ability to temporize in a conciliatory fashion seem supportive of the democratic peace proposition, as is the confidence we found on both sides of the "dovishness" of their counterparts.

Many comments in the literature in general, and in Maoz and Russett (1992) in particular, have emphasized the potentially important role of political stability in conflict processes. Commentators such as Doyle (1986) and Russett (1993) have expressed the opinion that democratic regimes must be stable if the pacifying effect of democracy is to be full-fledged, whereas Maoz and Russett (1992, 262) conclude that "stable states are far less likely to fight one another than expected, regardless of their regime type. This suggests that political stability, rather than or in addition to regime type, may account for the low rate of disputes between democracies."

The role of "stability" in the two disputes we have analyzed here has been an ambiguous one. Instability, or the threat of a coup, certainly did seem to make the Spanish regime more determined to fight for the sake of Cuba. Instability, in the shape of the Dreyfus affair in France, had countervailing effects, it seems, making the French government anxious to extract concessions from Great Britain but arguably making the French feel weak and conciliatory. Furthermore, there are hints in such sources as Bates (1984) that the British were concerned not to press the unstable situation in France too hard lest that pressure unseat their democratic counterparts in that country, thus suggesting in turn that the instability in France made a contribution to a peaceful resolution of the crisis. Then, too, in the United States, though the democratic regime had been in place for a long time (and thus was very stable by the operational definition utilized by Maoz and Russett, 1992), the particular government then in power under McKinley apparently felt itself quite vulnerable to defeat in the next election unless it pursued an assertive policy with respect to Spain over Cuba. In general, in any democratic regime, the particular government in power is virtually always "unstable" in the sense that there is at least some probability that it might lose the next election. Further, it could be argued that the instability of a particular government in that regard is higher within democratic regimes the more stable they (that is, the regimes) are. In short, the quasi-experiment here raised a lot more questions than it answered with respect to the role of "stability" in conflicts between democracies and between democratic and autocratic regimes, as well as with regard to the possible impact of stability on the relationship between regime type and conflict escalation.

Certainly the rival hypothesis that most plausibly challenges the democratic peace proposition as an explanation of the results of our pseudo-experiment focuses on the impact of power ratios and geopolitical calculations. More precisely, the plausible rival hypothesis fastens on the fact that France backed down in the Fashoda Crisis and war was avoided not because both France and Great Britain were democracies but because—in both tactical terms on the site at Fashoda and in strategic terms that would become relevant if a general war featuring naval battles were to break out—France was in a hopeless position. Russett (1993, 7–8) in his consideration of the relevance of the Fashoda Crisis to the democratic peace proposition, points out that the French "forces at Fashoda were far weaker, they had their hands full on the continent with Germany, and Britain held unquestioned naval superiority. . . . The French gave in because of their military weakness." Even so, Russett does not declare the democratic peace proposition irrelevant to an understanding of the outcome of the Fashoda Crisis. Hongying Wang (1992, 13) comes close to doing so. She declares that "in the end it was the French surrender that avoided a Franco-British War. And . . . at the heart of [France's] decision to give in on Fashoda was his realization of his country's obvious weakness vis-à-vis Britain. *The peaceful settlement of the Fashoda Crisis is better explained by a rational theory of strategic calculations than by the normative Kantian theory*" (emphasis added).

My first reaction to these arguments regarding the importance of traditional realpolitik calculations to the resolution of the Fashoda Crisis is to agree with them, up to a point, and even to elaborate on them. I agree that the calculations of Britain and especially France may have been influenced primarily by traditional realpolitik-type factors in the Fashoda Crisis. Furthermore, I would argue that a comparison of the Fashoda Crisis and the crisis leading up to the Spanish-American War suggests that perhaps the crucial difference between them that led the first to be resolved peacefully and the second to result in war was this: In the Fashoda Crisis, the state desiring a change in the status quo, France, was in the obviously weaker position, militarily, whereas in the crisis leading to the Spanish-American War, the state seeking a change in the status quo, the United States, was in the stronger position militarily. The logic here would be the same as that utilized by Paul Huth, Christopher Gelpi, and Scott Bennett (1993, 613) in their analysis of great power militarized disputes from 1816 to 1984 within the context of deterrence theory. They derive the hypothesis that "the more favorable the military capabilities for the challenger, the higher the probability that it will escalate a militarized dispute against the defender." They find evidence that "a change in the [power] balance from a three-to-one defender advantage to a three-to-one challenger advantage increases the probability of escalation by approximately 33%" (618). The admittedly modest evidence from our comparative case study supports a broader hypothesis regarding the probability of dispute escalation in other than deterrence situations and involving states other than major powers.

One of the purposes of comparative case studies of this kind is heuristic. They have the potential of bringing to light factors that have not hitherto been considered or emphasized. This comparative case study has highlighted the potentially central role of the distinction between that participant in an interstate dispute that seeks to change the status quo and the participant seeking to preserve it. It seems to me a distinction equivalent in importance to that between the initiator and the target of disputes in such analyses of international conflict as Maoz (1982), Bueno de Mesquita (1981), and Bueno de Mesquita and Lalman (1992). In fact, it seems that, for many purposes, such analysts as Maoz, Bueno Mesquita, and Lalman use the distinction between the initiator and the target of disputes as a kind of surrogate for the distinction between the state pushing for a change in the status quo and the state seeking to preserve the status quo. Patrick James (1988, 53–54) makes a similar point when he argues that "while [Bueno de Mesquita] has not made the error of attributing aggressor status to initiators as so defined, his expected utility model implies that they have planned their actions . . . [I]t would be illogical to expect initiators to win wars (as does Bueno de Mesquita) unless at some level they are thinking aggressively." In other words, it seems to me that a focus on the roles played by the dispute participants (i.e., either seeking a change in or defending the status quo) may be more relevant and more central to a clear understanding of the conflict processes being analyzed. Identification of the initiator of a conflict may be easier than the identification of the disputant seeking a change in the status quo, and that may be the reason that the distinction between the initiator and the target of disputes is more common in the literature. But the identity of the initiator of a dispute may be determined primarily by technical military considerations that have little to do with the theoretical considerations that lead to the interest in the distinction between the initiator and the target in a dispute or an international war. And previous experience, in Ray (1974), (as well as a similar strategy employed in James [1988], for example) suggests that though the task is difficult, it is not impossible to identify in at least a quasi-operational way, the dispute participant that seeks a change in the status quo and the disputant interested in preserving it.

In short, one idea that this comparative case study has brought to mind is that the analyses of disputes and conflict escalation might fruitfully focus on the distinction between the innovator (the state seeking a change in the status quo) and the defender (the state aiming to preserve the status quo). The analysis here of the Fashoda Crisis and the Spanish-American War suggests that the relationship between the power balance and the identities of the innovators and the defenders may have a crucial impact on the probability that a dispute will escalate to international war. As we have seen, Russell Leng (1973) reports that democratic states are more likely to select reciprocating influence strategies *if* they are defending the status quo. It is possible that distinguishing between innovators and defenders in serious disputes, or wars, will turn out to be crucial to a better understanding of the relationship between regime type, dispute involvement, and conflict escalation.

It might also be relevant to observe that Bueno de Mesquita, Siverson, and Woller (1992) and Bueno de Mesquita and Siverson (1993) show that the fate of political regimes is affected significantly by their fortunes in international wars and that this is particularly the case for democratic regimes. In addition, David Lake reports that democratic states are more likely than their autocratic counterparts to win the international wars in which they participate. Both Lake and Mark Brawley (1993) argue that democratic regimes have a tendency to avoid pervasive rent-seeking that will leave fewer resources available to devote to war-fighting efforts when the need arises, and thus are likely (according to Lake) to be more formidable opponents in war. France may, then, have been reluctant to take on Great Britain in a war over Fashoda in part because the British were perceived to be particularly difficult to defeat and in part also because England was democratic.

Having said (and in a way, conceded) all that credit to traditional, realpolitik, and realistic theoretical notions, I will also argue in conclusion, however, that analysts such as Hongying Wang (1992) go too far when they argue that the greater impact of France's strategic calculations over the joint democracy of England and France on the peaceful resolution of the Fashoda Crisis means that the crisis cannot be considered a source of evidence in support of the democratic peace proposition. Conceding that France's military inferiority to Britain was more important than the joint democracy of France and Britain in determining the outcome of the Fashoda Crisis does not necessitate the conclusion that joint democracy had *no* impact. Russett (1993, 85), for example, reports that since World War II, the ratio of capabilities between the disputants has had a much greater impact on the probability that a pair of states will become involved in serious disputes and on the probability that the dispute will escalate to war. But Russett also reports that even when controlling for the impact of capability ratios, regime type still has a visible impact on conflict involvement and conflict escalation. This reinforces findings in Bremer (1992, 1993), who focuses on a much longer time period, from 1816 to 1965, that contains the two disputes on which we focus here.

And the comparative case study here nicely reinforces the point that the important impact of geopolitical calculations and power ratios on conflict escalation need not be considered debilitating to the democratic peace proposition. This is because the capability ratios cannot explain the difference between the outcomes of the two disputes on which we focus. It is probably true that France capitulated in the Fashoda Crisis because its military position was bleak. But Spain's military position vis-à-vis the United States in the crisis leading up to the Spanish-American War was even bleaker. Offner (1992, 137), for example, points out that Spanish leaders such as "Sagasta, Moret and Gullon considered a war with the United States to be utterly hopeless, and Admiral Cerrara repeatedly warned against it." Recall our earlier discussion that a series of Correlates of War capability indicators reveal that whereas Britain enjoyed nearly a 2 to 1 power advantage over France, the ratio of American to Spanish capabilities was almost 12 to 1. The location of the conflict, compared to the locus of the Fashoda Crisis a long distance from Britain and France, reinforced that American power advantage. But Spain still did not capitulate. The Spanish government apparently felt that if it gave up Cuba without a fight, the regime would be overthrown. Recall also Offner's (1992) argument that McKinley and the Republican party fought the war against Spain primarily for domestic political reasons. The key role played by domestic political considerations on both sides in determining the outcome of this conflict is itself evidence in support of the democratic peace proposition that emphasizes the importance of such considerations and evidence against models relying solely on international power political calculations in the explanation of the outcomes of serious disputes.

Notes

1. Morgan and Campbell (1991) and Morgan and Schwebach (1992) adopt a strategy that might seem to be in the spirit of the strategy suggested by Przeworski and Teune. They suggest that it is not democracy per se that has a pacifying impact but more specific regime characteristics that might be present in either democratic or authoritarian political systems. However, this strategy does not involve a level of analysis transition of the type suggested by Przeworski and Teune. To the extent that the Morgan/Campbell and Morgan/Schwebach arguments are supported, they replace one national (or dyadic) level concept such as "democracy" or "autocracy" with another national (or dyadic) level concept such as "constraints on executive decision," or "constraints from political competition." In short, (as I have already indicated in chapter 1), Morgan and Campbell (1991) and Morgan and Schwebach (1992) both seem to me not to be, as they have sometimes been interpreted to be, elaborating on the democratic peace proposition, but instead to be trying to develop and defend competing, alternative hypotheses that would eliminate "democracy" as an explanatory variable without the kind of level of analysis transition advocated by Przeworski and Teune.

2. Russett and Starr cite Lave and March (1975) as a useful source on "thought experiments."

3. Campbell and Stanley (1963) refer to the static group comparison as a "preexperimental" design.

4. Oneal, Oneal, Maoz, and Russett (1993) brought the potential importance of interdependence through international trade to this pseudo-experiment to my attention at a point when deadlines and data problems made it difficult for me to deal with this factor in the manner that it probably deserves. I did establish that about 1898 France was England's second most important source of imports and third most important market for exports (not counting England's colonies; India was a very important trading partner at this time, too), whereas England was France's most important trading partner for exports and imports. For Spain, the United States was the third most important source of imports and the fourth most important export market, whereas for the United States, Spain was the fourth most important source of imports and the seventh most important export market. (See Keltie 1898, 80, 495, 956, 1096.) Although I would need data I do not have at hand regarding the importance of trade relative to the size of the total economies involved to calculate interdependence index scores such as those utilized by Oneal, Oneal, Maoz, and Russett, I can say almost certainly that this means that England and France were more interdependent than the United States and Spain, and thus interdependence is a factor that could also account for the difference in the outcomes of the disputes analyzed here instead of or in addition to joint democracy. (One might also argue, though, that in fact both of these pairs of states were quite interdependent in terms of international trade, so that a hypothesis based on interdependence might suggest that both of these disputes should have been resolved peacefully.)

5. "The correct figure," according to historian David Trask (1981, 9), "was closer to one hundred thousand."

6. The importance of this remark is reinforced by the fact that it is quoted by Russett (1993, 8).

7. In support of this assertion, Wilkerson (1932, 131–32) cites Oswald Garrison Villard to the effect that "it was by this appeal to the basest passions of the crowd that Mr. Pulitzer succeeded; like many another he deliberately stooped for success, and then, having achieved it, slowly put on the garment of righteousness."

8. Philip Foner (1972, 283) points out that Hobson concluded that the Spanish-American War was an imperialistic war and that "American imperialism was the natural product of the economic pressure of a sudden advance of capitalism which could not find occupation at home and needed foreign markets for goods and investments."

9. De Conde's (1963, 347) bottom line on this issue is that "McKinley headed a businessmen's administration that did not want war."

10. Even Foner (1972, 175–76) concludes from his analysis of the process leading to this war that "In whatever way they could, many Americans assisted the Cuban revolution. . . . To describe those activities as tantamount to jingoism and a desire for war or to view them as solely the result of the propaganda and machinations of the Cuban *junta,* the 'yellow press,' and the expansionist forces in the United States, is to denigrate the American people."

11. There is also, for those engaged in comparing the two events, interesting evidence that they impacted at least marginally on each other. Roger Glenn Brown (1969, 78–79), for example, reports: "The most urgent foreign policy question pending for both the British and the French cabinets was that of Egypt and the Upper Nile. In France, another question was occupying the new Minister of Foreign Affairs, however. Soon after taking office, Delcasse was caught up in the fanfare and the glory of mediating between the two belligerents in the Spanish-American War. Consequently, he had devoted little attention to the question of the approaching confrontation with Great Britain."

Chapter 6

The Democratic Peace Proposition: Past, Present, and Future

The democratic peace proposition asserts that, because they are democratic, democratic states will not fight (or initiate) international wars against each other. The proposition has philosophical roots that go back at least to Immanuel Kant. The roots of the current interest in it also can be traced in part to Georg Hegel, who anticipated that liberal values would ultimately predominate over their competitors. That idea, summarized in contemporary times by the phrase the "end of history," probably accounts for much of the current interest in the democratic peace proposition in the wake of the end of the Cold War. It now seems possible that the most powerful states in the international system, at least, will become uniformly democratic. If relationships among democratic states are fundamentally different from those among combinations of democratic and undemocratic states, as well as those among uniformly undemocratic states, then a significant trend toward democracy, even if it is restricted to the most powerful states in the international system, could transform international politics.

The Contemporary Origins of the Democratic Peace Proposition

Woodrow Wilson became an influential advocate of the pacifying potential of democracy in this century and might even be designated as a founder of the modern discipline of international relations. However, support for democracy as an important barrier against international war within the field of international politics soon all but disappeared. In the 1930s, Adolf Hitler was democratically elected, demonstrating that democracy is a fragile barrier to war and could even serve to bring to power extremely bellicose leaders. Then E. H. Carr warned against the presumption that the ethical prescriptions of the most powerful states in the world (which at the time were "English speaking" and democratic) were anything more than self-serving rationalizations. In the ten years immediately after World War II, Hans Morgenthau (1948) and Kenneth

Waltz (1954) wrote influential theoretical tracts arguing that the similarities in the foreign policies of all states, including democracies, were more fundamentally important than their differences.

Contemporary Research on the Democratic Peace Proposition

Nevertheless, in the 1960s, several of the earlier quantitative studies of international politics provided some evidence that the foreign policies of democratic states were less conflict prone than those of autocratic states, and then Dean Babst (1972) argued that democratic states have never fought interstate wars against each other. He also provided some systematic evidence in support of his argument. In the 1970s, too, R. J. Rummel began his five-volume effort (1975–1981), one major feature of which was the proposition that democratic (or "libertarian") states will not fight international wars against each other. He followed that with two articles (Rummel 1983, 1985) that generated and evaluated empirical evidence regarding the conflict and war proneness of democratic states compared to that of undemocratic states.

The earliest reactions to Rummel's two articles were arguments that democratic states were not less war prone than autocratic states (although not as persuasively as the current consensus would have it) and concessions almost as an aside that democratic states did seem to avoid wars against each other. Zeev Maoz and Nasrin Abdolali (1989) analyzed all pairs of states from 1817 to 1976; they also reported (with some significant qualifications) that democratic and autocratic states were equally war prone but that democratic states had demonstrated a "significant" tendency to avoid wars with each other. This has been followed by a series of impressive empirical analyses (e.g., Maoz and Russett 1992, 1993; Russett 1993; Bremer 1992, 1993), each of which suggests that democratic states have historically avoided wars against each other and that this absence of wars between democratic states is "significant" and not the result of a spurious relationship between regime type and international conflict.

Furthermore, despite rather common assertions to the contrary, this relationship between regime type and international conflict rests on a substantial theoretical base. Rummel (1976–1981) develops an extensive epistemological, metaphysical, as well as theoretical argument in defense of the democratic peace proposition. Bruce Bueno de Mesquita and David Lalman (1992) have developed a theory of international interactions in extended game form from which it is possible to derive the democratic peace proposition. Bruce Russett (1993) has articulated specifically the "cultural" and "structural" arguments on its behalf, and Spencer Weart (1994a, 1994b) provides a sweeping, historical defense of the assertion that political culture in "well-established" democratic states has always prevented them from going to war against each other. In addition, research indicating that the fate of political regimes depends to an important extent on their performance in international wars (Bueno de Mesquita, Siverson, and Woller 1992), especially for democratic regimes (Bueno de Mesquita and Siverson 1993), combined with evidence provided by David Lake (1992) that democratic states are particularly formidable opponents in international wars, provides intriguing empirical evidence in support of the idea that democratic states may avoid wars against each other in part because their war-fighting prowess makes them unattractive targets for military attack.

The more prevalent, orthodox theoretical arguments in defense of the democratic peace proposition, though, point first to the idea that public opinion in democracies will exert a pacifying impact, in part because the masses pay the heaviest cost of interstate wars. The possibility that the masses will retaliate at the polls against political leaders who get them involved in interstate wars is just one of the structural constraints that make it unlikely that democratic states will get involved in international wars, especially against each other. Symmetrical confidence that their counterparts would prefer to avoid war makes bargaining between democratic states especially likely to resolve disputes by preserving the status quo or through negotiations rather than military conflict. Finally, democratic values in favor of the peaceful resolution of conflicts, particularly when the conflicts are between democratic states, may also enhance the ability of democratic states to avoid international wars against each other.

Three Arguments against the Democratic Peace Proposition

In short, the theoretical arguments and the empirical evidence in support of the democratic peace proposition are persuasive. The case in favor of that proposition, though, is vulnerable to attack and criticism on at least three principal issues. The first two problems involve the fact that, statistically speaking, international wars and democratic regimes are relatively rare. About 99 percent of pairs of states in most years are not engaged in international wars against each other, and, until the last two or three decades at least, democratic states were far outnumbered by undemocratic states. This means that it is possible that the absence of wars between democratic states might require no explanation beyond the assertion that wars and democratic regimes are so rare that war between democratic states has been unlikely to occur for purely statistical reasons.

Several recent analyses suggest, however, that in fact it is statistically unlikely that democratic states would have avoided wars against each other entirely, *if* they were as likely to become involved in such wars as states in general. But those analyses have been based on quite interdependent annual observations of pairs of states, which make it fair to wonder whether the number of cases on which significance tests are based in these studies is in fact equivalent to the nominal N, or the very large number of dyad-years that serve as the objects of analysis. No matter how this issue is resolved, it is impossible to deny that the number of wars eliminated by the pacifying impact of democracy has been very small, making it especially desirable to supplement evidence from aggregate data analyses with complementary evidence from intensive analysis of crucial cases.

The second related issue on which the case for the democratic peace proposition is vulnerable to criticism persists even if we accept at face value the conclusions in several recent studies that the absence of international wars between democratic states is statistically significant. The rate of war involvements for pairs of states in general is so low that the absolute difference between the numbers of wars involving states in general and those involving democratic states will be very small even if the latter number is zero. This means that a relatively small number of exceptions to the rule that democratic states avoid wars against each other would reduce that difference to insignificance, both statistically and substantively. Therefore, it is arguably crucial to determine how many such exceptions there are.

The final issue on which the democratic peace proposition is, perhaps, most vulnerable to criticism involves the vulnerability of democratic regimes themselves. Democratic states can become undemocratic states. Therefore, *all* interactions among states involve states that are *potentially* autocratic. Logically, this potential must limit the impact of democracy on foreign policies and international politics. (Realists and neorealists argue that it reduces it to insignificance.) Democracy's impact is, in other words, a function to a crucial extent of its preservation in currently democratic states and its spread to currently autocratic states. This suggests in turn that analysts of international politics ought to pay more attention to a topic left until recently, at least, mostly to area specialists and analysts of comparative politics, i.e., regime transitions and, specifically, democratization.

Regime Transitions and International Politics

This book addresses each of these issues on which the democratic peace proposition may be particularly vulnerable to criticism. Global trends in democracy are analyzed, for example, in chapter 2. The basic argument in that chapter is that the international environment may play an important role in transitions toward or away from democracy within autocratic regimes and that such factors as political and economic competition among regimes of different types especially in the most powerful and influential states, as well as dramatic political events in those states, are among the most potent. The American Revolution, the French Revolution, and democratization throughout most of the nineteenth century in Great Britain, to cite three important examples of such international environmental factors, may have encouraged transitions to democracy throughout the international system up until World War I. The success of the democratic coalition in that war reinforced that trend. But then the Great Depression, and the concomitant apparent economic successes of the first Five-Year Plan in the Soviet Union and the Nazi's plan for dealing with the Depression in Germany, discredited democracy. The performance of the major democratic states in World War II restored, perhaps, some credibility to democracy, but the apparent successes of the Soviet Union, symbolized powerfully by the launching of the sputniks, helped to convince many, including leaders in a significant number of liberated colonies, that autocracy was the wave of the future. By the middle 1970s, though, earlier Soviet boasts that the autocratic, socialist system in the Soviet Union would lead that country to becoming the preeminent economy in the world were discredited. At the same time, all the richest countries in the world, with the highest standards of living as revealed in such indicators as life expectancy, were democratic.

If indices of democracy are calculated for virtually all states in the international system, and the average democracy index score in the international system traced over time, the trends in that average will conform to expectations based on the idea that crucial political and economic developments in and political and economic competition among the most powerful states in the system do play an important role in transitions toward and away from democracy in all of the states in the international system. The average level of democracy in the international system did, for example, increase throughout the nineteenth century (in the wake of the American Revolution, the French Revolution, and the continuing democratization in the preeminent state of Great Britain), and that trend was apparently reinforced after World War I. The various regimes of the world did become less democratic, on average, in the years immediately after the onset of the Great Depression and at a time when autocratic regimes in the Soviet Union and Germany were relatively successful in economic terms. The trend away from democracy was reversed briefly after World War II, but the launching of the sputniks by the Soviet Union did coincide with another significant decrease in the average level of democracy in the international system. Finally, the period of time marked by economic stagnation and ultimately the demise of the Soviet Union and relative economic and political successes in the major democratic states of the world was also marked by a substantial increase in the average level of democracy in the international system.

The extent to which such international environmental factors of the kind mentioned have an impact on regime transitions compared to the extent to which factors internal and peculiar to each state determine the direction of regime transitions can be ascertained by a technique referred to as decomposition, or partitioning of variance. The technique focuses on the extent to which changes toward or away from democracy in the all of the states of the international system are simultaneous and similar. The application of this technique to democracy index scores for virtually all states in the world from 1825 to 1993 reveals that *dis*similar changes toward or away from democracy have been, during that time period, substantially more common that transitions in tandem with changes in the system level average, in spite of the fact that those changes have seemed to reflect the impact of global, environmental factors.

This means that if system level forces have played an important role in regime transitions throughout the international system, those forces have usually operated in combination with characteristics peculiar to nation-states, or categories of states. In other words, the decomposition of variance technique is sensitive to the balance or net impact of system level forces. If the same system level factor affects different categories of states differently, or if different system level factors offset each other in their impacts, the *net* impact of system level forces on regime transitions will be (and apparently usually has been) negligible.

It should also be noted that the global trend toward democracy in place from the early 1970s to the early 1990s has apparently been reversed in the most recent two or three years. This reversal may be related to the fact that reforms in the direction of democracy have been accompanied by economic disasters in the Soviet Union while firm repression of democracy in the People's Republic of China has coincided with the fastest rates of growth in the GNP in the world. (Another way of saying the same thing would be that the "end of history" hypothesis may have underestimated the staying power of fascism.) In any case, if democracy is an important factor in the prevention of international war, the current global trend is not encouraging.

On Exceptions to the Rule of Democratic Peace

Although there is widespread agreement on the proposition that democratic states rarely fight international wars against each other, there are so many possible exceptions to that rule mentioned in prominent discussions of this proposition that even disinterested observers must wonder about its validity. This is particularly the case (to reiterate one last time) in light of the fact that the incidence of war for all states in the international system is so small that even a few exceptions to the rule regarding democratic peace could wipe out entirely the statistical significance of the difference between the rate of warfare among states in general and the incidence of wars among democratic states.

Most of the definitions of democracy and the operational indices used in research on democratic peace have been either too vague or too complex to allow significant progress in the direction of resolving disputes about just how many wars between democratic states have occurred. A resolution of such disputes must be based on a threshold of democracy defined according to important theoretical considerations and in accordance with widely accepted usage of the term "democracy." In addition, the threshold must be defined in a relatively simple, precise, and operational manner.

In chapter 3, democracy is defined as a political system in which the identities of leaders in the executive and legislative branches of government are determined in fair, competitive elections. It is stipulated that elections are competitive if at least two formally independent political parties participate in them. It is further stipulated that elections can be considered fair if at least 50 percent of the adult citizens in the country are given the right to vote and if it has been established by historical precedent that the political system in question can produce peaceful, constitutional transfers of power between different, formally independent political parties.

The most ambiguous cases in the controversy about whether there have ever been international wars between democratic states are arguably the War of 1812 between the United States and Great Britain, the War of the Roman Republic in 1849, the American Civil War, the Spanish-American War, the Boer War, and the war between Turkey and Cyprus in 1974. But the application of a threshold of democracy based on fair, competitive elections to these and other controversial cases mentioned most prominently in research on democratic peace reveals that none are necessarily or accurately categorized as wars between democratic states.

Case Studies, Covering Laws, and Pseudo-Experiments

Even if the argument that there has never been an international war between democratic states is accepted, and even if statistical estimates of the differences between rates of warfare among states in general and between democratic states are accurate, the number of wars that have been eliminated by the pacifying effect of democracy is very small. This is because, to repeat, wars are statistically rare, and until recently there have not been very many democratic regimes in the world.

This means that it is important to buttress statistical evidence in favor of the democratic peace proposition (because, statistically speaking, the impact of democracy on conflict proneness will always be small) with insights and persuasive power that can be generated only by intensive analyses of individual cases. The argument that small-n studies and analyses of large numbers of cases are complementary is widely agreed to. And yet the complementary character of these different types of studies is arguably underexploited, partly because those who prefer a case study approach and those who specialize in statistical or quantitative analyses of large numbers of cases have apparently incompatible notions about the key concepts of "cause" and "explanation."

For many (perhaps most) quantitatively oriented analysts, A may be said (tentatively) to be a cause of B if the temporal order between them is established, if A correlates with B, and if it can be determined (tentatively) that the correlation is not spurious. An "explanation" for such analysts is some kind of demonstration that a particular event is merely an example of an established general pattern (that is, a nonspurious correlation between factors for which temporal order has been established). For many historians, some who specialize in case studies, and scientific realists, this "covering law" notion of explanation is not acceptable. For them, to "explain" means to construct plausible descriptions of events that, for example, provide evidence of the *motives* and perceptions of the principal political agents in the event to be explained or ideas regarding *causal mechanisms* at work that determine that the event (or classes of events, in the case of scientific realists) turned out as it did.

However, an emphasis on the motives of political actors—as well as on connections between those motives and perceptions, on the one hand, and their behavior or actions, on the other—as "evidence" producing plausibility, which in turn produces the feeling that an event has been "explained," can be misleading. Motives are invisible, and the political actors in question may lie about them or not understand them, even if the motives in question are their own. Then, too, their motives may be irrelevant to the outcomes in question, which may be determined by political structures, for example, whose impact or even existence are only dimly perceived (if that) by those actors. *Mechanisms* can be made to appear causal (by citing confirmatory examples), especially within the confines of a single case (or a single system) even if they happen to focus on factors that actually militate against the outcome of an event that actually occurred. Subsumption of particular events within general patterns, which is only possible through the systematic comparison of events to be explained, offers the most promising route to the construction of "explanations" that contribute most effectively to our understanding of the political events and phenomena of concern to us.

The application of such notions regarding "causality" and "explanation" to particular cases can be demonstrated most effectively, perhaps, if comparative case studies are constructed according to an experimental logic. Analytical exercises based on such a logic, which might be labeled "pseudo-experimental," are most useful because they highlight plausible rival hypotheses and lead the investigator to focus on the most important factors on which those hypotheses are based. This is especially the case if one approaches such exercises with the "covering law" notion of explanation in mind, because that notion also highlights in turn the complementary nature of the results of analyses of large number of cases and the intensive analysis of one or two cases at hand.

Chapter 5 consists of a pseudo-experimental analysis of the Spanish-American War and the Fashoda Crisis. The Spanish-American War involved a pair of states that were almost uniformly democratic in a crisis that led to war, whereas the Fashoda Crisis involved a pair of states that were both democratic in a crisis that arguably came close to war but was resolved peacefully. This "most similar systems" design is adopted in the hope that the relatively low number of differences between the participants and the crises will facilitate the identification of those differences that had the most crucial impact on the differing outcomes of the crises in question.

The basic results of this pseudo-experiment support the democratic peace proposition, as the crisis involving the jointly democratic Great Britain and France was resolved peacefully, whereas the crisis involving the democratic United States and the not quite democratic Spain was not. But the results lend themselves to many alternative explanations. Some of these are based on factors contained within categories of confounding variables defined by Donald Campbell and John Stanley (1963). Additional potentially confounding variables, such as proximity, power ratios, alliances, levels of economic development, militarization, and political stability have been identified in previous theoretical and empirical investigations of the democratic peace proposition.

Our pseudo-experimental analysis allows us to eliminate, just to cite one example, what Campbell and Stanley (1963) refer to as "instrumentation" or "autonomous changes in the measurement instrument" as a factor rivaling joint democracy as an explanatory factor, because both of the crises we analyze occurred in the same year, in 1898. "Proximity" can also be ruled out as a rival explanatory factor, because the crisis participants that were contiguous to each other (Great Britain and France) were, contrary to the prevailing pattern regarding proximity and conflict, able to resolve their crisis peacefully. The weakness of France's military in comparison with Great Britain's almost certainly had something to do with the peaceful resolution of the Fashoda Crisis, thus conforming to the general rule that ratios of power or greater power discrepancies have an important impact on the outcomes of crises and the probability of war between pairs of states. Furthermore, the analyses of these two cases have convinced me that probably the most important factor leading to the different outcomes of these crises involved the relative military weakness of the state (France) attempting to change the status quo in the Fashoda Crisis and the military superiority of the state intent on changing the status quo (that is, the United States) in the crisis leading to the Spanish-American War.

But differences in the military capabilities, or power ratios, cannot account for the results of our pseudo-experiment. In general, greater differences in capabilities make pairs of states less likely to become involved in a war with each other. But in our pseudo-experiment, the pair of states with the greater gap in power between the disputants turned out to be the pair that ended up in a war.

That fact, plus our analysis of the processes leading to the outcomes of the two crises, which brought to light, for example, the apparent impact of joint democracy on bargaining and diplomatic negotiations between Great Britain and France during the Fashoda Crisis, leads to the conclusion that joint democracy does help to account for the peaceful outcome of the Fashoda Crisis compared to the conflict escalation and eventual international war resulting from the crisis between the United States and Spain in 1898.

An Optimistic but Cautionary Coda

The main strength of the democratic peace proposition is its simplicity. It is a relatively straightforward proposition, and the most important supporting evidence (the absence of war between democratic states) requires no complex technique to unearth. Yet the proposition is also able to withstand complex, powerful, and sophisticated theoretical as well as empirical scrutiny. The proposition is deserving of the attention it has received up to this point and promises to become a standard feature of the academic field of international politics, influential ultimately among policymakers as well as the general public.

But there are at least two serious threats, I believe, to its future viability. One of these is that the idea that "democracies never make war against each other" was practically part of Bill Clinton's standard campaign rhetoric in 1992, and at this writing, President Clinton is apparently giving serious consideration to an invasion of Haiti. One important ostensible purpose of such an invasion would be to "restore democracy" to that unfortunate island. The rationale for this policy choice will certainly implicate the democratic peace proposition. It might even imply by extension that the undoing of the Communist revolution of this era needs to be followed by the rolling back of the anticolonial revolution of the post–World War II period, (in places like Haiti, Rwanda, Somalia, the Sudan, Cambodia, for example), a proposition about which I am yet to be convinced. In any case, if an invasion of Haiti or some similar foreign policy project launched by Clinton or some future president should turn out badly, the democratic peace proposition, or at least its policy relevance, will be seriously undermined.

But probably the greatest future (and current) threat to the viability of the democratic peace proposition as a focal point for theory and research in the field of international politics involves the possible occurrence of several international wars between quasi-democratic states. In the eyes of one relatively prominent commentator, the democratic peace proposition has already been discredited by such wars. Michael Kinsley (1994, 68) observes that "it used to be said that democracies don't fight each other." By itself, such an observation might be taken as an encouraging indication of the extent to which this notion has permeated the popular culture. But Kinsley goes on to note the following about the idea that "democracies don't fight each other": "It's a nice thought. Unfortunately, it's been disproved in Yugoslavia, where the fall of communism has brought a vicious three-way war. Serbia and Croatia, both under democratically elected Presidents, intermittently fight each other while jointly dismembering Bosnia . . . [T]he most common cause of war is nationalist hatred—which democracy, far from suppressing, actually gives vent to" (Kinsley 1994, 68).

I can discount with relative ease the relevance of any war involving Serbia to any attempt to discredit the democratic peace proposition. The formerly Communist Slobodan Milosevic is in power there, and no peaceful constitutional transfer of power to one of his political rivals is in sight.

But it might be more difficult to discount the ongoing "war" between India and Pakistan (both arguably democratic) high in the Himalayas. "For about nine years, soldiers from Pakistan and India have battled the elements and each other to stake a claim on the Siachen Glacier . . . in the Himalayan Mountains. . . . The war has cost the two sides an estimated 2000 men and millions of dollars" (Associated Press circa May 3, 1993).

Perhaps more disconcerting, for the world in general and for advocates of the democratic peace proposition in particular, are even more recent reports that the Indian Army has assembled 400,000 soldiers to crush a rebellion in Kashmir and that "in Pakistan, determination to support the rebel cause in Kashmir appears . . . strong." The Clinton administration has identified the crisis in Kashmir as one of the world's most dangerous because of fears that it could trigger a nuclear war between India and Pakistan. "Western intelligence reports have concluded that New Delhi and Islamabad have secretly assembled small stockpiles of nuclear warheads . . . and that a race is on to deploy missiles capable of delivering the warheads" (Burns 1994, 4).

Supporters of the democratic peace proposition might also ponder reports that in July of 1991, the government of Pakistan "placed its intelligence agencies on heightened alert and tightened security around its largest nuclear reactor in response to what one newspaper termed the threat of a 'joint India and Israeli' attack on nuclear facilities" (*Freedom in the World* 1992, 359). It is rather difficult to imagine an event that would do more damage to the credibility of the democratic peace proposition (which is not to suggest that this would be the most tragic aspect of such an event) than a trilateral war among uniformly democratic states involving nuclear weapons.

I would not predict that such a war will take place. But in the not-too-distant future Greece might attack Macedonia or Albania (and either attack might ultimately bring in Turkey against Greece), Russia might get involved in a war with Ukraine (over the Crimea), the Slovak Republic might become embroiled in military conflict with Hungary, and so on. I hope that the pacifying impact of democracy is sufficiently strong and that all these countries (and others) are sufficiently democratic that none of these international wars will actually take place.

But I am not confident that all the current conflicts involving democratic and quasi-democratic states will be resolved peacefully. I am confident that if and when one of these conflicts does escalate to war, defenders of the democratic peace proposition will be quick to insist that one or both of the participants are not "really" democratic states. I will probably be among them. One of the most important themes of this book implies that it will be crucial to the viability of the democratic peace proposition to resolve issues regarding wars between reputedly "democratic" states on the basis of a definition and a threshold of democracy that is theoretically informed, intuitively appealing, simple, operational, and precise. To be frank, my reading of several contemporary crises makes me wonder if the threshold developed in chapter 3 will prove to be up to the task of identifying precisely those states that are sufficiently democratic to avoid wars against each other, *while* at the same time not restricting the category of democratic states so much that the absence of wars between them will become statistically insignificant and substantively rather meaningless. At the moment, I would argue that peaceful constitutional transfers of power between independent political parties should be *an* element of such a threshold but that it may prove necessary to add additional elements. Having said that, I think it is necessary to acknowledge that if future events dictate that more than *very* small number of ad hoc modifications in that threshold be made in order to save the democratic peace proposition, it will be discredited, and deservedly so.

I hope, instead, that defenders of the democratic peace proposition can move quickly to some consensus on a definition of a threshold of democracy appropriate to the evaluation of that proposition. I also believe that the "pseudo-experimental" comparative case studies (in chapter 5) of the Spanish-American War and the Fashoda Crisis may serve as a useful model for the analysis of "crucial" cases that are likely to emerge in the coming years. The approach in that chapter, for example, might be applied to the analysis of a war between Greece and Albania, compared to the peaceful resolution of a crisis, say, between Hungary and the Slovak Republic. That, at least, is one of the assumptions that motivated that "pseudo-experiment." In any case, these promise to be interesting times for the democratic peace proposition and those who care to defend it.

References

Achen, Christopher H., and Duncan Snidal. 1988. "Rational Deterrence Theory and Comparative Case Studies." *World Politics* 41 (January): 143–70.

Allison, Graham T. 1971. *Essence of Decision.* Boston: Little, Brown.

Amery, L. S., ed. 1900. *The Times History of the War in South Africa, 1899–1900.* London: Sampson Sons.

Anderson, Paul A., and Timothy J. McKeown. 1987. "Changing Aspirations, Limited Attention, and War." *World Politics* 40 (October): 1–29.

Apter, David. 1965. *The Politics of Modernization.* Chicago: University of Chicago Press.

Archer, J. Clark, and Fred M. Shelley. 1988. "The Geography of U.S. Presidential Elections." *Scientific American* 259 (July): 44–52.

Auxier, George W. 1940. "Middle Western Newspapers and the Spanish-American War, 1895–1898." *Mississippi Valley Historical Review* 26 (March): 523–34.

Babst, Dean V. 1972. "A Force for Peace." *Industrial Research* 14 (April): 55–58.

Baloyra, Enrique, ed. 1987a. *Comparing New Democracies.* Boulder, Colo.: Westview.

———. 1987b. "Democracy Despite Development." *World Affairs* 150:73–92.

Bates, Darrell. 1984. *The Fashoda Incident of 1898: Encounter on the Nile.* New York: Oxford University Press.

Becker, Howard S. 1992. "Cases, Causes, Conjunctures, Stories and Imagery." In Charles C. Ragin and Howard S. Becker, eds., *What Is a Case?,* 205–16. New York: Cambridge University Press.

Belfield, Eversley. 1925. *The Boer War.* London: Archon.

Bello, Walden. 1986. *Visions of a Warless World.* Washington, D.C.: FCNL Education Fund.

Bergeson, Albert. 1992. "Communism's Collapse: A World-Systemic Explanation." *Journal of Political and Military Sociology* 20 (Summer): 133–51.

Bernstein, Carl. 1990. "The Leisure Empire." *Time,* December 24, 1990, 56, 69.

Berry, Frances Stokes, and William D. Berry. 1990. "State Lottery Adoption as Policy Innovation: An Event History Analysis." *American Political Science Review* 84 (June): 395–415.

Binyan, Liu. 1989. "Deng's Pyrrhic Victory." *New Republic* (October 2): 21–24.

Blainey, Geoffrey. 1988. *The Causes of War.* 3d ed. New York: Free Press.

Bollen, Kenneth A. 1980. "Issues in Comparative Measurement of Political Democracy." *American Sociological Review* 45 (June): 370–90.

———. 1983. "World-System Position, Dependency, and Democracy: The Cross-National Evidence." *American Sociological Review* 48 (August): 468–79.

———. 1990. "Political Democracy: Conceptual and Measurement Traps." *Studies in Comparative International Development* 25 (Spring): 7–24.

Bourke, John. 1942. "Kant's Doctrine of Perpetual Peace." *Philosophy* 17:324–33.

Branegan, Jay. 1993. "Is Singapore a Model for the West?" *Time* January 18, 36–37.

Brawley, Mark R. 1993. "Regime Types, Markets, and War." *Comparative Political Studies* 26 (July): 178–97.

Bremer, Stuart A. 1992. "Dangerous Dyads: Conditions Affecting the Likelihood of Interstate War, 1816–1965." *Journal of Conflict Resolution* 36 (June): 309–41.

———. 1993. "Democracy and Militarized Interstate Conflict, 1816–1965." *International Interactions* 18 (No. 3): 231–50.

Brown, Chris. 1992. *International Relations Theory: New Normative Approaches.* New York: Columbia University Press, 1992.

Brown, Roger Hamilton. 1964. *The Republic in Peril: 1812.* New York: Columbia University Press.

Brown, Roger Glenn. 1969. *Fashoda Reconsidered.* Baltimore: Johns Hopkins University Press.

Brzezinski, Zbigniew. 1989. *The Grand Failure.* New York: Scribner's.

Bueno de Mesquita, Bruce. 1981. *The War Trap.* New Haven, Conn.: Yale University Press.

———. 1984. "A Critique of 'A Critique of *The War Trap.*'" *Journal of Conflict Resolution* 28 (June): 341–60.

———. 1985. "Toward A Scientific Understanding of International Conflict: A Personal View." *International Studies Quarterly* 29 (June): 121–36.

———. 1988. "The Contribution of Expected Utility Theory to the Study of International Conflict." *Journal of Interdisciplinary History* 18 (Spring): 629–57.

Bueno de Mesquita, Bruce, and David Lalman. 1988. "Empirical Support for Systemic and Dyadic Explanations of International Conflict." *World Politics* 41:1–20.

———. 1990. "Domestic Opposition and Foreign War." *American Political Science Review* 84 (September): 747–66.

———. 1992. *War and Reason.* New Haven, Conn.: Yale University Press.

Bueno de Mesquita, Bruce, and Randolph M. Siverson. 1993. "War and the Survival of Political Leaders: A Comparative Analysis." Paper presented at the Annual Meeting of the American Political Science Association, Washington, D.C., September 1–4.

Bueno de Mesquita, Bruce, Randolph M. Siverson, and Gary Woller. 1992. "War and the Fate of Regimes: A Comparative Analysis." *American Political Science Review* 86 (September): 638–46.

Burns, John F. 1994. "Rebels in Kashmir and Indian Army Ready for a Long Fight." *New York Times,* May 16, section A, p. 4.

Caldwell, Bruce J. 1982. *Beyond Positivism: Economic Methodology in the Twentieth Century.* London: Allen and Unwin.

Campbell, Donald T. 1988a. "Quasi-Experimental Designs." In E. Samuel Overman, ed., *Methodology and Epistemology for Social Science,* 191–221. Chicago: University of Chicago Press.

———. 1988b. "Factors Relevant to the Validity of Experiments in Social Settings." In E. Samuel Overman, ed., *Methodology and Epistemology for Social Science,* 151–67. Chicago: University of Chicago Press.

Campbell, Donald T., and John C. Stanley. 1963. *Experiments and Quasi-Experimental Designs for Research.* Chicago: Rand McNally.

Cardoso, Fernando Henrique, and Enzo Faletto. 1978. *Dependency and Development in Latin America.* Berkeley and Los Angeles: University of California Press.

Carr, Edward Hallet. 1939; reprint, 1946. *The Twenty Years' Crisis, 1919–1939.* New York: Harper Torchbooks.

Carr, Raymond. 1982. *Spain, 1808–1975.* Oxford: Clarendon.

Cecil, Evelyn. 1900. *On the Eve of the War.* London: John Murray.

Cefkin, J. Leo. 1992. "Africa: A Truly Historic Year." In R. Bruce McColm, ed., *Freedom in the World,* 22–27. New York: Freedom House.

Central Intelligence Agency. 1989. *The World Factbook 1989.* Washington, D.C.: U.S. Government Printing Office.

Chan, Steve. 1984. "Mirror, Mirror on the Wall . . . Are the Freer Countries More Pacific?" *Journal of Conflict Resolution* 28 (December): 617–48.

Chapman, Charles. 1948. *A History of Spain.* New York: Macmillan.

Claggett, William, William Flanagan, and Nancy Zingale. 1984. "Nationalization of the American Electorate." *American Political Science Review* 78 (March): 77–91.

"Cold Warriors." 1993. An Associated Press Report, circa May 3. Published in the *Tampa Tribune,* May 3, Nation/World, p. 5.

Cole, Timothy Michael. 1990. "Politics and Meaning: Explaining the Democratic Peace." Prepared for delivery at the annual meeting of the American Political Science Association, San Francisco, August 30–September 2.

Coles, Harry L. 1965. *The War of 1812.* Chicago: University of Chicago Press.

Collingwood, R. G. 1974. "Human Nature and Human History." In Patrick Gardiner, ed., *The Philosophy of History,* 1–16. London: Oxford University Press.

Cook, Thomas D., and Donald T. Campbell. 1979. *Quasi-Experimentation: Design and Analysis for Field Settings.* Boston: Houghton Mifflin.

Coulter, E. Merton. 1950. *The Confederate States of America, 1816–1865.* Baton Rouge: Louisiana State University Press.

Craig, Gordon A. 1988. *The Triumph of Liberalism.* New York: Scribner's.

Dahl, Robert. 1971. *Polyarchy: Participation and Opposition.* New Haven, Conn: Yale University Press.

De Conde, Alexander. 1963. *A History of American Foreign Policy.* New York: Scribner's.

De Luna, Frederick A. 1969. *The French Republic under Cavaignac.* Princeton: Princeton University Press.

Dessler, David. 1991. "Beyond Correlation: Toward a Causal Theory of War." *International Studies Quarterly* 35 (September): 337–55.

Deudney, Daniel, and G. John Ikenberry. 1991/92. "The International Sources of Soviet Change." *International Security* 16 (Winter): 74–118.

Diamond, Larry, Juan J. Linz, and Seymour Martin Lipset, eds. 1989. *Democracy in Developing Countries: Latin America.* Boulder, Colo.: Lynne Reinner.

Diamond, Larry, Juan J. Linz, and Seymour Martin Lipset. 1989. Preface. In Larry Diamond, Juan J. Linz, and Seymour Martin Lipset, eds., *Democracy in Developing Countries: Latin America,* 4:ix–xxviii. Boulder, Colo.: Lynne Reinner.

Dixon, William J. 1993a. "Democracy and the Management of International Conflict." *Journal of Conflict Resolution* 37 (March): 42–68.

———. 1993b. "Democracy and the Mediation of International Conflict." Presented to the Annual Meeting of the American Political Science Association, Chicago, September 3–6.

———. 1994. "Democracy and the Peaceful Settlement of International Conflict." *American Political Science Review* 88 (March): 14–32.

Domke, William. 1988. *War and the Changing Global System*. New Haven, Conn.: Yale University Press.

Dostert, Pierre Etienne. 1990. *Latin America 1990*. Harpers Ferry, W.V.: Stryker-Post.

Dougherty, James E., and Robert L. Pfaltzgraff. 1990. *Contending Theories of International Relations*. 3d ed. New York: Harper and Row.

Downs, George W. 1976. *Bureaucracy, Innovation, and Public Policy*. Lexington, Mass.: Lexington Books.

Downum, Garland. 1971. "Review of *Fashoda Reconsidered* by Roger Glenn Brown." *Annals of the American Academy* 393:162.

Doyle, Michael W. 1983a. "Kant, Liberal Legacies, and Foreign Affairs." *Philosophy and Public Affairs* 12 (Summer): 205–35.

———. 1983b. "Kant, Liberal Legacies, and Foreign Affairs, Part 2." *Philosophy and Public Affairs* 12 (Fall): 323–57.

———. 1986. "Liberalism and World Politics." *American Political Science Review* 80 (December): 1151–70.

Dray, William. 1974. "The Historical Explanation of Actions Reconsidered." In Patrick Gardiner, ed., *The Philosophy of History*, 66–89. London: Oxford University Press.

Durning, Alan B. 1990. "Ending Poverty." In Lester Brown et al., *State of the World 1990*, 135–53. New York: Norton.

Dye, Thomas R., and Harmon Ziegler. 1988. "Socialism and Equality in Cross-National Perspective." *PS: Political Science and Politics* 21:45–56.

East, Maurice, and Philip M. Gregg. 1967. "Factors Influencing Cooperation and Conflict in the International System." *International Studies Quarterly* 11 (September): 244–69.

East, Maurice, and Charles K. Hermann. 1974. "Do Nation-Types Account for Foreign Policy Behavior?" In James N. Rosenau, ed., *Comparing Foreign Policies*, 209–303. New York: Wiley.

Eckstein, Alexander, and Ted Robert Gurr. 1975. *Patterns of Authority*. New York: Wiley.

Eckstein, Harry. 1975. "Case Study and Theory in Political Science." In Fred I. Greenstein and Nelson W. Polsby, eds., *Handbook of Political Science*, 79–132. Reading, Mass.: Addison-Wesley.

Economist. 1994. May 7, p. 118.

Edler, Friedrich. 1911. *The Dutch Republic and the American Revolution*. Baltimore: Johns Hopkins Press.

Elson, Ruth Miller. 1964. *Guardians of Tradition: American Schoolbooks of the Nineteenth Century*. Lincoln: University of Nebraska Press.

Encyclopedia Britannica. 1990. Vol. 27. Chicago: Encyclopedia Britannica Inc.

Eskelinen, Heikki. 1973. "Independence and After." In Sylvie Nickels, Hillar Kollas and Philippa Friedman, *Finland: An Introduction*, 40–62. New York: Praeger.

Fagen, Richard. 1978. "A Funny Thing Happened on the Way to the Market." *International Organization* 32 (Winter): 287–300.

Fatton, Richard, Jr. 1990. "Liberal Democracy in Africa." *Political Science Quarterly* 105:455–74.

Fearon, James D. 1991. "Counterfactuals and Hypothesis Testing in Political Science." *World Politics* 43:169–95.

Fein, E. B. 1989. "Glasnost Is Opening the Door on Poverty." *New York Times,* January 29, section 1, p. 1.

Finley, M. I. 1973. *Democracy Ancient and Modern.* New Brunswick, N.J.: Rutgers University Press.

———. 1979. *Ancient Sicily.* London: Chatto and Windum.

Fisher, W. E. Garrett. 1900. *The Transvaal and the Boers.* London: Chapman and Hall.

Foner, Philip S. 1972. *The Spanish-Cuban-American War and the Birth of American Imperialism, 1895–1902.* New York: Monthly Review.

Forsythe, David P. 1992. "Democracy, War, and Covert Action." *Journal of Peace Research* 29 (November): 385–95.

Frank, Andre Gunder. 1968. *Development and Underdevelopment in Latin America.* New York: Monthly Review Press.

Freedom in the World, 1991–92. 1992. New York: Freedom House.

Friedman, Milton. 1953. "The Methodology of Positive Economics." *Essays in Positive Economics.* Chicago: University of Chicago Press.

Fukuyama, Francis. 1989. "The End of History?" *National Interest* No. 16 (Summer): 3–18.

———. 1992. *The End of History and the Last Man.* New York: Free Press.

Gaddis, John Lewis. 1986. "The Long Peace: Elements of Stability in the Postwar International System." *International Security* 10:99–142.

Galbraith, John Kenneth. 1975. *Money: Whence It Came, Where It Went.* New York: Bantam.

Garraty, John A., and Peter Gay, eds. 1972. *The Columbia History of the World.* New York: Harper and Row.

Gastil, Raymond Duncan. 1990. "The Comparative Survey of Freedom: Experiences and Suggestions." *Studies in Comparative International Development* 25 (Spring): 25–50.

Gaubatz, Kurt Taylor. 1993. "None Dare Call it Reason." Presented at the Annual Convention of the American Political Science Association, Washington, D. C., September 2–5.

Geller, Daniel S. 1985. *Domestic Factors in Foreign Policy.* Cambridge, Mass.: Schenkman.

George, Alexander. 1979. "Case Studies and Theory Development: The Method of Structured, Focused Comparisons," In Paul Gordon Lauren, ed., *Diplomacy: New Approaches in History, Theory, and Policy,* 43–68. New York: Free Press.

Gerschenkron, Alexander. 1962. *Economic Backwardness in Historical Perspective.* Cambridge: Belknap Press of Harvard University Press.

Geva, Nehemia, Karl R. DeRouen, and Alex Mintz. 1993. "The Political Incentive Explanation of 'Democratic Peace': Evidence from Experimental Research." *International Interactions* 18:215–30.

Gilbert, Alan. 1992. "Must Global Politics Constrain Democracy?" *Political Theory* 20 (February): 8–37.

Gillespie, Charles. 1987. "From Authoritarian Crisis to Democratic Transition." *Latin American Research Review* 22:165–85.

Gleditsch, Nils Petter. 1992. "Democracy and Peace." *Journal of Peace Research* 29 (November): 369–76.

———. 1993. "Democracy, Opportunity and War." Presented at the Annual Convention of the International Studies Association, Acapulco, Mexico, March 23–27.

Gurr, Ted Robert. 1974. "Persistence and Change in Political Systems, 1800–1971." *American Political Science Review* 48 (December): 1482–1504.

———. 1978. *Polity Data Handbook.* Ann Arbor, Mich.: Inter-University Consortium for Political and Social Research.

Gurr, Ted Robert, Keith Jaggers, and Will H. Moore. 1989. *Polity II Codebook.* Boulder, Colo.: Department of Political Science.

———. 1990. "The Transformation of the Western State: The Growth of Democracy, Autocracy, and State Power since 1800." *Studies in Comparative International Development* 25 (Spring): 73–108.

Haas, Michael. 1965. "Societal Approaches to the Study of War." *Journal of Peace Research* 2 (No. 4): 307–23.

Hale, William. 1990. "The Turkish Army in Politics, 1960–1973." In Andrew Finkel and Nukhet Sirman, eds., *Turkish State, Turkish Society,* 183–212. London: Routledge.

Harre, Rom, and Edward Madden. 1975. *Causal Powers.* Totowa, N.J.: Rowman and Littlefield.

Hausman, Daniel. 1983. "Are There Causal Relations among Dependent Variables?" *Philosophy of Science* 50:58–81.

Hayden, Joseph Ralston. 1942. *The Philippines: A Study in National Development.* New York: Macmillan.

Hearnshaw, F. J. C. 1919. *An Outline Sketch of the Political History of Europe.* London: Macmillan.

Heilbroner, Robert. 1959. *The Future as History.* New York: Harper and Row.

Heise, Lorie. 1989. "Life and Death in the USSR." *Worldwatch* 2:26–37.

Hempel, Carl. 1962. "Explanation in Science and History." In Robert G. Colodny, ed., *Frontiers of Science and Philosophy,* 7–34. Pittsburgh: University of Pittsburgh Press.

———. 1965. *Aspects of Scientific Explanation.* New York: Free Press.

———. 1974. "Reasons and Covering Laws in Historical Explanations." In Patrick Gardiner, ed., *The Philosophy of History,* 90–105. London: Oxford University Press.

Herr, Richard. 1971. *Spain.* Englewood Cliffs, N.J.: Prentice-Hall.

Herring, Hubert. 1972. *A History of Latin America.* New York: Knopf.

Hickey, Donald R. 1989. *The War of 1812.* Urbana: University of Illinois Press.

Historical Statistics of the United States: Colonial Times to 1970. 1975. Washington, D.C.: Bureau of the Census.

Holcombe, Randall G. 1992. "The Distributive Model of Government: Evidence From the Confederate Constitution." *Southern Economic Journal* 58 (January): 762–69.

Hollis, Martin, and Steve Smith. 1990. *Explaining and Understanding International Relations.* New York: Oxford University Press.

Hume, David. 1748; reprint, 1955. *An Inquiry Concerning Human Understanding.* Charles W. Hendel, ed. New York: Liberal Arts Press.

Huntington, Samuel P. 1968. *Political Order in Changing Societies.* New Haven, Conn.: Yale University Press.

———. 1991. *The Third Wave: Democratization in the Late Twentieth Century.* Norman: University of Oklahoma Press.

Huth, Paul, Christopher Gelpi, and D. Scott Bennett. 1993. "The Escalation of Great Power Militarized Disputes: Testing Rational Deterrence Theory and Structural Realism." *American Political Science Review* 87 (September): 609–23.

Inkeles, Alex. 1990. "Introduction: On Measuring Democracy." *Studies in Comparative International Development* 25 (Spring): 3–6.

Isaac, Jeffrey. 1987. "After Empiricism: The Realist Alternative." In Terence Ball, ed., *Idioms of Inquiry,* 187–205. Albany: State University of New York Press.

James, Patrick. 1988. *Crisis and War.* Kingston and Montreal: McGill-Queens University Press.

James, Patrick, and Glenn E. Mitchell. 1994. "Targets of Covert Pressure: The Hidden Victims of the Democratic Peace." Unpublished manuscript.

Jervis, Robert. 1985. "Pluralistic Rigor: A Comment on Bueno de Mesquita." *International Studies Quarterly* 29:145–50.

Johnson, Paul. 1983. *Modern Times.* New York: Harper and Row.

———. 1988. *Intellectuals.* New York: Harper and Row.

———. 1991. *Birth of the Modern.* New York: HarperCollins.

Jones, E. Terrence. 1971. *Conducting Political Research.* New York: Harper and Row.

Jonge, Alex de. 1986. *Stalin and the Shaping of the Soviet Union.* New York: William Morrow.

Kant, Immanuel. 1795; reprint, 1983. "To Perpetual Peace: A Philosophical Sketch." Translated by Ted Humphrey. Indianapolis, Ind.: Hackett.

Kantor, Harry. 1969. *Patterns of Politics and Political Systems in Latin America.* Chicago: Rand McNally.

Karatnycky, Adrian. 1993. "In Global Vacuum, Tyranny Advances." *Wall Street Journal,* December 16, section A, p. 16.

———. 1994. "Freedom in Retreat." *Freedom Review* (February): 4–9.

Karnow, Stanley. 1989. *In Our Image: American Empire in the Philippines.* New York: Random.

Kassmann, E. H. 1978 *The Low Countries, 1780–1940.* Oxford: Clarendon.

Katz, Richard S. 1973. "The Attribution of Variance in Electoral Returns: An Alternative Measurement Technique." *American Political Science Review* 67 (June): 817–28.

Keltie, J. S. 1898. *The Statesman's Year-book.* New York: St. Martin's Press.

Keohane, Robert O. 1983. "Theory of World Politics: Structural Realism and Beyond." In Ada Finifter, ed., *Political Science: The State of the Discipline,* 541–78. Washington, D.C.: American Political Science Association.

Kinsley, Michael. 1994. "Is Democracy Losing Its Romance?" *Time,* January 17, p. 68.

Kitschelt, Herbert. 1992. "Political Regime Change: Structure and Process-Driven Explanations?" *American Political Science Review* 86:1028–34.

Knutsen, Torbjorn. 1992. *A History of International Relations Theory.* Manchester: Manchester University Press.

Krasner, Stephen D. 1985. "Toward Understanding in International Relations." *International Studies Quarterly* 29:137–44.

Kristoff, Nicholas D. 1990. "A Mongolian Rock Group Fosters Democracy." *New York Times,* March 26, section B, p. 1.

―――. 1992. "China Sees Singapore as Model for Progress." *New York Times,* August 9, p. 4.

"Khrushchev Speaks on Economic and Technical Progress." 1957. *Bulletin of Atomic Scientists* 13 (December): 360.

LaFeber, Walter. 1963. *The New Empire: An Interpretation of American Expansion, 1860–1898.* Ithaca, N.Y.: Cornell University Press.

Lake, David. 1992. "Powerful Pacifists: Democratic States and War." *American Political Science Review* 86 (March): 24–37.

Langer, William. 1965. *The Diplomacy of Imperialism,* 2d ed. New York: Knopf.

Laski, Harold. 1932. "The Position and the Prospects of Communism." *Foreign Affairs* 11:94–108.

Lave, Charles, and James March. 1975. *An Introduction to Models in the Social Sciences.* New York: Harper and Row.

Leng, Russell J. 1993. "Reciprocating Influence Strategies in International Crisis Bargaining." *Journal of Conflict Resolution* 37 (March): 3–41.

Levine, Daniel. 1988. "Paradigm Lost: Dependence and Democracy." *World Politics* 40:377–94.

Levy, Jack S. 1983. *War in the Modern Great Power System, 1495–1975.* Lexington: University Press of Kentucky.

―――. 1988. "Domestic Politics and War." *Journal of Interdisciplinary History* 18 (Spring): 653–77.

―――. 1989. "The Causes of War: A Review of Theories and Evidence." In Philip E. Tetlock, Jo L. Husbands, Robert Jervis, Paul C. Stern, and Charles Tilly, eds., *Behavior, Society, and Nuclear War,* 174–208. New York: Oxford University Press.

Lijpart, Arendt. 1971. "Comparative Politics and the Comparative Method." *American Political Science Review* 45 (September): 682–93.

―――. 1974. "The Netherlands: Continuity and Change in Voting Behavior." In Richard Rose, ed., *Electoral Behavior: A Comparative Handbook,* 227–70. New York: Free Press.

Lincoln, Jennie K. 1984. "Peruvian Foreign Policy Since the Return to Democratic Rule." In Jennie K. Lincoln and Elizabeth G. Ferris, eds., *The Dynamics of Latin American Foreign Policies,* 137–49. Boulder, Colo.: Westview.

Linderman, Gerald F. 1974. *The Mirror of War: American Society and the Spanish-American War.* Ann Arbor: University of Michigan Press.

Lloyd, William Brass, Jr. 1958. *Waging Peace: The Swiss Experience.* Washington, D.C.: Public Affairs Press.

Lodge, Henry Cabot. 1899; reprint, 1970. *The War with Spain.* New York: Harper and Brothers; New York: Arno Press and the New York Times.

Luck, James Murray. 1985. *A History of Switzerland.* Palo Alto, Calif.: SPOSS Inc.

Maoz, Zeev. 1982. *Paths to Conflict: International Dispute Initiation.* Boulder, Colo.: Westview.

Maoz, Zeev, and Nasrin Abdolali. 1989. "Regime Types and International Conflict, 1817–1976." *Journal of Conflict Resolution* 33 (March): 3–35.

Maoz, Zeev, and Bruce Russett. 1992. "Alliance, Contiguity, Wealth, and Political Stability: Is the Lack of Conflict among Democracies a Statistical Artifact?" *International Interactions* 17 (No. 3): 245–67.

———. 1993. "Normative and Structural Causes of Democratic Peace, 1946–1986." *American Political Science Review* 87 (September): 624–38.

Markham, James M. 1989. "The East-West Flow of People and Ideas." *New York Times,* February 5, section 4, p. 5.

Markides, Kyriaros. 1977. *The Rise and Fall of the Cyprus Republic.* New Haven, Conn.: Yale University Press.

May, Ernest. 1961. *Imperial Democracy.* New York: Harcourt, Brace.

Mayes, Stanley. 1981. *Makarios: A Biography.* London: Macmillan.

McColm, R. Bruce. 1992. "The Comparative Survey of Freedom 1991–92: Between Two Worlds." In R. Bruce McColm, ed., *Freedom in the World,* 47–52. New York: Freedom House.

McCracken, William D. 1892. *The Rise of the Swiss Republic.* Boston, Mass.: Arena Publishing.

McGaw, Dickinson, and George Watson. 1976. *Political and Social Inquiry.* New York: Wiley.

McKay, Derek, and H. M. Scott. 1983. *The Rise of the Great Powers, 1648–1815.* New York: Longman.

McMullen, Ernan. 1984. "Two Ideals of Explanation in Natural Science." In Peter French, ed., *Causation and Causal Theories,* 205–20. Minneapolis: University of Minnesota Press.

Mead, W. R. 1968. *Finland.* New York: Praeger.

Mearsheimer, John J. 1990. "Back to the Future: Instability in Europe after the Cold War." *International Security* 15 (Summer): 5–56.

Meckstroth, Theodore W. 1975. "'Most Different Systems' and 'Most Similar Systems': A Study in the Logic of Comparative Inquiry." *Comparative Political Studies* 8 (July): 132–57.

Medhurst, Kenneth W. 1973. *Government in Spain.* Oxford: Pergamon.

Meigs, Russell. 1972. *The Athenian Empire.* Oxford: Clarendon.

Midlarsky, Manus I. 1989. "Introduction." In Manus I. Midlarsky, ed., *Handbook of War Studies,* xv–xxi. Boston: Unwin Hyman.

Miller, Stuart Creighton. 1982. *"Benevolent Assimilation": The American Conquest of the Philippines.* New Haven, Conn.: Yale University Press.

Miller, R. W. 1987. *Fact and Method: Explanation, Confirmation and Reality in the Natural and Social Sciences.* Princeton, N.J.: Princeton University Press.

Mintz, Alex, and Nehemia Geva. 1993. "Why Don't Democracies Fight Each Other?" *Journal of Conflict Resolution* 37 (September): 484–503.

Modelski, George. 1989. "Is America's Decline Inevitable?" *The Bridge* 19 (Summer): 1–18.

———. 1990. "Is World Politics Evolutionary Learning?" *International Organization* 44:1–24.

Modelski, George, and Gardner Perry III. 1991. "Democratization in Long Perspective." *Technological Forecasting and Social Change* 39:23–34.

Moe, Terry. 1979. "On the Scientific Status of Rational Models." *American Journal of Political Science* 23:215–43.

Mohr, Lawrence B. 1990. "Causality for the Social Sciences." Prepared for delivery at the annual meeting of the American Political Science Association, San Francisco, August 30–September 2.

————. 1992. "Causation and the Case Study." Paper delivered at the annual meeting of the World Association for Case Method Research and Application, Limerick, Ireland, June 21–24.

Moore, Barrington, Jr. 1966. *Social Origins of Dictatorship and Democracy.* Boston: Beacon.

Morgan, T. Clifton. 1993. "Democracy and War: Reflections in the Literature." *International Interactions* 18 (No. 3): 197–203.

Morgan, T. Clifton, and Sally Howard Campbell. 1991. "Domestic Structure, Decisional Constraints and War." *Journal of Conflict Resolution* 35 (June): 187–211.

Morgan, T. Clifton, and Valerie Schwebach. 1992. "Take Two Democracies and Call Me in the Morning: A Prescription for Peace?" *International Interactions* 17 (No. 4): 305–20.

Morgenthau, Hans J. 1948. *Politics among Nations.* New York: Knopf.

————. 1958. "Russian Technology and American Policy." *Current History* 34:133–34.

————. 1967. *Politics among Nations.* 4th ed. New York: Knopf.

Mueller, John 1989. *Retreat From Doomsday: The Obsolescence of Major War.* New York: Basic Books.

————. 1991. "Is War Still Becoming Obsolete?" Prepared for presentation at the annual meeting of the American Political Science Association, Washington, D.C. August 29–September 1.

Necatigil, Zaim. 1989. *The Cyprus Question and the Turkish Position in International Law.* Oxford: Oxford University Press.

Nef, Jorge. 1988. "The Trend Toward Democratization and Redemocratization in Latin America." *Latin American Research Review* 23:131–53.

New York Times. 1981a. January 30, section A, p. 6.

New York Times. 1981b. February 2, section A, p. 1.

New York Times. 1981c. February 10, section A, p. 2.

New York Times. 1992. June 1, section A, pp. 1, 8.

Newsweek. 1958. "A World at Stake." January 20, p. 69.

Newsweek. 1957. "Satellites and Our Safety: Stepping Up the Pace." October 21, p. 29.

Nye, Joseph S., Jr. 1993. *Understanding International Conflicts.* New York: HarperCollins.

O'Donnell, Guillermo. 1973. *Modernization and Bureaucratic-Authoritarianism.* Berkeley: Institute of International Studies, University of California.

O'Donnell, Guillermo, and Philippe C. Schmitter. 1986. "Tentative Conclusions about Uncertain Democracies." In Guillermo O'Donnell, Philippe C. Schmitter, and Laurence Whitehead, eds., *Transitions from Authoritarian Rule,* 1–78. Baltimore: Johns Hopkins University Press.

————, eds. 1986. *Transitions from Authoritarian Rule: Comparative Perspectives.* Baltimore: Johns Hopkins University Press, 1986.

Offner, John L. 1992. *An Unwanted War.* Chapel Hill: University of North Carolina Press.

Olson, Mancur. 1982. *The Rise and Decline of Nations*. New Haven, Conn.: Yale University Press.

Oneal, John R., Frances H. Oneal, Zeev Maoz, and Bruce Russett. 1993. "The Liberal Peace: Interdependence, Democracy, and International Conflict, 1950–1986." Unpublished manuscript.

Ortega, Jose Varela. 1980. "Aftermath of Splendid Disaster: Spanish Politics before and after the Spanish American War of 1898." *Journal of Contemporary History* 15:311–29.

Owen, John. 1993. "Public Opinion and the Democratic Peace: Two Cases." Chapter from "Developing the Democratic Peace: American Diplomatic Crises," Ph.D. diss., Harvard University, forthcoming.

Pacis, Vicente Abramo, Jose M. Aruego, Estaban de Ocampo, Carlos Quirinio, Jose Luna Castro, Marino Garcia, Isidrio Netizos, and D. M. Lariano. 1971. *Founders of Freedom: The History of the Three Philippine Constitutions*. Manila: Capital Publishing.

Packenham, Robert. 1973. *Liberal America in the Third World*. Princeton, N.J.: Princeton University Press.

Pakenham, Thomas. 1979. *The Boer War*. New York: Random.

Palmer, R. R. 1964. *The Age of Democratic Revolution*. Princeton: Princeton University Press.

Parish, Peter. 1975. *The American Civil War*. New York: Holmes and Meier.

Popper, Karl. 1963. *The Open Society and Its Enemies*. Vol. 1. Princeton, N.J.: Princeton University Press.

Przeworski, Adam, and Henry Teune. 1970. *The Logic of Social Inquiry*. New York: Wiley-Interscience.

Pye, Lucian. 1990. "Political Science and the Crisis of Authoritarianism." *American Political Science Review* 84:3–29.

Quester, George H. 1990. *The International Politics of Television*. Lexington, Mass.: Lexington Books.

Rapoport, Anatol. 1961. "Various Meanings of 'Theory.'" In James N. Rosenau, ed., *International Politics and Foreign Policy,* 44–52. New York: Free Press.

Ray, James Lee. 1974. *Status Inconsistency and War Involvement Among European States, 1816–1970*. Ph.D. diss., University of Michigan.

———. 1981. "Dependence, Political Compliance, and Economic Performance: Latin America and Eastern Europe." In Charles W. Kegley, Jr., and Pat McGowan, eds., *The Political Economy of Foreign Policy Behavior,* 111–36. Beverly Hills, Calif.: Sage.

———. 1982a. "Designing Research on the World-System." *Comparative Political Studies* 15:364–70.

———. 1982b. "Understanding Rummel." *Journal of Conflict Resolution* 26 (March): 161–87.

———. 1989. "The Abolition of Slavery and the End of International War." *International Organization* 43 (Summer): 405–39.

———. 1992. *Global Politics*. 5th ed. Boston: Houghton Mifflin.

———. 1995a. "The Future of International War: Global Trends and Middle Eastern Implications." In Mark Tessler and David Garnham, eds., *Democracy, War and Peace in the Middle East*. Bloomington: University of Indiana Press.

————. 1995b. "Promise or Peril? Neorealism, Neoliberalism, and the Future of International Politics." In Charles W. Kegley, ed., *Realism and the Neoliberal Challenge*. New York: St. Martin's.

Raymond, Gregory A. 1994. "Democracies, Disputes, and Third-Party Intermediaries." *Journal of Conflict Resolution* 38 (March): 24–42.

Reddaway, John. 1986. *Burdened With Cyprus*. London: Weidenfeld and Nicolson.

Reischauer, Edwin O. 1964. *Japan: Past and Present*. 3d ed. New York: Knopf.

Remmer, Karen. 1990. "Democracy and Economic Crisis: The Latin American Experience." *World Politics* 42:315–35.

————. 1992–93. "The Process of Democratization in Latin America." *Studies in Comparative International Development* 27:2–34.

Riker, T. W. 1929. "A Survey of British Policy in the Fashoda Crisis." *Political Science Quarterly* 44:54–78.

Rose, Richard. 1974. "Britain: Simple Abstractions and Complex Realities." In Richard Rose, ed., *Electoral Behavior: A Comparative Handbook*, 481–542. New York: Free Press.

Rosecrance, R., A. Alexandroff, W. Koehler, J. Kroll, S. Laqueuer, and J. Stocker. 1977. "Whither Interdependence?" *International Organization* 31 (Summer): 425–72.

Rosenau, James N. 1966. "Pre-Theories and Theories of Foreign Policy." In R. Barry Farrell, ed., *Approaches to Comparative and International Politics*, 27–92. Evanston, Ill.: Northwestern University Press.

————. 1990. *Turbulence in World Politics*. Princeton: Princeton University Press.

Rueshemeyer, Dietrich, Evelyne Huber Stephens, and John D. Stephens. 1992. *Capitalist Development and Democracy*. Chicago: University of Chicago Press.

Rummel, R. J. 1975. *Understanding Conflict and War: Volume 1, The Dynamic Psychological Field*. New York: Sage.

————. 1976. *Understanding Conflict and War: Volume 2, The Conflict Helix*. New York: Sage.

————. 1977. *Understanding Conflict and War: Volume 3, Conflict in Perspective*. New York: Sage.

————. 1979. *Understanding Conflict and War: Volume 4, War, Power, Peace*. New York: Sage.

————. 1981. *Understanding Conflict and War: Volume 5, The Just Peace*. New York: Sage.

————. 1983. "Libertarianism and Interstate Violence." *Journal of Conflict Resolution* 27 (March): 27–71.

————. 1984. "On Fostering a Just Peace." *International Journal on World Peace* 1 (Autumn): 4–15.

————. 1985. "Libertarian Propositions on Violence within and between Nations: A Test against Published Results." *Journal of Conflict Resolution* 29 (September): 419–55.

————. 1989. "Roots of Faith II." In Joseph Kruzel and James N. Rosenau, eds., *Journeys through World Politics*, 311–28. Lexington, Mass.: Lexington Books.

————. 1994. "The Most Important Fact of Our Time." Working draft of chapter 2 in *Power Kills: Democracy as Method of Nonviolence*. Forthcoming.

Russett, Bruce. 1970. "International Behavioral Research: Case Studies and Cumulation." In Michael Haas and Henry S. Kariel, eds., *Approaches in the Study of Political Science,* 425–43. Scranton, Penn.: Chandler.

——. 1983. "International Interactions and Processes: The Internal and External Debate Revisited." In Ada Finifter, ed., *Political Science: The State of the Discipline,* 541–78. Washington, D.C.: American Political Science Association.

——. 1985. "The Mysterious Case of Vanishing Hegemony: Or, Is Mark Twain Really Dead?" *International Organization* 39:207–32.

——. 1990. *Controlling the Sword.* Cambridge, Mass.: Harvard University Press.

——. 1993. *Grasping the Democratic Peace.* Princeton, N.J.: Princeton University Press.

Russett, Bruce, and William Antholis. 1992. "Do Democracies Fight Each Other? Evidence from the Peloponnesian War." *Journal of Peace Research* 29 (November): 415–34.

Russett, Bruce, with Zeev Maoz. 1993. "The Democratic Peace since World War II." Chapter 3 in *Grasping the Democratic Peace* by Bruce Russett. Princeton: Princeton University Press.

Russett, Bruce, and Harvey Starr. 1985. *World Politics: The Menu for Choice.* New York: Freeman.

Ryback, Timothy W. 1990. *Rock Around the Bloc.* New York: Oxford University Press.

Salmon, Wesley. 1985. "Conflicting Conceptions of Scientific Explanation." *Journal of Philosophy* 82:651–54.

Salmore, Stephen A., and Charles F. Hermann. 1969. "The Effect of Size, Development and Accountability on Foreign Policy." *Peace Science Society Papers* 14:16–30.

Schevill, Ferdinand. 1940. *A History of Europe.* New York: Harcourt Brace.

Schrodt, Philip A. 1990. "A Methodological Critique of a Test of the Effects of the Mararishi Technology of the Unified Field." *Journal of Conflict Resolution* 34:745–55.

Schweller, Randall L. 1992. "Domestic Structure and Preventive War." *World Politics* 44 (June): 235–69.

Share, Donald. 1986. *The Making of Spanish Democracy.* New York: Praeger.

Shearman, Hugh. 1950. *Finland: The Adventures of a Small Power.* New York: Praeger.

Shelley, Fred M. 1989. "Sectionalism and Presidential Politics." *Journal of Interdisciplinary History* 20 (Autumn): 227–56.

Simon, Julian L. 1969. *Basic Research Methods in Social Science.* New York: Random.

Singer, J. David. 1979. "Introduction." In J. David Singer, ed., *Explaining War: Selected Papers from the Correlates of War Project,* 11–20. Beverly Hills: Sage.

——. 1988. "Reconstructing the Correlates of War Dataset on Material Capabilities of States, 1816–1965." *International Interactions* 14 (No. 2): 115–31.

——. 1991. "Peace in the Global System: Displacement, Interregnum, or Transformation?" In Charles W. Kegley, Jr., ed., *The Long Peace,* 56–84. New York: HarperCollins.

Singer, Max, and Aaron Wildavsky. 1993. *The Real World Order.* Chatham, N.J.: Chatham House.

Siverson, Randolph M., and Harvey Starr. 1991. *The Diffusion of War.* Ann Arbor: University of Michigan Press.

Sorenson, Georg. 1992. "Kant and Processes of Democratization: Consequences of Neorealist Thought." *Journal of Peace Research* 29 (November): 397–414.

Small, Melvin, and J. David Singer. 1976. "The War-Proneness of Democratic Regimes, 1816–1965." *Jerusalem Journal of International Relations* 1 (Summer): 50–69.

———. 1982. *Resort to Arms.* Beverly Hills: Sage.

Smith, Dale L., and James Lee Ray. 1993. "European Integration: Gloomy Theory Versus Rosy Reality." In Dale L. Smith and James Lee Ray, eds., *The 1992 Project and the Future of Integration in Europe,* 19–44. Armonk, N.Y.: M. E. Sharpe.

Starr, Harvey. 1991. "Democratic Dominoes: Diffusion Approaches to the Spread of Democracy in the International System." *Journal of Conflict Resolution* 35:356–81.

———. 1992a. "Democracy and War: Choice, Learning, and Security Communities." *Journal of Peace Research* 29 (May): 207–14.

———. 1992b. "Why Don't Democracies Fight One Another—Evaluating the Theory-Findings Feedback Loop." *Jerusalem Journal of International Relations* 14 (No. 4): 41–59.

Stegler, Carl. 1962. "America: World Power by Accident." *New York Herald Tribune,* February 11, p. 8.

Stokes, Donald E. 1965. " A Variance Components Model of Political Effects." In J. M Claunch, ed., *Mathematical Applications in Political Science,* 61–85. Dallas: Arnold Foundation.

———. 1967. "Parties and the Nationalization of Electoral Forces." In W. N. Chambers and W. D. Burnham, eds., *The American Party Systems: Stages of Political Development,* 182–202. New York: Oxford University Press.

Sullivan, Michael. 1976. *International Relations: Theories and Evidence.* Englewood Cliffs, N.J.: Prentice-Hall.

Thompson, Leonard. 1990. *A History of South Africa.* New Haven, Conn.: Yale University Press.

Trask, David F. 1981. *The War with Spain in 1898.* New York: Macmillan.

Treadgold, Donald W. 1990. *Freedom: A History.* New York: New York University Press.

Tuchanski, Barbara. 1992. "What Is Explained in Science?" *Philosophy of Science* 59:102–19.

Tuchman, Barbara. 1966. *The Proud Tower.* New York: Bantam.

Ullman, O. 1990. "Soviet Economy in Ruins." *Albuquerque Tribune,* December 22, section A, pp. 1–3.

Van Schoor, M. C. E. 1986. "The Orange Free State." In C. F. J. Muller, ed., *Five Hundred Years: A History of South Africa,* 234–55. Pretoria: Academica.

Vandenbosch, Amry. 1959. *Dutch Foreign Policy since 1815.* The Hague: Martinus Nijhoff.

VanderEssen, Leon. 1916. *A Short History of Belgium.* Chicago: University of Chicago Press.

Vanhanen, Tatu. 1990. *The Process of Democratization.* New York: Crane Russak.

Verba, Sydney. 1967. "Some Dilemmas in Comparative Research." *World Politics* 20:111–27.

Verduin, Arnold. 1941. *Manual of Spanish Constitutions, 1808–1931: Translations and Introductions.* Ypsilanti, Mich.: University Lithoprinter.

Walker, Jack L. 1969. "The Diffusion of Innovations among the American States." *American Political Science Review* 63:880–99.

Wallace, Robert. 1957. "First Hard Facts on All Russian Science." *Life,* December 16, pp. 109–22.

Wallensteen, Peter. 1973. *Structure and War.* Stockhom: Raben & Sjogren.

Waltz, Kenneth N. 1954; reprint, 1959. *Man, the State and War.* New York: Columbia University Press.

———. 1962. "Kant, Liberalism, and War." *American Political Science Review* 56 (June): 331–40.

———. 1979. *Theory of International Politics.* New York: Random, 1979.

———. 1986. "Reductionist and Systemic Theories." In Robert O. Keohane, ed., *Neorealism and Its Critics,* 45–69. New York: Columbia University Press.

———. 1990. "On the Nature of States and Their Recourse to Violence." *United States Institute of Peace Journal* 3:6–7.

———. 1993. "The Emerging Structure of International Politics." *International Security* 18:44–79.

Wang, Hongying. 1992. "Liberal Peace? A Study of the Fashoda Crisis of 1898." Prepared for Delivery at the Annual Meeting of the American Political Science Association, Chicago, September 3–6.

Wang, Kevin, Noh Soon Chang, and James Lee Ray. 1992. "Democracy and the Use of Force in Militarized Disputes: A Subdyadic Level Analysis." Paper prepared for the Annual Meeting of the American Political Science Association. September 3–6, Chicago, Illinois.

Ward, Michael. 1978. *The Political Economy of Distribution.* New York: Elsevier.

Weart, Spencer. 1991. "Why Don't Democracies Make War on One Another?" Manuscript.

———. 1994a. "Peace Among Democratic and Oligarchic Republics." *Journal of Peace Research* 31 (August): 299–316.

———. 1994b. *Never at War.* Manuscript.

Weede, Erich. 1984. "Democracy and War Involvement." *Journal of Peace Research* 28 (December): 649–64.

———. 1992. "Some Simple Calculations on Democracy and War Involvement." *Journal of Peace Research* 29 (November): 377–83.

Wendt, Alexander. 1987. "The Agent-Structure Problem in International Relations Theory." *International Organization* 41 (Summer): 335–70.

Whitehead, Laurence. 1986. "International Aspects of Democratization." In Guillermo O'Donnell, Philippe C. Schmitter, and Laurence Whitehead, eds., *Transitions from Authoritarian Rule,* 3–46. Baltimore: Johns Hopkins University Press.

Wilkenfeld, Jonathan, Michael Brecher, and Sheila Moses. 1988. *Crises in the Twentieth Century.* New York: Pergamon.

Wilkerson, Marcus M. 1932. *Public Opinion and the Spanish-American War.* Baton Rouge: Louisiana State University Press.

Wilson, Monica, and Leonard Thompson. 1971. *The Oxford History of South Africa.* Oxford: Clarendon.

Winch, Robert F., and Donald T. Campbell. 1969. "Proof? No. Evidence? Yes. The Significance of Tests of Significance." *American Sociologist* 4 (May): 140–43.

Wisan, Joseph E. 1934. *The Cuban Crisis as Reflected in the New York Press, 1895–1898*. New York: Octagon.

World Bank. 1990. *World Development Report 1990*. New York: Oxford University Press.

———. 1992. *World Development Report 1992*. New York: Oxford University Press.

Wright, Patricia. 1972. *Conflict on the Nile: The Fashoda Incident of 1898*. London: Heinemann.

Wright, Quincy. 1942; reprint, 1965. *A Study of War.* Chicago: University of Chicago Press.

Wright, Robin. 1992. "Islam, Democracy and the West." *Foreign Affairs* 71:131–45.

Wylie, Alison. 1986. "Arguments for Scientific Realism: The Ascending Spiral." *American Philosophical Quarterly* 23:287–97.

Zinnes, Dina, and Jonathan Wilkenfeld. 1971. "An Analysis of Foreign Conflict Behavior of Nations." In Wolfram F. Hanreider, ed., *Comparative Foreign Policy,* 200–16. New York: McKay.

Name Index

Abdolali, Nasrin, 19, 21–22, 23–24, 44n13, 86, 125, 158, 188, 202
Achen, Christopher H., 157n16
Adams, John, 175
Allison, Graham T., 133–34
Amery, L. S., 129n32
Anderson, Paul A., 170
Antholis, William, 86, 104
Apter, David, 83n13
Archer, J. Clark, 80
Aruego, Jose M., 115
Auxier, George W., 182

Babst, Dean V., 11–12, 13, 43n6, 43n7, 86, 202
Baloyra, Enrique, 50
Bates, Darrell, 177, 179, 183, 184, 191, 192, 194–95
Becker, Howard S., 140–41
Belfield, Eversley, 117, 129n32
Bello, Walden, 87
Bennett, D. Scott 196,
Bergeson, Albert, 64, 80
Bernstein, Carl, 62
Berry, Frances Stokes, 53
Berry, William D., 53
Binyan, Liu, 63
Blainey, Geoffrey, 87, 110
Bollen, Kenneth A., 56–57, 80, 90, 96, 97
Bourke, John, 1
Branegan, Jay, 63
Brawley, Mark R., 28, 197
Brecher, Michael, 87, 120
Bremer, Stuart A., 13, 20, 26–27, 44n12, 44n14, 44n16, 44n17, 90, 152–53, 158, 159, 170–72, 173, 188, 198, 202
Brown, Chris, 1, 127n13
Brown, Roger Hamilton, 107

Brown, Roger Glenn, 177, 187, 200n11
Brzezinski, Zbigniew, 54
Bueno de Mesquita, Bruce, 18, 19–20, 21, 23, 30–31, 32–33, 35, 37, 38–39, 40, 41, 43n1, 43n5, 44n16, 79, 87, 91–92, 101, 105, 112, 119, 124, 131, 134, 144, 145, 146, 147, 150–51, 155n1, 155n4, 156n15, 157n17, 158–59, 171, 183, 188, 192, 193, 196, 197, 202, 203
Burns, John F., 211

Caldwell, Bruce J., 140
Campbell, Donald T., 22–23, 31–32, 33, 45n22, 45n22, 45n23, 163–69, 199n1, 199n3, 209
Cardoso, Fernando Henrique, 83n13
Carr, Edward Hallet, 8, 201
Carr, Raymond, 114, 128n27, 129n28
Castro, Jose Luna, 115
Cecil, Evelyn, 117
Cefkin, J. Leo, 48
Chang, Noh Soon, 20
Chan, Steve, 17, 18, 19, 44n14, 76, 87, 96, 108, 114–15, 120, 125
Chapman, Charles, 114
Claggett, William, 64, 68, 69, 80
Coles, Harry L., 127n17
Cole, Timothy Michael, 86, 87, 114–15
Collingwood, R. G., 137, 141
Cook, Thomas D., 164
Coulter, E. Merton, 87, 111, 128n24
Craig, Gordon A., 108

Dahl, Robert, 97, 98
De Conde, Alexander, 110, 112, 163, 184, 200n9
de Jonge, Alex, 82n10
de Luna, Frederick A., 109, 128n21

229

Subject Index

Africa, 173, 176–77
    sub-Saharan, 48–49
aggression, military, 37
Ahmed, Muhammad, 176
Albania, 211, 212
Algeria, 48
alliance, 170
    bonds, 171
    ties, 25, 26
analysis
    correlational, 165n12
    large-N. *See* studies, large-N
    world-system, 50, 59, 64
Angola, 59
antiauthoritarianism, 60, 62
Arguilero, Jaime Roldos, 122
Arguinaldo, Emilio, 115
arguments, cultural, 91
Armenia, 87, 122, 123–24, 130n43
arms race, 79
Asia, 47
Athens, 87, 104, 105
Austria, 134
authoritarianism, 58
autocracy, 1, 10, 60, 70, 80, 90, 92, 169,
    184, 188, 205
    as a cause of war, 1
    indicators of, 66–67
    institutionalized, 66
    scores, 67
    Spanish, 189–90
Azerbaijan, 87, 122, 123–24, 130n43

Bailey, Joe, 185
Bangladesh, 47
bargaining
    and negotiations, 174
    between states, 101, 192
    crisis, 190–91

    impact of joint democracy on, 33,
        40, 191, 210
    impact of structural constraints on,
        31
    pacifying effect on, 124
Battle of Omdurman, 176
Beatles, 61
Belaunde, Fernando, 122
Belgium, 87, 107–8, 128n19
Benin, 48
Boer War, 12, 36, 87, 115–18, 124, 207
bomb, atomic, 54. *See also* war, nuclear
Bongo, Omar, 48
Bosnia-Herzegovina, 87, 122, 123
bourgeoisie, 51
    in France, 184
Brazil, 36
British Broadcasting Corp., 61
British Guiana, 162
Bryan, William Jennings, 185–86
Burma, 47
business
    class, 183
    community, 186
    groups, 184, 193

Cambodia, 210
capability ratios. *See* ratios, capability
capitalism, 53–54, 59, 60, 183, 184
    expansionist, 193
case studies. *See* studies, case
Catholic Church, 51–52, 136
causality, 133, 135, 139, 140, 141, 152,
    156n12, 159, 166, 168, 208
causal mechanisms, 141–44, 147, 149,
    151, 154, 160, 208
    and "as if" assumptions, 144, 149–
        51
    and covering laws, 144–47